ATLA BIBLIOGRAPHY SERIES
edited by Dr. Kenneth E. Rowe

29. *Rediscovery of Creation: A Bibliographical Study of the Church's Response to the Environmental Crisis*, by Joseph K. Sheldon. 1992.

30. *The Charismatic Movement: A Guide to the Study of Neo-Pentecostalism with Emphasis on Anglo-American Sources*, by Charles Edwin Jones. 1995.

31. *Cities and Churches: An International Bibliography* (3 vols.), by Loyde H. Hartley. 1992.

32. *A Bibliography of the Samaritans*, 2nd ed., by Alan David Crown. 1993.

33. *The Early Church: An Annotated Bibliography of Literature in English*, by Thomas A. Robinson. 1993.

34. *Holiness Manuscripts: A Guide to Sources Documenting the Wesleyan Holiness Movement in the United States and Canada*, by William Kostlevy. 1994.

35. *Of Spirituality: A Feminist Perspective*, by Clare B. Fischer. 1995.

36. *Evangelical Sectarianism in the Russian Empire and the USSR: A Bibliographic Guide*, by Albert Wardin, Jr. 1995.

37. *Hermann Sasse: A Bibliography*, by Ronald R. Feuerhahn. 1995.

OF SPIRITUALITY
A Feminist Perspective

by
Clare B. Fischer

ATLA Bibliography Series, No. 35

The American Theological Library Association
and
The Scarecrow Press, Inc.
Lanham, Md., & London
1995

SCARECROW PRESS, INC.

Published in the United States of America
by Scarecrow Press, Inc.
4720 Boston Way
Lanham, Maryland 20706

4 Pleydell Gardens, Folkestone
Kent CT20 2DN, England

British Cataloguing-in-Publication Information Available.

Library of Congress Cataloging-in-Publication Data
Fischer, Clare Benedicks.
    Of spirituality : a feminist perspective / Clare B. Fischer
      p.   cm. — (ATLA bibliographica series ; no. 35)
    Includes bibliographical references and index.
    1. Women and religion—Bibliography.   2. Women—Religious life—
Bibliography.   I. Title.   II. Series.
    z7833.F57   1995   [BL458]   95-5660   016.2′0082—dc20   CIP

ISBN 0-8108-3006-X (cloth : alk. paper)

♾The paper used in this publication meets the minimum requirements of
American National Standard for Information Sciences—Permanence of
Paper for Printed Library Materials, ANSI Z39.48–1984.
Manufactured in the United States of America.

CONTENTS

EDITOR'S FOREWORD

Since 1974 the American Theological Library Association has been publishing this bibliography series with the Scarecrow Press. Guidelines for projects and selections for publication are made by the ATLA Publications Section in consultation with the editor. Our goal is to stimulate and encourage the preparation and publication of reliable bibliographies and guides to the literature of religious studies in all of its scope and variety. Compilers are free to define their fields, to make their own selections, and to work out internal organization as the unique demands of the subjects indicate.

We are pleased to publish Clare Fischer's *Of Spirituality: A Feminist Bibliography* as number 35 in the ATLA Bibliography Series.

Clare Benedicks Fischer (A.B. Hunter College; M.A. Syracuse University; Ph.D., Religion and Society, Graduate Theological Union) is on the faculty of the Starr King School for the Ministry, which is a member of the Graduate Theological Union in Berkeley, California. She holds the Aurelia Reinhardt Chair in Religion and Culture and has served as convenor of the History of Religions area of the consortium. For the past decade she has taught classes in comparative feminist approaches to religion, feminist theology, and feminist theory. She published *Breaking Through: A Feminist Bibliography in Theology* in 1980 and is currently doing research on Indonesian women and work.

Kenneth E. Rowe
Series Editor

Drew University Library
Madison, NJ

INTRODUCTION

When this bibliography was first conceived as a viable project ten years ago, I was eager to explore the relationship between two important fields of study for students of religion: feminism and spirituality. I was well aware of the dramatic increase in published titles in both fields of endeavor and was certain that a bibliographic index bringing the two into a formal relationship would be helpful. This focus was a departure from earlier bibliographies I had undertaken in the general area of women and religion. A decade ago with the Graduate Theological Union, through its Library and the Center of Women and Religion, I had published an index of books entitled *Breaking Through*. In that editing effort, I was determined to make women's scholarship accessible to both general and academic readers. It became obvious after a few years that the document, as useful as it might have been, was dated and no longer representative of women's work in theology and religion.

No mere revision of the earlier project would suffice. However straightforward an updating and supplementary process might have been, I had already committed myself to a new bibliography as such. This new vision assumed an openness to the subject matter. I followed the inspiration of the poet H.D., who wrote in her poem *Trilogy:* "we know no rules of procedure, we are voyagers, discoverers of the not-known." In short, I pursued the task of collecting and organizing as a cartographer of new terrain—eager to locate important sites but without attachment to prior locations (or conceptions).

The title of this new bibliography reveals something of this spirit of adventure in my effort. "Of" spirituality refers, for me, to the open character of the many voices which speak to this reality. It does not suggest that spirituality is any particular activity or field of study. It demands curiosity and a tilting forward toward a literature that is paradoxically new and old at the same time: new in its fresh interpretation, old in its rootedness in both Western and non-Western religious lives.

My continued interest in women's studies and religion over the years, in both research and teaching, has kept me relatively informed about the publications available in feminist studies. I routinely collected titles for syllabi and general knowledge. Thus, the second half of my title indicates that I have approached the "merger" of feminism and spirituality with a perspective. This, most certainly, does not mean that I hold to a position that forecloses the posture of curiosity which I took toward spirituality; rather, my classification of materials reflects a perspective embedded in the currents of contemporary feminism.

In the earlier bibliography I constructed a trio of organizing rubrics to order the materials found therein. This scheme reflected my commitment to the infusion of women's studies literature into theology and religious studies. I chose a linear design that progressed from traditional approaches to women's scholarship on religion through a quasifeminist to a feminist writing of the same. In retrospect my design is naïve, assuming a definitive feminism that can be clustered in one place. Just as there are many voices in spiritual writing, so, too, there are in feminism. This realization initially overwhelmed me with the thought that both fields—spirituality and feminist studies—could be approached with an inclusivity that would have no boundaries. The final organization of this work reveals my solution.

Feminist Spirituality

Although I undertook this project with a concern about the relationship between feminism and spirituality, I was not without guidance on the subject. A number of women writers had published material on the connection, and I sought out early their respective understandings in order to secure a sense of the geography. Charlene Spretnak's now-classic anthology entitled *The Politics of Women's Spirituality*[1] proved to be an excellent point of departure for my mapping work. Her introduction insists upon the connection of "spiritual power" and feminism, and she provides an effective defense of women's spirituality as attached to the concerns of the polity. She further suggests a "cluster" of spiritual ways which distinguish traditional, patriarchal religious practices and beliefs from a feminist spirituality.

Reading from other authors I was convinced that the spirituality to be incorporated into this bibliography would not refer to the disembodied, distant understanding that Western Christianity had seemingly promoted. Practices of devotion and aspirations for release from this world could not effectively meet feminism and its embodied, radically democratic perspective on liberation. One cue I was able to take and elaborate upon emerged from my experience with the Ph.D. program in Christian Spirituality at the Graduate Theological Union in Berkeley. Although requiring scholarly education in the tradition, including comprehensive examinations in biblical and theological spirituality, the program fosters an embrace of spirituality that is neither other-worldly nor body-rejecting. Faculty and students appropriate an authentic spirituality from the tradition and dismiss the vulgarization of spirituality that is so often associated with patriarchal religion. A useful essay by my colleague Sr. Sandra Schneiders describes the significance of spirituality as a disciplined study ("Spirituality in the Academy," *Theological Studies* 50 [1989]).

In 1986 Anne Carson published a bibliography on feminist spirituality (*Feminist Spirituality and the Feminine Divine*[2]). Her perspective has been clarifying for me, indicating that feminist spirituality covers a wide expanse. It "touches the fields of history, religion, mythology and folklore, anthropology and archaeology, psychology, witchcraft and occult science, New Age studies, parapsychology, lesbian-feminism, health, literature, and the arts." In effect, most of human enterprise is relevant to the subject. Recently, the same author has published an up-to-date annotated bibliography entitled *Goddesses and Wise Women*.[3]

In considering the scope of the bibliography, then, feminist spirituality was not to be confused with a dominant but distorted historical view of spirituality which narrows human possibility and fragments the spirit. Perceiving that wholeness, complexity, and a good deal of tension characterize feminist spirituality, I proceeded in my work with a commitment to inclusiveness. This approach has meant that I continually have had to ask myself why a title is appropriate, what material is unsuitable, irrelevant, or confusing. The boundaries are decidedly elastic and the embrace generous.

I was comforted by the introductory words of Judith Plascow and Carol Christ in their anthology, *Weaving the Visions.*[4] In determining how they would select essays for inclusion in their volume, they were compelled to recast an earlier understanding of feminist spirituality. Theirs was a position that shifted from a somewhat generalized and "universalizing" feminism to an appreciation of diversity and difference. Their discernment with respect to material reflected this historical and deepening transformation of meaning. In other words, the pluralization of feminism and spirituality permits the reader to understand feminisms and spiritualities.

A Moveable Feast

I eventually found the largeness of my subject was not cause for panic. My delight in the cross-disciplinary and multivariant expression of feminist spirituality brought me to a celebratory mood and this, in turn, to a metaphor which serves as the organizing scheme of this bibliography. In 1979 I had viewed Judy Chicago's art event entitled "The Dinner Party." At the time, I was impressed with the project and its use of women's artistic expression, including china painting, embroidery, and weaving. The subject of the event, perhaps somewhat ambitiously conceived, was the presence of women in history (that is, *at* the table and not in the kitchen) and the long struggle for liberation. Chicago's project and mine resemble one another. The published presence of women in spirituality (as subjects and authors) requires recognition and celebration.

A banner hung at the entrance of Chicago's "Dinner Party" which announced a vision, including the promise that "all that has divided us will merge." I have taken this promise as my principal motivation in assembling the materials of the bibliography. Ironic as it may seem, because classifications, by definition, separate what may not warrant separation, the division of my work is meant to suggest places in a continuous flow of material. Specifically, the bibliography is to be seen as a pilgrimage through published sources which takes the reader closer to understanding an elemental connection.

The "Dinner Party" metaphor underlies the thirteen chapter headings of my bibliography; each is related to all the others but not in a linear manner. While Chicago's artistic creation suggested movement from earliest times (the first setting representing the "primordial goddess") to the twentieth century (with the Georgia O'Keeffe plate as the last of the thirteen), my classification of material is not historically progressive, nor do I suggest a movement toward greater liberation as the reader approaches the later listings of the bibliography. The thirteen headings can be understood as "way stations" along a pilgrimage route which invite the traveller to pause and take respite. The stations, or sites, are clusters of material that enable the reader to find a path through the plethora of documents. Yet within each site there are other sites which further nourish and refresh the reader.

Following the metaphor inspired by the Chicago work, I believe the various classifications permit the reader to get a sense of the abundance of material within any one site, to experience the visibility of many women writing from most parts of the world and through history. Just as Chicago's dinner guests began to rise off the plates upon which they were images as they came closer to human liberation, I would like the reader to recognize that the writers in this bibliography have veritably lifted and changed the ways in which we will see spiritual life from this time forth.

Organization and Further Explanation

In the creation of thirteen sites I have attempted to organize material in such a way that both the structure and its internal classification make sense to the reader. As I have already indicated, all of the thirteen headings are interdependent and point to a notion of comprehensiveness that includes both scholarly and more general resources available to the reader. I have placed each of the thirteen headings with intentionality, beginning with feminist theology and scriptural studies and ending with a list of women's resources. Although there is no movement as such, from heading to heading, I would like to believe that the first twelve headings invite readers to pursue active connection with one or another center or press listed in the thirteenth section.

Each of the thirteen sections is introduced by a verbal statement. I have provided a brief overview of each chapter in order to clarify how I understand the cluster of materials. I had considered an annotated scheme, but early in my work abandoned this idea, hoping to keep the list sufficiently coherent and representative within the particular sites. I believe that the reader who wants to research a specific issue—for example, Australian aboriginal women—will find sufficient information (in this case, in the site entitled "Primal" within the "Cross-Cultural" section that constitutes the third chapter of the bibliography).

I approached the various headings with a sense of conversation between and among the several authors both within the particular cluster and across the headings I had created. The first and third headings were meant to hold the second in tension. The "classic" material and titles which reflected a more traditional positioning between feminist theology (the first) and "cross-cultural" material (the third) seemed entirely appropriate. Similarly, the section on feminist theory was located as a point of departure from the more practical dimensions of women's spirituality ("Ministry and Spiritual Practice") and an entry to those activities and realities of women in the everyday world: home, family, environment.

The section on "Global Community" moves the bibliography toward the vision of a large and active relationship, and the last section invites further work by offering lists of resources.

Although the project has been designed to identify women authors and women's spiritual endeavors, I have included a representative number of male authors whose works were sufficiently relevant and prominent to warrant consideration. I hasten to add that I am aware that many contributors to the list are not perceived as feminist writers; this does not modify my intent. I have a perspective which I believe to be feminist (note my title) and assumes an inclusivity of subject and person where I believe material to be especially useful.

I am very clear that the work of organizing and editing this bibliography has been gratifying precisely because it has been an educational venture for me during all phases of the project's development. It is my hope that the bibliography will serve as a meaningful educational opportunity for its readers. The questions of inclusivity and particular placement never became entirely comfortable. In truth, many volumes belonged in many places; similarly, many authors could have been placed under several subheadings. This is proof, in a way, of the multidisciplinary character of both spirituality and feminist studies. My ambivalence is even more heightened by the creation of subheadings around women's color or cultural or sexual identity. I settled on this arrangement in spite of the philosophical violence which underlies such separation. My reason: that the clustering of material would enhance recognition of the particularity that belongs to women's experience.

My approach to the specific question of scope is based upon a method of discernment that privileges accessibility and relevance. For example, English language titles are the rule yet I have included several authors who originally published in another language but have been translated into English. My discernment reflects the decision to exclude titles which have been published in other bibliographies treating a particular subject (for example, sexual abuse and recovery, women's work aspirations and experiences). My rationale for incorporation has everything to do with the spiritual implications of the subject and how the particular publication reflects a position which deepens this perspective. It should be noted here that I have excluded books that are generally perceived as "self-help" studies or popular religious commentaries. There is a fine line in this discernment and I am certain that I have omitted some salient works and included others that may be marginal to the subject.

I want to take note of the fact that there are several bibliographies and presses that enable further research on women in the area of history and religion. Scarecrow Press is a leader in reference publications. Its catalogues offer a variety of bibliographic materials which I believe to be outstanding. In addition, Garland Press has published a bibliography by Inger Marie Ruud, *Women and Judaism,*[5] which includes many relevant titles. Dorothy C. Bass and Sandra Boyd edited a bibliography on *Women in American Religious History* (published by G. K. Hall in 1986) that is also valuable to the researcher. I have referred earlier to Anne Carson's edited bibliography, *Feminist Spirituality and the Feminine Divine* published in 1986 by Crossing Press, and her recent volume *Goddesses and Wise Women*. In all cases, these bibliographies are annotated guides and serve as excellent resources.

One publication which I have found invaluable for feminist study is *Feminist Collections,* a listing edited by Phyllis Holman Weisbard and Linda Shult. It can be subscribed to for $25 a year for individuals; and $46 for institutions, from 430 Memorial Library, 728 State Street, Madison, Wisconsin 53706.)

Two publishing houses are instrumental in offering women's history texts that are fine additions to a library collection. Garland has published a 36-volume reprint collection, *Women in American Protestant Religion, 1800–1930,* edited by Caroline De Swarte Gifford. And, a series on black women in American history is edited by Darlene Clark Hine and published by Carson Publishing.

Acknowledgements

I have been involved in the tasks of editing, organizing, and administering this bibliography for many years and can honestly say that the project has been a challenge with the mark of a good deal of collaborative investment. For all the interest and excitement in this work evinced by my friends and colleagues, I am very grateful.

From the first days of the project my institution has shown unwavering commitment to this effort. Starr King School for the Ministry has expressed interest most concretely in offering me its computer system and the helpful advice of many persons. Beverly Smhra, who was a staff member some years ago, helped introduce me to a technology that seemed awesome and convinced me that I would find working on a computer program entirely non-threatening. I am thankful to her in more ways than one. Patti Lawrence provided computer advice and support in the final editing of this work. Art Ungar might be called the midwife of this bibliography. He designed the program, followed along through each step of the organization and editing of the data, and assured me along the way that the tasks would all get done. He has demonstrated the value of perseverance and patience, offering wisdom and skill without reservation or complaint. A simple thank you to him does not suffice. His investment of imagination and time is threaded through the pages of this volume.

The generosity of spirit and care for the project which I experienced from staff and colleagues at Starr King School for the Ministry was found in other settings of the Graduate Theological Union as well. Staff at the Graduate Theological Union Bookstore were always ready to assist and answer inquiries. Help was offered by personnel at the Library of the Graduate Theological Union in assisting my searches. I wish to thank Judy Clarence, formerly reference librarian at the G.T.U. Library, and James Else, Oscar Burdick, and Gilles Poitras in particular.

This bibliography was conceived as a joint effort originally. In its earliest development I worked closely with a graduate student at the Graduate Theological Union. Judith Chendo and I sent off a grant application to the American Theological Library Association for preliminary assistance. Her help in the formative stages was essential. Several women have been crucial to this work, and I cannot praise them too much. Kali Halverson worked with the text of the bibliography in its middle period—editing, criticizing classifications, and so on. Marie deYoung was involved in a later phase of this project, and she routinely gave proof of the worth of collaboration. Dee Graham provided intelligent commentary about the editorial process and indicated that "the little bugs" were mere distractions easily overcome. In sum, I am satisfied that "sisterhood is powerful" in the work of creating this document.

In 1984 the Publication Committee of the American Theological Library Association provided a grant to get the project started. For this first indication of support for the bibliography I am grateful. Claude Welch (formerly dean of the G.T.U.) has also been supportive. Through his auspices I received a faculty enhancement grant from the Graduate Theological Union.

Notes

1. Charlene Spretnak, ed., *The Politics of Women's Spirituality* (New York: Doubleday & Co., 1982).
2. Anne Carson, *Feminist Spirituality and the Feminine Divine* (New York: Crossing Press, 1986).
3. Anne Carson, *Goddesses and Wise Women* (New York: Crossing Press, 1992).
4. Judith Plaskow and Carol Christ, eds., *Weaving the Visions: New Patterns in Feminist Spirituality* San Francisco: Harper & Row, 1989).
5. Inger Marie Ruud, ed., *Women and Judaism: A Selected Annotated Bibliography* (New York: Garland Press, 1988), vol. 316.

1. FEMINIST THEO/ALOGY, SCRIPTURE STUDY, AND HISTORY

Titles are offered in this first of thirteen sections which introduce the general subject of feminist theo/alogy. I have created the spelling of this discipline with a slash to indicate that women are working within and between these orientations. A decade ago, few authors were accessible to the general reader who had developed a critique of the traditional "guild" disciplines of theology, and fewer yet would be identified with an approach that used a spelling that refers explicitly to woman (that is, "thealogy"). Over the years, Rosemary Ruether, Mary Daly, and Dorothee Soelle have been joined by both "academic" and noninstitutionally associated theologians who have understood their respective efforts as part of the larger feminist movement. This first section of the bibliography attempts to identify those writers who provide us with a critique of patriarchal religious culture and the inequities of institutions alleged to be committed to justice.

Elisabeth Schuessler Fiorenza's now well recognized study of textual interpretation and woman—church, *In Memory of Her,* provides an excellent illustration of the cross-disciplinary character of feminist theo/alogy. She presents an argument that fits in well with any one of the three subsections under this rubric, indicating the overlap of biblical analysis, historical interpretation, and theological purpose.

In each section of this chapter there are books which speak to some of the trends I perceive as important to women's spirituality. The recovery of our foremothers in the publications of Pauli Murray, Nelle Morton, and Anne McGrew Bennett points to the commitment feminists have to rootedness and historical connection. Moreover, womanist theology (for example, the work of Katie Cannon and Delores Williams)

1

reveals the current and long overdue recognition of black women's religious experiences and reflections. Related to this new accessibility to writings heretofore unknown, voices hidden by assumptions of canon, is the corpus of material written by women from Asia, Africa, and Latin America.

The quest for human justice has been addressed by feminist ethicists within the Christian tradition. Beverly Harrison, Carter Heyward, and Mary E. Hunt are but a few who approach the subject from differing angles, sharing a vision which presents women and men in a new relationship.

Among the contributors to biblical scholarship and historical analysis represented in this section are writers who reveal the reality of human violence and suffering and discern patterns of women's resistance. Trible and Bal have specifically studied this vulnerability of women through their scriptural lens. Gerda Lerner's popular study of archaic and ancient women, *The Creation of Patriarchy,* is a singular effort to make more precise the meaning of this asymmetry in sexual relationships: probing the reasons for women's alleged victimization within patriarchal culture. Lerner's quest for historical understanding of subordination introduces the importance of the concept of agency and its meaning for women in all times.

In all three sections of this chapter hiddenness from history and the ideology of a natural subordination are taken to task. The feminist writers incorporated here sing in many voices about woman's liberation from the repressiveness of male-dominated institutions. Theirs is a rich chorus which invites us to appreciate the breadth and depth of contemporary theo/alogical endeavor.

Theology/Thealogy

1.   Andolsen, Barbara H., C. Gudorf, and M. Pellauer, eds.
     Women's Consciousness, Women's Conscience: A Reader in Feminist Ethics
     San Francisco, CA: Harper & Row, 1987. 310 pp.

2. Aquino, Maria Pilar, trans. Dinah Livingston
   Our Cry for Life: Feminist Theology for Latin America
   Maryknoll, NY: Orbis Books, 1993. 254 pp.

3. Atkinson, Clarissa, C. Buchanan, and M. Miles, eds.
   *Immaculate and Powerful: The Female in Sacred Image and
       Social Reality*
   Boston, MA: Beacon Press, 1985. 330 pp.

4. Atkinson, Clarissa, C. Buchanan, and M. Miles, eds.
   Shaping New Vision: Gender and Values in American Culture
   Ann Arbor, MI: UMI Research Press, 1987. 218 pp.

5. Barciauskas, Rosemary Curran, and Debra B. Hull
   Am I My Sister's Keeper? Reweaving Private and Public Lives
   Oak Park, IL: Meyer-Stone, 1989. 216 pp.

6. Becher, Jeanne, ed.
   *Women, Religion, and Sexuality: Studies on the Impact of
       Religious Teachings on Women*
   Philadelphia, PA: Trinity International Press, 1991. 278
   pp.

7. Bennett, Anne McGrew, ed. Mary E. Hunt
   *From Woman-Pain to Woman-Vision: Writings in Feminist
       Theology*
   Philadelphia, PA: Fortress Press, 1989. 192 pp.

8. Bloomquist, Karen L.
   The Dream Betrayed: Religious Challenge of the Working Class
   Philadelphia, PA: Fortress Press, 1989. 130 pp.

9. Brock, Rita Nakashima
   Journeys by Heart: A Christology of Erotic Power
   New York, NY: Crossroad Publishing, 1988. 130 pp.

10. Brown, Joanne Carlson, and Carole R. Bohn, eds.
    Christianity, Patriarchy, and Abuse: A Feminist Critique
    New York, NY: Pilgrim Press, 1989. 208 pp.

11. Bulkin, Elly, Minnie B. Pratt, and Barbara Smith
     Yours in Struggle: Three Feminist Perspectives on Anti-Semitism and Racism
     New York, NY: Long Haul Press, 1984. 233 pp.

12. Burke, Mary P.
     Reaching for Justice: The Women's Movement
     Washington, DC: Center for Concern, 1984. 162 pp.

13. Cahill, Lisa Sowle
     Between the Sexes: Foundations for a Christian Ethic of Sexuality
     Philadelphia, PA: Fortress Press, 1985. 166 pp.

14. Cannon, Katie G.
     Black Womanist Ethics
     Alpharetta, GA: Scholars Press, 1988. 183 pp.

15. Carmody, Denise Lardner
     Feminism and Christianity: A Two-Way Reflection
     Nashville, TN: Abingdon Press, 1982. 188 pp.

16. Carmody, Denise Lardner
     The Double Cross: Ordination, Abortion, and Catholic Feminism
     New York, NY: Crossroad Publishing, 1986. 158 pp.

17. Carr, Anne, and Elisabeth Schuessler Fiorenza, eds.
     The Special Nature of Women?
     New York, NY: Pilgrim Press, 1991. 128 pp.

18. Carr, Anne E.
     Transforming Grace: Christian Tradition and Women's Experience
     San Francisco, CA: Harper & Row, 1988. 272 pp.

19. Case-Winters, Anna
     God's Power: Traditional Understandings and Contemporary Challenges

Louisville, KY: Westminster/John Knox Press, 1990. 276 pp.

20. Chopp, Rebecca S.
The Praxis of Suffering: An Interpretation of Liberation and Political Theologies
Maryknoll, NY: Orbis Books, 1986. 178 pp.

21. Chopp, Rebecca S.
The Power to Speak: Feminism, Language, God
New York, NY: Crossroad Publishing, 1989. 224 pp.

22. Christ, Carol P., and Judith Plaskow, eds.
Womanspirit Rising: A Feminist Reader in Religion
San Francisco, CA: Harper & Row, 1979. 287 pp.

23. Clanton, Jann Aldredge
In Whose Image? God and Gender
New York, NY: Crossroad Publishing, 1990. 144 pp.

24. Clark, Elizabeth, and Herbert Richardson, eds.
Women and Religion: A Feminist Sourcebook of Christian Thought
New York, NY: Harper & Row, 1977. 296 pp.

25. Coll, Regina, ed.
Women and Religion
Ramsey, NJ: Paulist Press, 1982. 140 pp.

26. Daly, Mary
Beyond God the Father (with original reintroduction)
Boston, MA: Beacon Press, 1985. 225 pp.

27. Daly, Mary
The Church and the Second Sex
Boston, MA: Beacon Press, 1985. 229 pp.

28. Daly, Mary
Outercourse: The Be-Dazzling Voyage
San Francisco, CA: Harper & Row, 1992. 480 pp.

29. Davies, Susan B., and Eleanor Haney, eds.
     *Redefining Sexual Ethics: A Sourcebook of Essays, Stories, and
        Poems*
     New York, NY: Pilgrim Press, 1991. 576 pp.

30. Douglass, Jane Dempsey
     Women, Freedom and Calvin
     Louisville, KY: Westminster/John Knox Press, 1985. 155
        pp.

31. Downing, Christine
     Psyche's Sisters: Re-Imagining the Meaning of Sisterhood
     San Francisco, CA: Harper & Row, 1987. 192 pp.

32. Duck, Ruth
     *Gender and the Name of God: The Trinitarian Baptismal
        Formula*
     New York, NY: Pilgrim Press, 1991. 192 pp.

33. Elwes, Teresa, ed.
     Women's Voices: Essays in Contemporary Feminist Theology
     Maryknoll, NY: Orbis Books, 1988. 192 pp.

34. Fabella, Virginia, and Mercy A. Oduyoye, eds.
     *With Passion and Compassion: Third World Women Doing
        Theology*
     Maryknoll, NY: Orbis Books, 1988. 192 pp.

35. Farley, Margaret
     Personal Commitments: Making, Keeping, Breaking
     San Francisco, CA: Harper & Row, 1986. 148 pp.

36. Fiorenza, Elisabeth Schuessler, and Mary Collins, eds.
     Women: Invisible in Church and Theology
     Philadelphia, PA: Fortress Press, 1986. 126 pp.

37. Fiorenza, Elisabeth Schuessler
     *Claiming the Center: A Feminist Critical Theology of Libera-
        tion*
     Somers, CT: Seabury Press, 1987.

38. Fiorenza, Elisabeth Schuessler
    Revelation: Vision of a Just World
    Philadelphia, PA: Fortress Press, 1991. 160 pp.

39. Fiorenza, Elisabeth Schuessler
    *Discipleship of Equals: A Critical Feminist Ek-klesialogy of
    Liberation*
    New York, NY: Crossroad Publishing, 1993. 372 pp.

40. Gerstenberger, Erhard, and W. Schrage, trans. D. Stott
    Woman and Man
    Nashville, TN: Abingdon Press, 1981. 252 pp.

41. Goldenberg, Naomi
    Changing of the Gods
    Boston, MA: Beacon Press, 1979. 152 pp.

42. Grey, Mary C.
    Feminism, Redemption, and the Christian Tradition
    Mystic, CT: Twenty-Third Publications, 1990. 251 pp.

43. Hampson, Daphne
    Theology and Feminism
    Cambridge, MA: Blackwell, 1990. 192 pp.

44. Harrison, Beverly Wildung, ed. Carol Robb
    Making the Connections: Essays in Feminist Social Ethics
    Boston, MA: Beacon Press, 1985. 312 pp.

45. Hellwig, Monika K.
    Christian Women in a Troubled World
    Ramsey, NJ: Paulist Press, 1985. 57 pp.

46. Heyward, Carter
    The Redemption of God: A Theology of Mutual Relation
    Washington, DC: University Press of America, 1982. 240
    pp.

47. Heyward, Carter
    *Our Passion for Justice: Images of Power, Sexuality, and
    Liberation*
    New York, NY: Pilgrim Press, 1984. 264 pp.

48. Heyward, Carter
     *Touching Our Strength: The Erotic as Power and the Love of
        God*
     San Francisco, CA: Harper & Row, 1989. 160 pp.

49. Heyward, Carter, ed. Ellen C. Davis
     Speaking of Christ: A Lesbian Feminist Voice
     New York, NY: Pilgrim Press, 1989. 96 pp.

50. Hosmer, Rachel
     Gender and God
     Cambridge, MA: Cowley Publishing, 1986. 142 pp.

51. Hunt, Mary E.
     Fierce Tenderness: Toward a Feminist Theology of Friendship
     New York, NY: Crossroad Publishing, 1990. 216 pp.

52. Isasi-Diaz, Ada Maria, and Yolanda Tarango
     Hispanic Women: Prophetic Voice in the Church
     Philadelphia, PA: Fortress Press, 1992. 144 pp.

53. Jantzen, Grace
     God's World, God's Body
     Louisville, KY: Westminster/John Knox Press, 1984. 173
        pp.

54. Johnson, Elizabeth A.
     Consider Jesus: Waves of Renewal in Christology
     New York, NY: Crossroad Publishing, 1990. 128 pp.

55. Johnson, Elizabeth A.
     *She Who Is: The Mystery of God in a Feminist Theological
        Perspective*
     New York, NY: Crossroad/Continuum, 1992. 304 pp.

56. Kalven, Janet, and Mary I. Buckley, eds.
     Women's Spirit Bonding
     New York, NY: Pilgrim Press, 1984. 389 pp.

57. Katoppo, Marianne
     Compassionate and Free: An Asian Woman's Theology
     Maryknoll, NY: Orbis Books, 1981. 96 pp.

58. Keller, Catherine
     From a Broken Web: Separation, Sexism and Self
     Boston, MA: Beacon Press, 1986. 277 pp.

59. LaCugna, Catherine Mowry, ed.
     Freeing Theology: The Essentials of Theology in Feminist Perspective
     San Francisco, CA: Harper & Row, 1993. 266 pp.

60. Loades, Ann
     Searching for Lost Coins: Explorations in Christianity and Feminism
     London, U.K.: S.P.C.K., 1987. 118 pp.

61. Loades, Ann, ed.
     Feminist Theology: A Reader
     Louisville, KY: Westminster/John Knox Press, 1990. 324 pp.

62. Long, Asphodel P.
     In a Chariot Drawn by Lions: The Search for the Female in Deity
     London, U.K.: Women's Press, 1992. 220 pp.

63. Maitland, Sara
     A Map of the New Country: Women and Christianity
     Boston, MA: Routledge & Kegan Paul, 1983. 218 pp.

64. Massey, Marilyn C.
     Feminine Soul: The Fate of an Ideal
     Boston, MA: Beacon Press, 1985. 218 pp.

65. McFague, Sallie
     Metaphysical Theology: Models of God in Religious Language
     Philadelphia, PA: Fortress Press, 1982. 240 pp.

66. McFague, Sallie
    Models of God: Theology for an Ecological, Nuclear Age
    Philadelphia, PA: Fortress Press, 1987. 240 pp.

67. Miles, Margaret R.
    Desire and Delight: A New Reading of Augustine's Confessions
    New York, NY: Crossroad/Continuum, 1992. 126 pp.

68. Moltmann-Wendel, Elisabeth
    A Land Flowing with Milk and Honey: Perspectives on Feminist Theology
    New York, NY: Crossroad Publishing, 1988. 224 pp.

69. Moltmann-Wendel, Elisabeth, and Jurgen Moltmann
    Humanity in God
    New York, NY: Pilgrim Press, 1983. 133 pp.

70. Morton, Nelle
    The Journey Is Home
    Boston, MA: Beacon Press, 1985. 255 pp.

71. Mud Flower Collective, ed. Carter Heyward
    God's Fierce Whimsy: Christian Feminism and Theological Education
    New York, NY: Pilgrim Press, 1985. 226 pp.

72. O'Neill, Maura
    Women Speaking, Women Listening: Women in Interreligious Dialogue
    Maryknoll, NY: Orbis Books, 1990. 131 pp.

73. Oduyoye, Mercy Amba
    Hearing and Knowing: Theological Reflections on Christianity in Africa
    Maryknoll, NY: Orbis Books, 1986. 168 pp.

74. Papa, Mary Bader
    Christian Feminism: Completing the Subtotal Woman
    Chicago, IL: Fides/Claretian, 1981. 186 pp.

75. Phipps, William E., ed.
    Influential Theologians on Wo/Man
    Washington, DC: University Press of America, 1981. 135
    pp.

76. Plaskow, Judith
    Sex, Sin and Grace
    Washington, DC: University Press of America, 1980. 216
    pp.

77. Plaskow, Judith
    Standing Again at Sinai
    San Francisco, CA: Harper & Row, 1990. 272 pp.

78. Pobee, John, and Barbel von Wartenberg-Potter, eds.
    *New Eyes for Reading: Biblical and Theological Reflections—
    Women of the Third World*
    Oak Park, IL: Meyer-Stone, 1987. 112 pp.

79. Purvis, Sally B.
    *The Power of the Cross: Foundations for a Christian Feminist
    Ethic of Community*
    Nashville, TN: Abingdon Press, 1993. 15 pp.

80. Rabuzzi, Kathryn A.
    *The Sacred and the Feminine: Toward a Theology of House-
    work*
    Somers, CT: Seabury Press, 1982. 215 pp.

81. Ranke-Heinemann, Uta
    Eunuchs for the Kingdom of Heaven
    Garden City, NY: Doubleday & Co., 1990. 360 pp.

82. Rosenblatt, Marie-Eloise, ed.
    *Where Can We Find Her? Searching for Women's Identity in
    the New Church*
    Ramsey, NJ: Paulist Press, 1991. 166 pp.

83. Ruether, Rosemary Radford
    *New Woman New Earth: Sexist Ideologies and Human Libera-
    tion*
    Somers, CT: Seabury Press, 1975. 221 pp.

84.   Ruether, Rosemary Radford
      Mary, the Feminine Face of the Church
      Louisville, KY: Westminster/John Knox Press, 1977. 106
      pp.

85.   Ruether, Rosemary Radford
      Sexism and God—Talk: Toward a Feminist Theology
      Boston, MA: Beacon Press, 1983. 289 pp.

86.   Ruether, Rosemary Radford
      Woman—Guides: Readings Toward a Feminist Theology
      Boston, MA: Beacon Press, 1985. 274 pp.

87.   Ruether, Rosemary Radford
      Woman—Church: Theology and Practice
      San Francisco, CA: Harper & Row, 1988. 306 pp.

88.   Ruether, Rosemary Radford
      Contemporary Roman Catholicism: Crises and Challenges
      Kansas City, MO: Sheed & Ward, 1988. 81 pp.

89.   Russell, Letty, et al., eds.
      *Inheriting Our Mothers' Gardens: Feminist Theology in Third
          World Perspective*
      Louisville, KY: Westminster/John Knox Press, 1988. 168
      pp.

90.   Russell, Letty M.
      Household of Freedom: Authority in Feminist Theology
      Louisville, KY: Westminster/John Knox Press, 1987. 116
      pp.

91.   Russell, Letty M.
      Church in the Round: Feminist Interpretation of the Church
      Louisville, KY: Westminster/John Knox Press, 1993. 272
      pp.

92.   Say, Elizabeth A.
      *Evidence on Her Own Behalf: Women's Narrative as Theologi-
          cal Voice*
      Totowa, NJ: Rowman & Allanheld, 1990. 151 pp.

93. Schneiders, Sandra M.
     *Beyond Patching: Faith and Feminism in the Catholic
         Church*
     Ramsey, NJ: Paulist Press, 1991. 136 pp.

94. Snyder, Mary H.
     The Christology of Rosemary Radford Ruether
     Mystic, CT: Twenty-Third Publications, 1988. 176 pp.

95. Soelle, Dorothee
     Choosing Life
     Philadelphia, PA: Fortress Press, 1981. 116 pp.

96. Soelle, Dorothee
     Beyond Mere Obedience
     New York, NY: Pilgrim Press, 1982. 73 pp.

97. Soelle, Dorothee
     *The Strength of the Weak: Toward a Christian Feminist
         Identity*
     Louisville, KY: Westminster/John Knox Press, 1984.
         184 pp.

98. Soelle, Dorothee
     Thinking About God
     New York, NY: Pilgrim Press, 1991. 210 pp.

99. Soelle, Dorothee, with Shirley A. Cloyes
     To Work and to Love
     Philadelphia, PA: Fortress Press, 1984. 165 pp.

100. Soelle, Dorothee, trans. Linda Maloney
     The Window of Vulnerability: A Political Spirituality
     Philadelphia, PA: Fortress Press, 1990. 176 pp.

101. Tamez, Elsa
     Against Machismo (interviews about liberation theol-
         ogy)
     Oak Park, IL: Meyer-Stone, 1988. 160 pp.

102.   Tamez, Elsa, ed.
       The Feminist Face of Theology
       Maryknoll, NY: Orbis Books, 1989. 140 pp.

103.   Tennis, Diane
       Is God the Only Reliable Father?
       Louisville, KY: Westminster/John Knox Press, 1985.
          117 pp.

104.   Thistlethwaite, Susan
       Sex, Race, and God
       New York, NY: Crossroad Publishing, 1991. 192 pp.

105.   Townes, Emilie, ed.
       *A Troubling in My Soul: Womanist Perspectives on Evil and
          Suffering*
       Maryknoll, NY: Orbis Books, 1993. 300 pp.

106.   Vaughan, Judith
       Sociality, Ethics, and Social Change (on R. Niebuhr and
          R. R. Ruether)
       Washington, DC: University Press of America, 1983.
          220 pp.

107.   Wartenberg-Potter, Barbel von
       *We Will Not Hang Our Harps on the Willows: Global
          Sisterhood and God's Story*
       Geneva, Switz.: World Council of Churches, 1987. 144
          pp.

108.   Weidman, Judith, ed.
       Christian Feminism: Visions of a New Humanity
       San Francisco, CA: Harper & Row, 1984. 179 pp.

109.   Welch, Sharon D.
       *Communities of Resistance and Solidarity: A Feminist Theol-
          ogy of Liberation*
       Maryknoll, NY: Orbis Books, 1985. 102 pp.

110.   Welch, Sharon D.
        A Feminist Ethic of Risk
        Philadelphia, PA: Fortress Press, 1989. 176 pp.

111.   Williams, Delores
        Sisters in the Wilderness: The Challenge of Womanist God-Talk
        Maryknoll, NY: Orbis Books, 1992. 287 pp.

112.   Wilson-Kastner, Patricia
        Faith, Feminism and the Christ
        Philadelphia, PA: Fortress Press, 1983. 141 pp.

113.   Young, Pamela Dickey
        Feminist Theology/Christian Theology: In Search of Method
        Philadelphia, PA: Fortress Press, 1990. 112 pp.

Scriptural Analysis

114.   Bach, Alice, ed.
        The Pleasure of Her Text: Feminist Readings of Biblical and Historical Texts
        Philadelphia, PA: Trinity International Press, 1990. 144 pp.

115.   Bal, Mieke
        Lethal Love: Feminist Literary Readings of Biblical Love Stories
        Bloomington, IN: Indiana University Press, 1987. 141 pp.

116.   Bal, Mieke
        Murder and Difference: Gender, Genre and Scholarship
        Bloomington, IN: Indiana University Press, 1988. 150 pp.

117. Brooten, Bernadette
Women Leaders in the Ancient Synagogue: Inscription Evidence and Background Issues
Alpharetta, GA: Scholars Press, 1986. 281 pp.

118. Bundesen, Lynne
The Women's Guide to the Bible
New York, NY: Crossroad Publishing, 1993. 278 pp.

119. Burns, Rita J.
Has the Lord Indeed Spoken Only Through Moses? A Study of the Biblical Portrait of Miriam
Alpharetta, GA: Scholars Press, 1987. 142 pp.

120. Callaway, Mary
Sing, O Barren One: A Study in Comparative Midrash
Alpharetta, GA: Scholars Press, 1987. 157 pp.

121. Carmody, Denise Lardner
Biblical Woman: Contemporary Reflections on Scriptural Texts
New York, NY: Crossroad Publishing, 1988. 168 pp.

122. Collins, Adela Yarbro, ed.
Feminist Perspectives on Biblical Scholarship
Alpharetta, GA: Scholars Press, 1985. 144 pp.

123. Darr, Katheryn Pfisterer
Far More Precious Than Jewels: Perspectives on Biblical Women
Louisville, KY: Westminster/John Knox Press, 1991. 224 pp.

124. Demers, Patricia
Women as Interpreters of the Bible
Ramsey, NJ: Paulist Press, 1992. 192 pp.

125. Exum, J. Cheryl, and Johanna W. H. Bos, eds.
Reasoning with the Foxes: Female Wit in a World of Male Power
Alpharetta, GA: Scholars Press, 1988. 146 pp.

126. Fiorenza, Elisabeth Schuessler
     The Book of Revelation: Justice and Judgment
     Philadelphia, PA: Fortress Press, 1984. 211 pp.

127. Fiorenza, Elisabeth Schuessler
     *Bread Not Stone: The Challenge of Feminist Biblical Interpre-
     tation*
     Boston, MA: Beacon Press, 1984. 182 pp.

128. Fiorenza, Elisabeth Schuessler
     But SHE Said: Feminist Practices of Biblical Interpretation
     Boston, MA: Beacon Press, 1992. 262 pp.

129. Fiorenza, Elisabeth Schuessler, ed.
     Searching the Scriptures
     New York, NY: Crossroad Publishing, 1993. 372 pp.

130. Frymer-Kensky, Tikva Simone
     *In the Wake of the Goddesses: Women, Culture, and Biblical
     Transformation of Pagan Myth*
     New York, NY: The Free Press, 1991. 292 pp.

131. Gibbons, Joan Lyon, ed. Elizabeth Howes and R.
     Naegle
     The Courage of Questions
     San Francisco, CA: Guild for Psychological Studies
     Publishing House, 1989. 125 pp.

132. Good, Deidre J.
     Reconstructing the Tradition of Sophia in Gnostic Literature
     Alpharetta, GA: Scholars Press, 1987. 103 pp.

133. Gregory, Sadie
     A New Dimension in Old Testament Study
     San Francisco, CA: Guild for Psychological Studies
     Publishing House, 1980. 103 pp.

134. Handelman, Susan A.
     *The Slayers of Moses: The Emergence of Rabbinic Interpreta-
     tion in Modern Literary Theory*

Albany, NY: State University of New York Press, 1982.
267 pp.

135. Hareven, Shulamith
      The Miracle Hater (Exodus myth)
      Berkeley, CA: North Point, 1988. 96 pp.

136. Jeansonne, Sharon Pace
      The Women of Genesis: From Sarah to Potiphar's Wife
      Philadelphia, PA: Fortress Press, 1990. 160 pp.

137. Koontz, Gayle G., and W. Swartley, eds.
      Perspectives on Feminist Hermeneutics
      Elkhart, IN: Institute of Mennonite Studies, 1987. 128
      pp.

138. Laffey, Alice L.
      An Introduction to the Old Testament: A Feminist Perspective
      Philadelphia, PA: Fortress Press, 1988. 243 pp.

139. Mollenkott, Virginia Ramey
      The Divine Feminine: The Biblical Imagery of God as Female
      New York, NY: Crossroad Publishing, 1984. 128 pp.

140. Mollenkott, Virginia Ramey
      Godding: Human Responsibility and the Bible
      New York, NY: Crossroad Publishing, 1987. 176 pp.

141. Mollenkott, Virginia Ramey
      Women, Men and the Bible
      New York, NY: Crossroad Publishing, 1988. 160 pp.

142. Moltmann-Wendel, Elisabeth
      The Women Around Jesus
      New York, NY: Crossroad Publishing, 1982. 160 pp.

143. Niditch, Susan
      Chaos to Cosmos: Studies in Biblical Patterns of Creation
      Alpharetta, GA: Scholars Press, 1985. 114 pp.

144. Nunnally-Cox, Janice
     Foremothers: Women of the Bible
     New York, NY: Winston/Seabury, 1985. 167 pp.

145. Pagels, Elaine
     The Gnostic Gospels
     New York, NY: Random House, 1979. 214 pp.

146. Perkins, Pheme
     *Resurrection: New Testament Witness and Contemporary
     Reflection*
     Garden City, NY: Doubleday & Co., 1984. 504 pp.

147. Phipps, William E.
     *Genesis and Gender: Biblical Myths of Sexuality and Their
     Cultural Impact*
     New York, NY: Praeger, 1989. 141 pp.

148. Russell, Letty M., ed.
     Feminist Interpretation of the Bible
     Louisville, KY: Westminster/John Knox Press, 1985.
     168 pp.

149. Russell, Letty M., ed.
     Changing Contexts of Our Faith
     Philadelphia, PA: Fortress Press, 1985. 112 pp.

150. Sakenfeld, Katharine D.
     Faithfulness in Action: Loyalty in Biblical Perspective
     Philadelphia, PA: Fortress Press, 1985. 158 pp.

151. Schaberg, Jane
     *The Illegitimacy of Jesus: A Feminist Theological Interpreta-
     tion of the Infancy Narratives*
     New York, NY: Crossroad Publishing, 1990. 272 pp.

152. Schottroff, Luise
     *Let the Oppressed Go Free: Feminist Perspectives on the New
     Testament*

Louisville, KY: Westminster/John Knox Press, 1993.
192 pp.

153.   Shenk, Barbara K.
The God of Sarah, Rebekah and Rachel
Scottdale, PA: Herald Press, 1985. 132 pp.

154.   Sheres, Ita
Dinah's Rebellion: A Biblical Parable for Our Time
New York, NY: Crossroad Publishing, 1990. 176 pp.

155.   Tetlow, Elisabeth Meier
Women and Ministry in the New Testament: Called to Serve
Washington, DC: University Press of America, 1980.
164 pp.

156.   Teubal, Savina
Sarah the Priestess: The First Matriarch of Genesis
Athens, OH: Ohio University Press, 1985. 199 pp.

157.   Tolbert, Mary Ann, ed.
The Bible and Feminist Hermeneutics
Alpharetta, GA: Scholars Press, 1984. 126 pp.

158.   Trible, Phyllis
God and the Rhetoric of Sexuality
Philadelphia, PA: Fortress Press, 1978. 228 pp.

159.   Trible, Phyllis
*Texts of Terror: Literary—Feminist Readings of Biblical
Narratives*
Philadelphia, PA: Fortress Press, 1984. 128 pp.

160.   VanderKam, James C., ed.
"No One Spoke Ill of Her": Essays on Judith
Alpharetta, GA: Scholars Press, 1992. 106 pp.

161.   Weems, Renita J.
*Just a Sister Away: A Womanist Vision of Women's Relation-
ship to the Bible*
San Diego, CA: LuraMedia, 1988. 147 pp.

162. Wire, Antoinette Clark
      The Corinthian Women Prophets: A Reconstruction Through Paul's Rhetoric
      Philadelphia, PA: Fortress Press, 1990. 320 pp.

Femininist Historical Analysis

163. Allen, Prudence
      The Concept of Woman: The Aristotelian Revolution, 750 BC–AD 1250
      Toronto, Ont.: Eden Press, University of Toronto Press, 1985. 544 pp.

164. Anderson, Bonnie S., and Judith P. Zinsser
      A History of Their Own: From Prehistory to the Present, vol. 1
      New York, NY: Harper & Row, 1989. 594 pp.

165. Andolsen, Barbara H.
      "Daughters of Jefferson, Daughters of Bootblacks": Racism and American Feminism
      Macon, GA: Mercer University Press, 1986. 130 pp.

166. Armstrong, Karen
      The Gospel According to Woman: Christianity's Creation of the Sex War in the West
      Garden City, NY: Doubleday & Co., 1987. 323 pp.

167. Boulding, Elise
      The Underside of History: A View of Women Through Time, vol. 1
      Newbury Park, CA: Sage Publishers, 1992. 392 pp.

168. Boulding, Elise
      The Underside of History: A View of Women Through Time, vol. 2
      Newbury Park, CA: Sage Publishers, 1992. 372 pp.

169. Brown, Judith C.
      *Immodest Acts: The Life of a Lesbian Nun in Renaissance
         Italy*
      Oxford, U.K.: Oxford University Press, 1986. 222 pp.

170. Chance, Jane
      Women as Hero in Old English Literature
      Syracuse, NY: Syracuse University Press, 1985. 192 pp.

171. Cott, Nancy
      The Grounding of Modern Feminism
      New Haven, CT: Yale University Press, 1987. 372 pp.

172. Ehrenreich, Barbara, and Deirdre English
      Witches, Midwives, and Nurses: A History of Women Healers
      Old Westbury, NY: The Feminist Press, 1973. 48 pp.

173. Eisler, Riane
      The Chalice and the Blade: Our History, Our Future
      San Francisco, CA: Harper & Row, 1987. 288 pp.

174. Fiorenza, Elisabeth Schuessler
      *In Memory of Her: A Feminist Theological Reconstruction of
         Christian Origins*
      New York, NY: Crossroad Publishing, 1984. 357 pp.

175. Hayden, Dolores
      *The Grand Domestic Revolution: A History of Feminist
         Designs for American Homes*
      Cambridge, MA: M.I.T. Press, 1982. 367 pp.

176. Huber, Elaine C.
      *Women and the Authority of Inspiration: Two Prophetic
         Movements*
      Washington, DC: University Press of America, 1985.
         252 pp.

177. Hunter, Jane
      *The Gospel of Gentility: American Women Missionaries in
         China*
      New Haven, CT: Yale University Press, 1984. 318 pp.

178.   Kelley, Mary
       *Private Woman, Public Stage: Literary Domesticity in Nine-
       teenth-Century America*
       Oxford, U.K.: Oxford University Press, 1984. 409 pp.

179.   Kelly, Joan
       Women, History and Theory: Essays
       Chicago, IL: University of Chicago Press, 1984. 193 pp.

180.   Kleinbaum, Abby Wettan
       The War Against the Amazons
       New York, NY: McGraw-Hill Book Co., 1983. 240 pp.

181.   Kolodny, Annette
       *The Land Before Her: Fantasy and Experience of the Ameri-
       can Frontiers, 1630–1860*
       Chapel Hill, NC: University of North Carolina Press,
       1984. 293 pp.

182.   Labalme, Patricia, ed.
       Beyond Their Sex: Learned Women of the European Past
       New York, NY: New York University Press, 1980. 188 pp.

183.   Lerner, Gerda
       The Creation of Patriarchy
       Oxford, U.K.: Oxford University Press, 1986. 250 pp.

184.   Lerner, Gerda
       *The Creation of Feminist Consciousness: From the Middle
       Ages to 1870*
       Oxford, U.K.: Oxford University Press, 1993. 395 pp.

185.   Machaffie, Barbara, ed.
       Readings in Her Story: Women in Christian Tradition
       Philadelphia, PA: Fortress Press, 1992. 256 pp.

186.   Malmgreen, Gail, ed.
       Religion in the Lives of English Women, 1760–1930
       Bloomington, IN: Indiana University Press, 1986. 295
       pp.

187. Mayeski, Marie Anne
Women: Models of Liberation
Kansas City, MO: Sheed & Ward, 1989. 256 pp.

188. Miles, Margaret R.
Image as Insight: Visual Understanding in Western Christianity and Secular Culture
Boston, MA: Beacon Press, 1985. 304 pp.

189. Miles, Margaret R.
Carnal Knowing: Female Nakedness and Religious Meaning in the Christian West
New York, NY: Vintage Books, 1991. 254 pp.

190. Nicholson, Linda
Gender and History: The Limits of Social Theory in the Age of the Family
New York, NY: Columbia University Press, 1986. 238 pp.

191. Pagels, Elaine
Adam, Eve, and the Serpent
New York, NY: Random House, 1988. 189 pp.

192. Pantel, Pauline Schmitt, ed.
A History of Women in the West, vol. 1: From Ancient Goddesses to Christian Saints
Cambridge, MA: Harvard University Press, 1992. 642 pp.

193. Phillips, John A.
Eve: The History of an Idea
San Francisco, CA: Harper & Row, 1983. 201 pp.

194. Rader, Rosemary
Breaking Boundaries: Male/Female Friendships in Early Church Communities
Ramsey, NJ: Paulist Press, 1983. 117 pp.

195. Rosenberg, Rosalind
      Beyond Separate Spheres: Intellectual Roots of Modern Feminism
      New Haven, CT: Yale University Press, 1982. 289 pp.

196. Ruether, Rosemary Radford, and Rosemary S. Keller, eds.
      Women and Religion in America, vol. 1: The Nineteenth Century
      San Francisco, CA: Harper & Row, 1982. 353 pp.

197. Ruether, Rosemary Radford, and Rosemary S. Keller, eds.
      Women and Religion in America, vol. 2: The Colonial and Revolutionary Periods
      San Francisco, CA: Harper & Row, 1983. 464 pp.

198. Ruether, Rosemary Radford, and Rosemary S. Keller, eds.
      Women and Religion in America, vol. 3: The Twentieth Century, 1900–1968
      San Francisco, CA: Harper & Row, 1986. 434 pp.

199. Schmidt, Alvin J.
      Veiled and Silenced: How Culture Shaped Sexist Theology
      Macon, GA: Mercer University Press, 1990. 238 pp.

200. Solomon, Dorothy
      In My Father's House
      New York, NY: Franklin Watts, 1985. 312 pp.

201. Torjessen, Karen Jo
      When Women Were Priests: Women's Leadership in the Early Church and the Scandal of Their Subordination in Rise of Early Christianity
      San Francisco, CA: Harper & Row, 1993. 278 pp.

202. Warner, Marina
      Joan of Arc: The Image of Female Heroism
      New York, NY: Random House, 1982. 349 pp.

203.   Warner, Marina
       *Alone of All Her Sex: The Myth and the Cult of the Virgin
          Mary*
       New York, NY: Random House, 1983. 419 pp.

204.   Warner, Marina
       Monuments and Maidens: The Allegory of the Female Form
       New York, NY: Atheneum, 1985. 417 pp.

2. CLASSICS IN SPIRITUALITY AND THE HISTORICAL APPROACH TO THE PREMODERN PERIOD

The scope of this chapter indicates my recognition of continuity in women's expression of spirituality through Western history. I have divided the material into three sections to distinguish texts of particular historical figures from analyses of women's lives in premodern times. Under the heading of "Classics" I have assembled books that provide the reader with "holy women," that is, women who have written of extraordinary religious experience and have, in some cases, been recognized by religious structures as gifted religious persons (for example, St. Teresa of Avila). In recent years, the contributions of women less known to the lay reader have come to general attention, notably Julian of Norwich and Hildegard of Bingen. I have also located modern holy women in this section. These women may not figure as feminist thinkers, but they clearly advance women's presence in the discussion of spirituality. I refer, for example, to Dorothy Day and Simone Weil, whose lives are exemplary (if not difficult to follow) and whose writings deepen our grasp of spiritual endeavor.

Women's ordinary activity has been more difficult to document; however, recent historical work by and about women has enlarged the picture of woman's place in premodern culture. Many of the titles in this section invite the reader to enter the routine experience of women who lived centuries ago. They are not presented through a feminist lens which provides a specific critique of male/female roles, but these writings enable the reader to appreciate women's activities in spite of inequity in the social and cultural structures of the time.

Classic Voices

205. Allchin, A. M.
      *Songs to Her God: Spirituality of Ann Griffiths (eighteenth-
      century hymns)*
      Cambridge, MA: Cowley Publishing, 1987. 132 pp.

206. Brock, Sebastian, and Susan Harvey, eds. and trans.
      *Holy Women of the Syrian Orient (15 hagiographies, 5th–7th
      centuries A.D.)*
      Berkeley, CA: University of California Press, 1987. 197
      pp.

207. Campbell, Karen J., ed.
      *German Mystical Writings: Hildegard of Bingen, Meister
      Eckhart, Jacob Boehme and Others*
      New York, NY: Crossroad/Continuum, 1991. 324 pp.

208. Catherine of Genoa, trans. Serge Hughes
      *Catherine of Genoa: Purgation and Purgatory—The Spiri-
      tual Dialogue*
      Ramsey, NJ: Paulist Press, 1979. 163 pp.

209. Catherine of Siena, trans. Suzanne Noffke
      The Dialogue
      Ramsey, NJ: Paulist Press, 1980. 398 pp.

210. Catherine of Siena, trans. Suzanne Noffke
      The Prayers of Catherine of Siena
      Ramsey, NJ: Paulist Press, 1983. 257 pp.

211. Celeste, Marie
      The Intimate Friendships of Elizabeth Ann Bayley Seton
      Dearborn, MI: Alba, 1989. 250 pp.

212. Clare of Assisi, ed. and trans. Regis Armstrong
      Early Documents
      Ramsey, NJ: Paulist Press, 1988. 345 pp.

213. Cooper, Austin, ed.
Julian of Norwich: Reflections on Selected Texts
Mystic, CT: Twenty-Third Publications, 1988. 144 pp.

214. Curtayne, Alice
Saint Catherine of Siena
Rockford, IL: Tan Books & Publishers, 1980. 268 pp.

215. Dreyer, Elizabeth
Passionate Women: Two Medieval Mystics (Hildegard and Hadewijch)
Ramsey, NJ: Paulist Press, 1989. 88 pp.

216. Egeria, trans. G. Gingras
Egeria: Diary of a Pilgrimage
New York, NY: Newman Press, 1970. 287 pp.

217. Flanagan, Sabina
Hildegard of Bingen, 1098–1179: A Visionary Life
New York, NY: Routledge, 1989. 224 pp.

218. Francis and Clare, ed. Regis Armstrong and Ignatius C. Brady
Francis and Clare: The Complete Works
Ramsey, NJ: Paulist Press, 1982. 256 pp.

219. Franklin, James C.
Mystical Transformation: The Imagery of Liquids in the Work of Mechtilde von Magdeburg
Cranbury, NJ: Fairleigh Dickinson University Press, 1978. 192 pp.

220. Freemantle, Anne
The Protestant Mystics
New York, NY: New American Library, 1965. 317 pp.

221. Furlong, Monica
Therese of Lisieux
New York, NY: Pantheon Books, 1987. 144 pp.

222.   Gertrude the Great, trans. G. Lewis and J. Lewis
       Spiritual Exercises
       Kalamazoo, MI: Cistercian, 1989. 165 pp.

223.   Green, Deidre
       *Gold in the Crucible: Teresa of Avila and the Western
          Mystical Tradition*
       Rockport, MA: Element Books, 1989. 215 pp.

224.   Hadewijch, trans. Mother Columba Hart
       Hadewijch: The Complete Works
       Ramsey, NJ: Paulist Press, 1980. 412 pp.

225.   Harley, Marta P., ed. and trans.
       *A Revelation of Purgatory by Unknown Woman Fifteenth-
          Century Visionary*
       Lewiston, NY: The Edwin Mellen Press, 1985. 149 pp.

226.   Hildegard of Bingen
       Illuminations
       Santa Fe, NM: Bear & Co., 1985. 111 pp.

227.   Hildegard of Bingen
       *Symphonia: A Critical Edition of the Symphony of Harmony
          of Celestial Revelation*
       Ithaca, NY: Cornell University Press, 1988. 330 pp.

228.   Hildegard of Bingen, trans. Bruce Hozeski
       Scivas/Know the Ways
       Santa Fe, NM: Bear & Co., 1986. 310 pp.

229.   Jantzen, Grace
       Julian of Norwich: Mystic and Theologian
       Ramsey, NJ: Paulist Press, 1988. 230 pp.

230.   Julian of Norwich
       Enfolded in Love: Daily Readings
       London, U.K.: Darton, Longman, & Todd, 1980. 72
          pp.

231. Julian of Norwich, trans. Edmond Colledge and James
     Walsh
     Showings
     Ramsey, NJ: Paulist Press, 1978. 369 pp.

232. Llewelyn, Robert, ed.
     Julian: Woman of Our Day
     Mystic, CT: Twenty-Third Publications, 1988. 160 pp.

233. Maria, Sor of Santo Domingo, trans. Mary Giles
     *The Book of Prayer of Sor Maria of Santo Domingo: A Study
     and Translation*
     Albany, NY: State University of New York Press, 1990.
     192 pp.

234. Marie of the Incarnation, ed. and trans. I. Mahoney
     *Selected Writings: The Balance Between Contemplation and
     Action*
     Ramsey, NJ: Paulist Press, 1989. 285 pp.

235. Mechtilde of Magdeburg
     The Revelations
     White Plains, NY: Longman, 1953. 263 pp.

236. Mechtilde of Magdeburg, Beatrice of Nazareth, and
     Hadewijch of Brabant
     Beguine Spirituality
     New York, NY: Crossroad/Continuum, 1990. 144 pp.

237. Newman, Barbara
     Sister of Wisdom: St. Hildegard's Theology of the Feminine
     Berkeley, CA: University of California Press, 1987. 289
     pp.

238. Nuth, Joan M.
     Wisdom's Daughter: The Theology of Julian of Norwich
     New York, NY: Crossroad/Continuum, 1991. 256 pp.

239. Pelphrey, Brian
     Christ Our Mother: Julian of Norwich
     Wilmington, DE: Michael Glazier, 1990. 271 pp.

240. Petroff, Elizabeth A., ed.
      Medieval Women's Visionary Literature
      Oxford, U.K.: Oxford University Press, 1986. 416 pp.

241. Porete, Marguerite
      *A Mirror for Simple Souls: The Mystical Works of Marguerite
      Porete*
      New York, NY: Crossroad/Continuum, 1990. 160 pp.

242. Savage, Anne, and Nicholas Watson, trans.
      Anchoritic Spirituality: Ancrene Wisse and Associated Works
      Ramsey, NJ: Paulist Press, 1991. 487 pp.

243. Seraphim, Mary
      Clare: Her Light and Her Song
      Chicago, IL.: Franciscan Herald Press, 1984. 44 pp.

244. Seton, Elizabeth, ed. E. M. Kelly and A. Melville
      Elizabeth Seton: Selected Writings
      Ramsey, NJ: Paulist Press, 1987. 377 pp.

245. Tavard, George
      Juana Ines de la Cruz and the Theology of Beauty
      Notre Dame, IN: Notre Dame University Press, 1991.
      224 pp.

246. Teresa of Avila, ed. E. Allison Peers
      The Way of Perfection
      Garden City, NJ: Image Books, Doubleday & Co.,
      1964. 280 pp.

247. Teresa of Avila, trans. John Venard, O.C.D.
      The Way of Perfection
      Oak Park, IL: Meyer-Stone, 1989. 155 pp.

248. Teresa of Avila, trans. John Venard, O.C.D.
      The Interior Castle
      Oak Park, IL: Meyer-Stone, 1989. 121 pp.

249.   Teresa of Avila, trans. Kieran Kavanaugh
       Teresa of Avila: Interior Castle
       Ramsey, NJ: Paulist Press, 1979. 235 pp.

250.   Uhlein, Gabriele, ed.
       Meditations with Hildegard of Bingen
       Santa Fe, NM: Bear & Co., 1982. 128 pp.

251.   Weber, Alison
       Teresa of Avila and the Rhetoric of Femininity
       Oxford, U.K.: Oxford University Press, 1990. 206 pp.

252.   Whitson, Robley Edward, ed.
       Shakers: Two Centuries of Spiritual Reflection
       Ramsey, NJ: Paulist Press, 1983. 370 pp.

253.   Wilson, Katharina, ed.
       The Plays of Hrotsvit of Gandersheim
       New York, NY: Garland Publications, 1989. 198 pp.

254.   Woodruff, Sue
       Meditations with Mechtilde of Magdeburg
       Santa Fe, NM: Bear & Co., 1982. 132 pp.

Modern Expressions

255.   Addams, Jane
       Newer Ideals of Peace
       1907. Reprint.
       Englewood, NJ: Ozer, 1972. 243 pp.

256.   Addams, Jane
       Peace and Bread in Time of War
       1922. Reprint.
       Englewood, NJ: Ozer, 1972. 269 pp.

257. Addams, Jane
      Twenty Years at Hull House
      1910. Reprint.
      Urbana, IL: University of Illinois Press, 1989. 350
        pp.

258. Addams, Jane
      The Spirit of Youth and the City Streets
      1916. Reprint.
      Urbana, IL: University of Illinois Press, 1989. 192 pp.

259. Addams, Jane, ed. Christopher Lash
      Social Thoughts of Jane Addams
      New York, NY: Irvington Books, 1982. 300 pp.

260. Bell, Richard H., ed.
      Simone Weil's Philosophy of Culture
      Cambridge, U.K.: Cambridge University Press, 1993.
        353 pp.

261. Brittain, Vera
      Testament of Youth
      New York, NY: Penguin Books, 1989. 672 pp.

262. David-Neel, Alexandra
      Magic and Mystery in Tibet
      Ithaca, NY: Snow Lion Publishers, 1991. 321 pp.

263. Day, Dorothy
      From Union Square to Rome
      Salem, NH: Ayer Company Publications, 1938. 173 pp.

264. Day, Dorothy
      From Union Square to Rome
      Salem, NH: Ayer Company Publications, 1938. 173 pp.

265. Day, Dorothy
      Therese: The Life of Therese of Lisieux
      Springfield, IL: Templegate, 1985. 178 pp.

266. Day, Dorothy, ed. Robert Ellsberg
      By Little and by Little: The Selected Writings
      New York, NY: Alfred A. Knopf, 1983. 371 pp.

267. Doherty, Catherine de Hueck
      *Poustinia: Christian Spirituality of the East for Western
      Man*
      Notre Dame, IN: Ave Maria Press, 1975. 216 pp.

268. Doherty, Catherine de Hueck
      *Sobornost: Eastern Unity of Mind and Heart for Western
      Man*
      Notre Dame, IN: Ave Maria Press, 1977. 110 pp.

269. Doherty, Catherine de Hueck
      Strannick: The Call to Pilgrimage for Western Man
      Notre Dame, IN: Ave Maria Press, 1978. 84 pp.

270. Doherty, Catherine de Hueck
      Molchanie: The Silence of God
      New York, NY: Crossroad Publishing, 1982. 100 pp.

271. Doherty, Catherine de Hueck
      Urodivoi: Fools for God
      New York, NY: Crossroad Publishing, 1983. 94 pp.

272. Doherty, Catherine de Hueck
      Journey Inward: Conversations, 1960 to the Present
      Dearborn, MI: Alba, 1984. 116 pp.

273. Fuller, Margaret
      Woman in the Nineteenth Century
      New York, NY: W. W. Norton, 1971. 212 pp.

274. Green, Dana, ed.
      *Suffrage and Religious Principles: Speeches and Writings of
      Olympia Brown*
      Metuchen, NJ: Scarecrow Press, 1983. 192 pp.

275.   Haughton, Rosemary
        *Tales from Eternity: The World of Faerie and the Spiritual
        Search*
        London, U.K.: Allen & Unwin, 1973. 191 pp.

276.   Haughton, Rosemary
        *Feminine Spirituality: Reflections on the Mysteries of the
        Rosary*
        Ramsey, NJ: Paulist Press, 1976. 93 pp.

277.   Haughton, Rosemary
        The Passionate God
        Ramsey, NJ: Paulist Press, 1981. 344 pp.

278.   Haughton, Rosemary
        Song in a Strange Land
        Springfield, IL: Templegate, 1990. 180 pp.

279.   Hurston, Zora Neale
        Tell My Horse
        Berkeley, CA: Turtle Island Press, 1981. 301 pp.

280.   Juana, Sor, trans. Alan Trueblood
        A Sor Juana Anthology
        Cambridge, MA: Harvard University Press, 1988. 560
        pp.

281.   Koeppel, Josephine
        Edith Stein
        Wilmington, DE: Michael Glazier, 1990. 196 pp.

282.   Little, J. P.
        Simone Weil: Waiting on Truth
        New York, NY: Berg, 1988. 170 pp.

283.   Nevin, Thomas R.
        Simone Weil: Portrait of a Self-Exiled Jew
        Chapel Hill, NC: University of North Carolina Press,
        1991. 480 pp.

284. O'Connor, June
      The Moral Vision of Dorothy Day: A Feminist Perspective
      New York, NY: Crossroad Publishing, 1991. 210 pp.

285. Paz, Octavio
      Sor Juana; or, The Traps of Faith
      Cambridge, MA: Harvard University Press, 1988. 560
      pp.

286. Russell, Dora
      The Religion of the Machine Age
      Boston, MA: Routledge & Kegan Paul, 1985. 232 pp.

287. Sayers, Dorothy L.
      The Mind of the Maker
      San Francisco, CA: Harper & Row, 1956. 229 pp.

288. Sayers, Dorothy L.
      Are Women Human?
      Grand Rapids, MI: William B. Eerdmans Publishing
      Co., 1971. 47 pp.

289. Sayers, Dorothy, ed. Ann Loades
      Spritual Writings
      Cambridge, MA: Cowley Publishing, 1993. 184 pp.

290. Sayers, Dorothy, ed. Rosamond Kent Sprague
      A Matter of Eternity
      Grand Rapids, MI: William B. Eerdmans Publishing
      Co., 1973. 139 pp.

291. Springsted, Eric
      Simone Weil and the Suffering of Love
      Cambridge, MA: Cowley Publishing, 1986. 140 pp.

292. Stanton, Elizabeth Cady
      The Woman's Bible (originally published 1895–98)
      Boston, MA: Northeastern University Press, 1993. 217
      pp.

293. Stein, Edith, ed. and trans. Hilda Graef
     The Scholar and the Cross: The Life and Works of Edith Stein
     New York, NY: Newman Press, 1955. 234 pp.

294. Stein, Edith, trans. Freda Oben, ed. L. Gelber and R.
     Leuven
     Essays on Woman
     Washington, DC: Institute of Carmelite Studies, 1987.
     290 pp.

295. Stein, Edith, trans. J. Koppel, ed. L. Gelber and R.
     Leuven
     Life in a Jewish Family: Her Unfinished Autobiography
     Washington, DC: Institute of Carmelite Studies, 1986.
     548 pp.

296. Teresa, Mother of Calcutta and Kathryn Spink
     I Need Souls Like You: Sharing in the Work of Charity
     San Francisco, CA: Harper & Row, 1984. 96 pp.

297. Underhill, Evelyn
     An Anthology of the Love of God
     Wilton, CT: Morehouse, 1984. 220 pp.

298. Underhill, Evelyn
     The House of the Soul and Concerning the Inner Life
     New York, NY: Winston/Seabury, 1984. 119 pp.

299. Underhill, Evelyn
     The Spiritual Life
     Wilton, CT: Morehouse, 1984. 127 pp.

300. Underhill, Evelyn
     The Mystics of the Church
     Wilton, CT: Morehouse, 1988. 259 pp.

301. Underhill, Evelyn
     Worship
     New York, NY: Crossroad Publishing, 1989. 350 pp.

302. Underhill, Evelyn
      The School of Charity: Meditations on the Christian Creed
      Wilton, CT: Morehouse, 1990. 124 pp.

303. Underhill, Evelyn
      The Mystery of Sacrifice
      Wilton, CT: Morehouse, 1990. 96 pp.

304. Underhill, Evelyn, ed. Dana Greene
      Modern Guide to the Ancient Quest for the Holy
      Albany, NY: State University of New York Press, 1989.
         220 pp.

305. Underhill, Evelyn, ed. Grace A. Brame
      The Ways of the Spirit
      New York, NY: Crossroad/Continuum, 1990. 252 pp.

306. Weil, Simone, ed. and trans. D. T. McFarland and W.
         V. Van Ness
      Formative Writings, 1929–1941
      Amherst, MA: University of Massachusetts Press, 1988.
         306 pp.

307. Weil, Simone, ed. George Panichas
      The Simone Weil Reader
      New York, NY: David McKay Company, 1977. 529 pp.

308. Weil, Simone, ed. Sian Miles
      Simone Weil: An Anthology
      London, U.K.: Virago Press, 1986. 256 pp.

309. Weil, Simone, trans. Arthur F. Wills
      *The Need for Roots: Prelude to a Declaration of Duties
         Towards Mankind*
      New York, NY: ARK Publishing, Routledge, Chapman
         & Hall, 1987. 288 pp.

310. Weil, Simone, trans. Arthur Wills and John Petrie
      Oppression and Liberty
      Amherst, MA: University of Massachusetts Press, 1973.
         216 pp.

311.   Weil, Simone, trans. Arthur Wills
       Gravity and Grace
       New York, NY: ARK Publishing, Routledge, Chapman
          & Hall, 1988. 200 pp.

312.   Weil, Simone, trans. Hugh Price
       Lectures on Philosophy
       Cambridge, U.K.: Cambridge University Press, 1978.
          232 pp.

313.   Weil, Simone, trans. Richard Rees
       On Science, Necessity and the Core of God
       Oxford, U.K.: Oxford University Press, 1968. 201 pp.

314.   Weil, Simone, trans. Richard Rees
       First and Last Notebooks
       Oxford, U.K.: Oxford University Press, 1970. 368 pp.

315.   White, George Abbott, ed.
       Simone Weil: Interpretations of a Life
       Amherst, MA: University of Massachusetts Press, 1981.
          224 pp.

316.   Wilson-Kastner, Patricia, and R. Rader, eds.
       A Lost Tradition: Women Writers of the Early Church
       Washington, DC: University Press of America, 1981.
          180 pp.

317.   Winch, Peter
       Simone Weil: "The Just Balance"
       Cambridge, U.K.: Cambridge University Press, 1989.
          234 pp.

Historical Sources

318.   Arenal, Electra, and Stacey Schlau, trans. A Powell
       Untold Sisters: Hispanic Nuns in Their Own Works

Albuquerque, NM: University of New Mexico Press, 1989. 450 pp.

319. Atkinson, Clarissa
Mystic and Pilgrim: The "Book" and the World of Margery Kempe
Ithaca, NY: Cornell University Press, 1983. 241 pp.

320. Atkinson, Clarissa W.
The Oldest Vocation: Christian Motherhood in the Middle Ages
Ithaca, NY: Cornell University Press, 1991. 272 pp.

321. Barstow, Anne
Joan of Arc: Heretic, Mystic, Shaman
Lewiston, NY: The Edwin Mellen Press, 1985. 167 pp.

322. Berger, Pamela
The Goddess Obscured: Transformation of the Grain Protectress from Goddess to Saint
Boston, MA: Beacon Press, 1985. 173 pp.

323. Bilinkoff, Jodi
The Avila of Saint Teresa: Religious Reform in a Sixteenth-Century City
Ithaca, NY: Cornell University Press, 1990. 218 pp.

324. Blumenfeld-Kosinki, Renate, and Timea Szell, eds.
Images of Sainthood in Medieval Europe
Ithaca, NY: Cornell University Press, 1991. 320 pp.

325. Bradley, Ritamary
Julian's Way: A Practical Commentary on Jualian of Norwich
New York, NY: HarperCollins, 1992. 231 pp.

326. Brunn, Emily Zum, and Georgette Epiney-Burgard
Women Mystics in Medieval Europe
New York, NY: Paragon, 1989. 233 pp.

327. Buckley, Joruna Jacobsen
Female Fault and Fulfillment in Gnosticism
Chapel Hill, NC: University of North Carolina Press,
1986. 220 pp.

328. Bynum, Caroline Walker
*Jesus as Mother: Studies in the Spirituality of the High
Middle Ages*
Berkeley, CA: University of California Press, 1982. 279
pp.

329. Bynum, Caroline Walker
*Holy Feast and Holy Fast: The Religious Significance of Food
to Medieval Women*
Berkeley, CA: University of California Press, 1987. 444
pp.

330. Bynum, Caroline Walker
*Fragmentation and Redemption: Essays on Gender and the
Human Body in Medieval Religion*
New York, NY: Zone Books, 1990. 384 pp.

331. Carney, Margaret
*The First Franciscan Woman: Clare of Assisi and Her Form
of Life*
Quincy, IL: Franciscan Press, 1993. 261 pp.

332. Cherewatuk, Karen, and Ulrike Wiethaus, eds.
Dear Sisters: Medieval Women and the Epistolary Genre
Philadelphia, PA: University of Pennsylvania Press,
1993. 224 pp.

333. Clark, Elizabeth A.
*Ascetic Piety and Women's Faith: Essays in Late Ancient
Christianity*
Lewiston, NY: The Edwin Mellen Press, 1986. 427 pp.

334. Clayton, Mary
The Cult of the Virgin Mary in Anglo-Saxon England
Cambridge, U.K.: Cambridge University Press, 1990.
300 pp.

335. Collis, Louise
The Life and Times of Margery Kempe
San Francisco, CA: Harper & Row, 1982. 269 pp.

336. Cox, Patricia
Biography in Late Antiquity: The Quest for the Holy Man
Berkeley, CA: University of California Press, 1983. 166 pp.

337. Daichman, Graciela
Wayward Nuns in Medieval Literature
Syracuse, NY: Syracuse University Press, 1987. 223 pp.

338. Day, Dorothy
Loaves and Fishes: The Story of the Catholic Worker Movement
New York, NY: Harper & Row, 1983. 240 pp.

339. Dillard, Heath
Daughters of the Covenant: Women in Castilian Town Society, 1100–1300
Cambridge, U.K.: Cambridge University Press, 1985. 272 pp.

340. Dronke, Peter
Women Writers of the Middle Ages: A Critical Study of Texts
Cambridge, U.K.: Cambridge University Press, 1984. 338 pp.

341. Eckenstein, Lina
Women Under Monasticism: Chapters on Saint-Lore and Convent Life (500–1500)
New York, NY: Russell, 1963. 496 pp.

342. Elkins, Sharon K.
Holy Women of Twelfth-Century England
Chapel Hill, NC: University of North Carolina Press, 1988. 268 pp.

343. Elliott, Dyan
    *Spiritual Marriage: Sexual Abstinence in the Medieval
        Wedlock*
    Princeton, NJ: Princeton University Press, 1993. 328
    pp.

344. Erler, Mary, and MaryAnne Kowaleski, eds.
    Women and Power in the Middle Ages
    Athens, GA: University of Georgia Press, 1988. 277 pp.

345. Flinders, Carol Lee
    Enduring Grace: Living Portraits of Seven Women Mystics
    San Francisco, CA: Harper & Row, 1993. 256 pp.

346. Gold, Penny Shine
    *The Lady and the Virgin: Image, Attitude and Experience in
        Twelfth-Century France*
    Chicago, IL: University of Chicago Press, 1985. 182 pp.

347. Grassi, Joseph A., and Carolyn M. Grassi
    Mary Magdalene and the Women in Jesus' Life
    Kansas City, MO: Sheed & Ward, 1986. 158 pp.

348. Gross, Frances, with Toni Gross
    *The Making of a Mystic: Seasons in the Life of Teresa of
        Avila*
    Albany, NY: State University of New York Press, 1993.
    285 pp.

349. Gross, Susan H., and Marjorie W. Bingham
    Women in Medieval-Renaissance Europe
    St. Louis Park, MN: Glenhurst Publishers, 1984. 198
    pp.

350. Hamburger, Jeffrey
    *The Rothschild Canticles: Art and Mysticism in Flanders
        and the Rhineland Circa 1300* (religious women)
    New Haven, CT: Yale University Press, 1990. 324 pp.

351. Haskins, Susan
      Mary Magdalen: Myth and Metaphor
      New York, NY: Harcourt Brace Jovanovich, 1993. 518
      pp.

352. Hickey, Anne Ewing
      Women of the Roman Aristocracy as Christian Monastics
      Ann Arbor, MI: UMI Research Press, 1986. 159 pp.

353. Hughes, Kathleen, and Ann Hamlin
      The Modern Traveler to the Early Irish Church
      Somers, CT: Seabury Press, 1981. 131 pp.

354. Johnson, Penelope D.
      *Equal in Monastic Profession: Religious Women in Medieval
      France*
      Chicago, IL: University of Chicago Press, 1990. 312 pp.

355. King, Karen L., ed.
      Images of the Feminine in Gnosticism
      Minneapolis, MN: Fortress/Augsburg, 1988. 455 pp.

356. Kirscher, Julius, and Suzanne Wempel, eds.
      Women of the Medieval World
      Oxford, U.K.: Oxford University Press, 1987. 390 pp.

357. Knowles, David
      The English Mystical Tradition
      New York, NY: Harper & Row, 1961. 197 pp.

358. Kuryluk, Ewa
      *Veronica and her Cloth: History, Symbolism, and Structure of
      a 'True' Image*
      Cambridge, MA: Blackwell, 1991. 256 pp.

359. Labarge, Margaret Wade
      A Small Sound of the Trumpet: Women in Medieval Life
      Boston, MA: Beacon Press, 1986. 271 pp.

360.   Larner, Christine
        Witchcraft and Religion: The Politics of Popular Belief
        Cambridge, MA: Blackwell, 1984. 172 pp.

361.   Levin, Carole, and Jeanie Watson, eds.
        Ambiguous Realities: Women in the Middle Ages and Renais-
        sance
        Detroit, MI: Wayne State University Press, 1987. 263
        pp.

362.   Lucas, Angela
        Women in the Middle Ages: Religion, Marriage, and Letters
        New York, NY: St. Martin's Press, 1983. 214 pp.

363.   Machaffie, Barbara J.
        Her Story: Women in Christian Tradition
        Philadelphia, PA: Fortress Press, 1986. 183 pp.

364.   Mack Phyllis
        Visionary Women: Ecstatic Prophecy in Seventeenth-Century
        England
        Berkeley, CA: University of California Press, 1992. 433
        pp.

365.   Marshall, Sherrin, ed.
        Women in Reformation and Counter-Reformation Europe:
        Private and Public Worlds
        Bloomington, IN: Indiana University Press, 1989. 224
        pp.

366.   Martimont, Georges Aime, ed. K. D. Whitehead
        Deaconesses: An Historical Study
        San Francisco, CA: Ignatius Press, 1986. 268 pp.

367.   Matter, E. Ann
        The Voice of My Beloved: The Song of Songs in Western
        Medieval Christianity
        Philadelphia, PA: University of Pennsylvania Press,
        1990. 264 pp.

368. McNamara, Jo Ann
      *A New Song: Celibate Women in the First Three Christian
          Centuries*
      New York, NY: Haworth Press, 1983. 154 pp.

369. McNamara, Jo Ann, and John Hallborg, with E. G.
          Whatley, eds.
      Sainted Women of the Dark Ages
      Durham, NC: Duke University Press, 1992. 369 pp.

370. Miles, Margaret R.
      Fullness of Life
      Louisville, KY: Westminster/John Knox Press, 1981.
          186 pp.

371. Monson, Craig A., ed.
      *The Crannied Wall: Women, Religion, and the Arts in Early
          Modern Europe*
      Ann Arbor, MI: University of Michigan Press, 1992.
          300 pp.

372. Mycoff, David, ed. and trans.
      *The Life of Saint Mary Magdeline and Her Sister Martha: A
          Medieval Biography*
      Kalamazoo, MI: Cistercian, 1989. 166 pp.

373. Nichols, John, and Lillian T. Shank, eds.
      Peace Weavers: Medieval Religious Women
      Kalamazoo, MI: Cistercian, 1987. 396 pp.

374. Nichols, John, and Lillian T. Shank, eds.
      Distant Echoes: Medieval Religious Women
      Kalamazoo, MI: Cistercian, 1984. 299 pp.

375. Paden, William, ed.
      *The Voice of the Trobairitz: Perspectives on the Women
          Troubadours*
      Philadelphia, PA: University of Pennsylvania Press,
          1989. 264 pp.

376. Rengers, Christopher
      Mary of the Americas: Our Lady of Guadalupe
      Dearborn, MI: Alba, 1990. 154 pp.

376a. Roper, Lyndal
       *The Holy Household: Women and Morals in Reformation
          Augsburg*
       Oxford, U.K.: Oxford University Press, 1989. 300 pp.

377. Rose, Mary Beth, ed.
      Women in the Middle Ages and the Renaissance
      Syracuse, NY: Syracuse University Press, 1986. 288 pp.

378. Salisbury, Joyce E.
      Church Fathers, Independent Virgins (seven women saints)
      New York, NY: Verso/Cond, 1991. 176 pp.

379. Shahar, Shulamith, trans. Chaya Galan
      The Fourth Estate: A History of Women in the Middle Ages
      New York, NY: Methuen, 1984. 351 pp.

380. Smith, Margaret
      The Way of the Mystics
      London, U.K.: Sheldon Press, 1976. 276 pp.

381. Surtz, Ronald E.
      *The Guitar of God: Gender, Power and Authority in the
          Visionary World of Mother Juana de la Cruz (1481–1534)*
      Philadelphia, PA: University of Pennsylvania Press,
          1990. 192 pp.

382. Thurston, Bonnie Bowman
      The Widows: A Woman's Ministry in the Early Church
      Philadelphia, PA: Fortress Press, 1989. 144 pp.

383. Waithe, Mary Ellen, ed.
      *The History of Women Philosophers, vol. 2: Renaissance and
          Enlightenment, A.D. 500–1600*
      Norwell, MA: Kluwer Academic Books, 1989. 349 pp.

384. Warnicke, Retha M.
     Women of the English Renaissance and Reformation
     Westport, CT: Greenwood Press, 1983. 228 pp.

385. Willard, Charity Cannon
     Christine de Pizan: Her Life and Works
     New York, NY: Persea Books, 1985. 266 pp.

386. Yates, Gale G., ed.
     Harriet Martineau on Women
     New Brunswick, NJ: Rutgers University Press, 1985.
        183 pp.

3. CROSS-CULTURAL SPIRITUALITY

In a genuine sense, this chapter offers a bibliography within the bibliography, taking up the question of women's multicultural expressions of spirituality. The authors and titles here belong together as a statement about an emerging global community of women that recognizes diversity in experience. Thirteen subsections serve to organize the titles associated with cross-cultural spirituality, suggesting a parallel with the thirteen chapters of the complete bibliography.

In the introductory section, general publications are enumerated, including anthologies, encyclopedias, and broadly conceived statements regarding the spiritual dimension. In large measure, these volumes inform the reader about what spirituality is and how spirituality infuses women's lives. There are many voices in this assembly of writers and, remarkably, they share in mapping a terrain. This map includes collected essays in world religions and comparative analyses from feminist perspectives.

The arrangement of the other twelve categories refers to large cultural spheres (for example, antiquity, Asian women) and religious traditions. Buddhism, Hinduism, Islam and Judaism offer classificatory headings; Native American and African-American are distinguished from other materials, as are titles associated with primal (that is, preliterate or nonhistoric) and African women's spirituality. In many ways, this section of the bibliography demonstrates the vulnerability of arrangements by cultural label, separating the religious worlds of women by categories that divide. But the distinctiveness of women's experiences deserves to be raised, and I have chosen to classify publications with an eye to this reality.

General

387. Anderson, Sherry Ruth, and Patricia Hopkins
      The Feminine Face of God: The Unfolding of the Sacred in Women
      New York, NY: Bantam Books, 1991. 253 pp.

388. Anzaldua, Gloria, ed.
      Making Face, Making Soul: Haciendo Caras—Creative and Critical Perspectives by Women of Color
      San Francisco, CA: Aunt Lute Press, 1990. 402 pp.

389. Bancroft, Anne
      Weavers of Wisdom: Women Mystics of the Twentieth Century
      Harmondsworth, U.K.: Penguin, 1990. 192 pp.

390. Borrowdale, Anne
      Distorted Images: Misunderstandings Between Men and Women
      Louisville, KY: Westminster/John Knox Press, 1991. 160 pp.

391. Bozarth, Alla Renee
      Love's Prism: Reflections from the Heart of a Woman
      Kansas City, MO: Sheed & Ward, 1987. 76 pp.

392. Brereton, Virginia L.
      From Sin to Salvation: Stories of Women's Conversions, 1800 to the Present
      Bloomington, IN: Indiana University Press, 1991. 153 pp.

393. Bynum, Caroline Walker, S. Harrell, and P. Richman, eds.
      Gender and Religion: On the Complexity of Symbols
      Boston, MA: Beacon Press, 1986. 326 pp.

394. Byrne, Lavinia
      Women Before God: Our Own Spirituality

Mystic, CT: Twenty-Third Publications, 1988. 144 pp.

395. Cady, Susan, Marian Ronan, and Hal Taussig
Sophia: The Future of Feminist Spirituality
Boston, MA: Beacon Press, 1986. 120 pp.

396. Callahan, Annice
Spiritual Guides for Today
New York, NY: Crossroad/Continuum, 1991. 160 pp.

397. Carmody, Denise Lardner
Seizing the Apple: A Feminist Spirituality of Personal Growth
New York, NY: Crossroad Publishing, 1984. 184 pp.

398. Carmody, Denise Lardner
Women and World Religions
Englewood Cliffs, NJ: Prentice-Hall, 1989. 254 pp.

399. Chernin, Kim
Reinventing Eve: Modern Woman in Search of Herself
San Francisco, CA: Harper & Row, 1987. 191 pp.

400. Chervin, Ronda
Feminine, Free and Faithful
San Francisco, CA: Ignatius Press, 1986. 143 pp.

401. Christ, Carol P.
Diving Deep and Surfacing: Women Writers on Spiritual Quest
Boston, MA: Beacon Press, 1980. 159 pp.

402. Coakley, Mary Lewis
Long Liberated Ladies
San Francisco, CA: Ignatius Press, 1988. 168 pp.

403. Coles, Robert, and Jane H. Coles
Women of Crisis: Lives of Struggle and Hope, vol. 1
New York, NY: Delacort Press/Seymour Lawrence, 1978. 291 pp.

404.   Coles, Robert, and Jane H. Coles
       Women of Crisis: Lives of Struggle and Hope, vol. 2
       New York, NY: Delacort Press/Seymour Lawrence,
          1979. 236 pp.

405.   Conn, Joann Wolski, ed.
       Women's Spirituality: Resources of Christian Development
       Ramsey, NJ: Paulist Press, 1986. 327 pp.

406.   Cooey, Paula M., William Eakin, and Joy McDaniel,
          eds.
       *After Patriarchy: Feminist Transformations of the World
          Religions*
       Maryknoll, NY: Orbis Books, 1991. 169 pp.

407.   Crawford, Janet, and Michael Kinnamon, eds.
       In God's Image
       Geneva, Switz.: World Council of Churches, 1983. 108
          pp.

408.   Dicken, Helene
       Full Face to God
       London, U.K.: S.P.C.K., 1971. 118 pp.

409.   Eller, Cynthia
       *Living in the Lap of the Goddess: The Feminist Spirituality
          Movement in America*
       New York, NY: Crossroad Publishing, 1993. 276 pp.

410.   Falk, Nancy A., and Rita Gross, eds.
       *Unspoken Worlds: Women's Religious Lives in Non-Western
          Cultures*
       San Francisco, CA: Harper & Row, 1980. 292 pp.

411.   Fischer, Kathleen
       Women at the Well
       Ramsey, NJ: Paulist Press, 1989. 215 pp.

412.   Fischer, Kathleen R.
       Winter Grace: Spirituality for the Later Years (aging)
       Ramsey, NJ: Paulist Press, 1985. 170 pp.

413. Fischer, Kathleen R.
Reclaiming the Connections: A Contemporary Spirituality
Kansas City, MO: Sheed & Ward, 1990. 104 pp.

414. Furlong, Monica
Christian Uncertainties
Cambridge, MA: Cowley Publishing, 1982. 128 pp.

415. Garcia, Jo, and Sara Maitland, eds.
Walking on the Water: Women Talk About Spirituality
London, U.K.: Virago Press, 1983. 214 pp.

416. Giles, Mary, ed.
*The Feminist Mystic and Other Essays on Women and
    Spirituality*
New York, NY: Crossroad Publishing, 1982. 159 pp.

417. Golden, Renny
The Hour of the Poor: The Hour of Women
New York, NY: Crossroad/Continuum, 1991. 200 pp.

418. Goodrich, Norma Lorre
Priestesses (tales and myths)
New York, NY: Franklin Watts, 1989. 428 pp.

419. Gray, Elizabeth Dodson, ed.
Sacred Dimensions of Women's Experience
Wellesley, MA: Roundtable Press, 1988. 244 pp.

420. Griffin, David, ed.
Spirituality and Society: Postmodern Visions
Albany, NY: State University of New York Press, 1988.
    192 pp.

421. Grob, Leonard, Riffat Hassan, and Haim Gordon, eds.
Women's and Men's Liberation: Testimonies of Spirit
Westport, CT: Greenwood Press, 1991. 232 pp.

422. Gross, Rita M., ed.
Beyond Androcentrism: New Essays on Women and Religion
Alpharetta, GA: Scholars Press, 1977. 347 pp.

423.   Gupta, Bina, ed.
        Sexual Archetypes, East and West
        New York, NY: ERA Books, 1989. 247 pp.

424.   Haddad, Yvonne Y., and Ellison B. Findley, eds.
        Women, Religion and Social Change
        Albany, NY: State University of New York Press, 1985.
        508 pp.

425.   Haddon, Genia Pauli
        Body Metaphors: Releasing the God-Feminine in Us All
        New York, NY: Crossroad Publishing, 1988. 288 pp.

426.   Hagan, June Steffenson, ed.
        *Gender Matters: Women's Studies for the Christian Commu-
        nity*
        Grand Rapids, MI: Zondervan Press, 1989. 288 pp.

427.   Haney, Eleanor Humes
        *Vision and Struggle: Meditations on Feminist Spirituality
        and Politics*
        Portland, ME: Astarte Shell Press, 1989. 135 pp.

428.   Harris, Maria
        Dance of the Spirit: The Seven Steps of Women's Spirituality
        New York, NY: Bantam Books, 1989. 224 pp.

429.   Holden, Pat, ed.
        Women's Religious Experience
        New York, NY: Barnes & Noble, 1983. 205 pp.

430.   Hurcombe, Linda, ed.
        Sex and God: Some Varieties of Women's Religious Experience
        Boston, MA: Routledge & Kegan Paul, 1987. 296 pp.

431.   Jergen, Carol Frances, ed.
        Mary According to Women
        Kansas City, MO: Sheed & Ward, 1985. 163 pp.

432. Johnson, Sonia
Going Out of Our Minds: The Metaphysics of Liberation
Trumansburg, NY: Crossing Press, 1987. 359 pp.

433. Kimball, Gayle, ed.
Women's Culture: The Women's Renaissance of the Seventies
Metuchen, NJ: Scarecrow Press, 1980. 296 pp.

434. King, Ursala
*The Spirit of One Earth: Reflections on Teilhard de Chardin
and Global Spirituality*
New York, NY: Paragon, 1988. 198 pp.

435. King, Ursala
Women and Spirituality: Voice of Protest and Promise
Philadelphia, PA: University of Pennsylvania Press,
1993. 268 pp.

436. King, Ursala, ed.
Women and World Religions
New York, NY: Paragon, 1986. 261 pp.

437. Kolbenschlag, Madonna
*Lost in the Land of Oz: The Search for Identity in American
Life*
San Francisco, CA: Harper & Row, 1988. 256 pp.

438. Lechman, Judith
*The Spirituality of Gentleness: A Journey Toward Christian
Wholeness*
San Francisco, CA: Harper & Row, 1987. 192 pp.

439. Leckey, Dolores
Women and Creativity (Maldeva Lecture, 1991)
Ramsey, NJ: Paulist Press, 1991. 182 pp.

440. Leddy, Mary Jo
Reweaving Religious Life: Beyond the Liberal Model
Mystic, CT: Twenty-Third Publications, 1990. 208 pp.

441.   Meehan, Brenda
       Holy Women of Russia
       San Francisco, CA: Harper & Row, 1993. 224 pp.

441a.   Miles, Margaret R.
       *Practicing Christianity: Critical Perspectives for an Embod-
       ied Christianity*
       New York, NY: Crossroad/Continuum, 1989. 256 pp.

442.   Mollenkott, Virginia Ramey, ed.
       Women of Faith in Dialogue
       New York, NY: Crossroad Publishing, 1987. 144 pp.

443.   Moraga, Cherrie, and Gloria Anzaldua, eds.
       *This Bridge Called My Back: Writings by Radical Women of
       Color*
       Watertown, NY: Persephone Press, 1981. 261 pp.

444.   Muto, Susan
       *Womanspirit: Reclaiming the Deep Feminine in Our Human
       Spirituality*
       New York, NY: Crossroad/Continuum, 1991. 180 pp.

445.   Ochs, Carol
       Women and Spirituality
       Totowa, NJ: Rowman & Allanheld, 1983. 156 pp.

446.   Ochs, Carol
       An Ascent to Joy: Transforming Deadness of Spirit
       Oak Park, IL: Meyer-Stone, 1989. 144 pp.

447.   Parbury, Kathleen
       *Women of Grace: A Biographical Dictionary of British
       Women Saints, Martyrs and Reformers*
       Boston, MA: Oriel Press, Routledge & Kegan Paul,
       1985. 199 pp.

448.   Phillips, Dorothy, E. B. Howes, and Lucille Nixon, eds.
       *The Choice Is Always Ours: An Anthology on the Religious
       Way*

Wheaton, IL: Theosophical Publishing House, 1982. 493 pp.

449. Plaskow, Judith and Carol P. Christ, eds.
Weaving the Visions: New Patterns in Feminist Spirituality
San Francisco, CA: Harper & Row, 1989. 359 pp.

450. Puls, Joan
Every Bush Is Burning: A Spirituality for Our Times
Mystic, CT: Twenty-Third Publications, 1986. 120 pp.

451. Puls, Joan
A Spirituality of Compassion
Mystic, CT: Twenty-Third Publications, 1988. 144 pp.

452. Puls, Joan
Hearts Set on the Pilgrimage: The Challenge of Discipleship in a World Church
Mystic, CT: Twenty-Third Publications, 1989. 128 pp.

453. Racette, Catherine, and Peg Reynolds, eds.
American Women: Our Spirituality in Our Own Words
Oakland, CA: Friends of Creation Spirituality, 1985. 210 pp.

454. Rae, Eleanor, and Bernice Marie-Daly
Created in Her Image: Models of the Feminine Divine
New York, NY: Crossroad Publishing, 1990. 250 pp.

455. Randour, Mary Lou
Women's Psyche, Women's Spirit: The Reality of Relationships
New York, NY: Columbia University Press, 1986. 240 pp.

456. Rupp, Joyce
The Star in My Heart: Experiencing Sophia, Inner Wisdom
San Diego, CA: LuraMedia, 1990. 96 pp.

457.   Sharma, Arvind, ed.
       Women in World Religions
       Albany, NY: State University of New York Press, 1986.
       256 pp.

458.   Spretnak, Charlene
       States of Grace: Spiritual Grounding in the Postmodern Age
       San Francisco, CA: Harper & Row, 1991. 320 pp.

459.   Spretnak, Charlene, ed.
       *The Politics of Women's Spirituality: Essays on the Rise of
       Spiritual Power Within the Feminist Movement*
       Garden City, NY: Anchor Press, Doubleday, 1982. 623
       pp.

460.   Walker, Barbara G.
       The Woman's Encyclopedia of Myths and Secrets
       New York, NY: Harper & Row, 1983. 1,124 pp.

461.   Walker, Barbara G.
       Women's Dictionary of Symbols and Sacred Objects
       San Francisco, CA: Harper & Row, 1988. 640 pp.

462.   Washbourn, Penelope
       *Becoming Woman: The Quest for Wholeness in Female
       Experience*
       San Francisco, CA: Harper & Row, 1977. 174 pp.

463.   Washbourn, Penelope, ed.
       *The Seasons of Woman: Song, Poetry, Ritual, Prayer, Myth,
       Story*
       San Francisco, CA: Harper & Row, 1979. 176 pp.

464.   Weaver, Mary Jo
       *Springs of Water in a Dry Land: Spiritual Survival for
       Catholic Women Today*
       Boston, MA: Beacon Press, 1993. 224 pp.

465.   Weber, Christin Lore
       WomanChrist: A New Vision of Femininist Spirituality
       San Francisco, CA: Harper & Row, 1987. 256 pp.

466. Wynne, Patrice
The Womanspirit Sourcebook
San Francisco, CA: Harper & Row, 1988. 277 pp.

467. Young, Serenity, ed.
*Sacred Writings by and About Women: Sources from World's
Religion—A Universal Anthology*
New York, NY: Crossroad/Continuum, 1992. 448 pp.

468. Zagano, Phyllis
Woman to Woman: An Anthology of Women's Spiritualities
Collegeville, MN: Liturgical Press, 1993. 115 pp.

469. Zappone, Katherine
The Hope for Wholeness: A Spirituality for Feminists
Mystic, CT: Twenty-Third Publications, 1991. 208 pp.

Archaic and Ancient Women

470. Boyce, Mary
Zoroastrians: Their Religious Beliefs and Practices
Boston, MA: Routledge & Kegan Paul, 1979. 252 pp.

471. Cameron, Averil, and Amelie Kuhrt, eds.
Images of Women in Antiquity
Detroit, MI: Wayne State University Press, 1983. 323 pp.

472. Cantarella, Eva, trans. M. Fant
*Pandora's Daughters: The Role and Status of Women in
Greek and Roman Antiquity*
Baltimore, MD: Johns Hopkins University Press, 1986.
229 pp.

473. Carmody, Denise Lardner
The Oldest God: Archaic Religion Yesterday and Today
Nashville, TN: Abingdon Press, 1981. 190 pp.

474. Carson, Anne
Eros the Bittersweet: An Essay
Princeton, NJ: Princeton University Press, 1989. 201 pp.

475. Demand, Nancy
Thebes in the Fifth Century
Boston, MA: Routledge & Kegan Paul, 1983. 196 pp.

476. Dowden, Ken
Death and the Maiden: Girls' Initiation Rites in Greek Mythology
New York, NY: Routledge, 1989. 256 pp.

477. DuBois, Page
Centaurs and Amazons: Women and the Prehistory of the Great Chain of Being
Ann Arbor, MI: University of Michigan Press, 1982. 161 pp.

478. DuBois, Page
Sowing the Body: Psychoanalysis and Ancient Representations of Women
Chicago, IL: University of Chicago Press, 1988. 227 pp.

479. Ehrenberg, Margaret
Women in Prehistory
Norman, OK: University of Oklahoma Press, 1989. 192 pp.

480. Evans, Arthur
The God of Ecstasy: Sex Roles and the Madness of Dionysos
New York, NY: St. Martin's Press, 1988. 286 pp.

481. Fierz-David, Linda
Women's Dionysian Initiation: The Villa of Mysteries in Pompeii
New York, NY: Spring Publishing, 1988. 166 pp.

482. Gero, Joan, and Margaret Conkey, eds.
Women and Prehistory: Engendering Archaelogy
Cambridge, MA: Blackwell, 1990. 250 pp.

483. Hall, Nor
Those Women (including H.D. and Fierz-David, on ancient Greece)
New York, NY: Spring Publishing, 1988. 93 pp.

484. Hallett, Judith P.
Fathers and Daughters in Roman Society: Women and the Elite Family
Princeton, NJ: Princeton University Press, 1984. 423 pp.

485. Harrison, Jane Ellen
Epilegomena to the Study of Greek Religion
New Hyde Park, NY: University Books, 1962. 600 pp.

486. Harrison, Jane Ellen
Prolegomena to the Study of Greek Religion
Atlantic Highlands, NJ: Humanities Press, 1981. 682 pp.

487. Heyob, Sharon Kelly
The Cult of Isis Among Women in the Graeco-Roman World
Leiden, Neth.: E. J. Brill, 1975. 140 pp.

488. Holum, Kenneth
Theodosian Empresses: Women and the Imperial Dominion in Late Antiquity
Berkeley, CA: University of California Press, 1982. 258 pp.

489. Houston, Jean
Soulcycle: The Mythic World of the Odyssey
Warwick, NY: Amity House, 1988. 160 pp.

490. Johns, Catherine
Sex or Symbol: Erotic Images of Greece and Rome

Austin, TX: University of Texas Press, 1982. 160 pp.

491. Johnston, Sarah Iles
Hekate Soteria: A Study of Hekate's Roles in the Chaldean Oracles and Related Literature
Alpharetta, GA: Scholars Press, 1990. 192 pp.

492. Keuls, Eva C.
The Reign of the Phallus: Sexual Politics in Ancient Greece
New York, NY: Harper & Row, 1985. 452 pp.

493. Kraemer, Ross, ed.
Maenads, Martyrs, Matrons, Monastics: A Sourcebook on Women's Religions
Minneapolis, MN: Fortress/Augsburg, 1988. 432 pp.

494. Lefkowitz, Mary R.
Heroines and Hysterics
New York, NY: St. Martin's Press, 1981. 96 pp.

495. Lefkowitz, Mary R.
Women in Greek Myth
Baltimore, MD: Johns Hopkins University Press, 1986. 158 pp.

496. Lefkowitz, Mary R., and Maureen B. Fant, eds.
Women's Life in Greece and Rome
Baltimore, MD: Johns Hopkins University Press, 1982. 294 pp.

497. Lesko, Barbara S., ed.
Woman's Earliest Records: From Ancient Egypt and Western Asia
Alpharetta, GA: Scholars Press, 1989. 350 pp.

498. Loraux, Nicole, trans. A. Forster
Tragic Ways of Killing a Woman
Cambridge, MA: Harvard University Press, 1987. 100 pp.

499. Meyers, Carol
     Discovering Eve: Ancient Israelite Women in Context
     Oxford, U.K.: Oxford University Press, 1991. 256 pp.

500. Ochshorn, Judith
     The Female Experience and the Nature of the Divine
     Bloomington, IN: Indiana University Press, 1981. 269
     pp.

501. Pomeroy, Sarah
     Women in Hellenistic Egypt: From Alexander to Cleopatra
     New York, NY: Schocken Books, 1984. 241 pp.

502. Rousselle, Aline, trans. Felina Pheasant
     Porneia: The Meaning of Desire in Late Antiquity
     Oxford, U.K.: Oxford University Press, 1988. 224 pp.

503. Sissa, Giulia, trans. Arthur Goldhammer
     Greek Virginity
     Cambridge, MA: Harvard University Press, 1990. 240
     pp.

504. Skinner, Marilyn, ed.
     *Rescuing Creusea: New Methodological Approaches to
     Women in Antiquity*
     Lubbock, TX: Texas Tech University Press, 1987. 175
     pp.

505. Sly, Dorothy
     Philo's Perception of Women
     Alpharetta, GA: Scholars Press, 1990. 237 pp.

506. Tyrrell, William Blake
     Amazons: A Study in Athenian Mythmaking
     Baltimore, MD: Johns Hopkins University Press, 1989.
     192 pp.

507. Waithe, Mary Ellen, ed.
     *The History of Women Philosophers, vol. 1: Ancient Women,
     600 B.C.–A.D. 500*
     Norwell, MA: Kluwer Academic Books, 1987. 256 pp.

508. Watterson, Barbara
      Women in Ancient Egypt
      New York, NY: St. Martin's Press, 1992. 224 pp.

509. Winkler, John J.
      Constraints of Desire: The Anthropology of Sex and Gender in Ancient Greece
      New York, NY: Routledge, 1989. 288 pp.

Jewish Women

510. Adler, Ruth
      Women of the Shtetl: Through the Eyes of Y. L. Peretz
      Cranbury, NJ: Fairleigh Dickinson University Press, 1979. 144 pp.

511. Aschkenasy, Nehama
      Eve's Journey: Feminine Images in Hebraic Literary Tradition
      Philadelphia, PA: University of Pennsylvania Press, 1986. 269 pp.

512. Aviad, Janet
      Return to Judaism: Religious Renewal in Israel
      Chicago, IL: University of Chicago Press, 1983. 194 pp.

513. Azmon, Yael, and Dafna Izraeli, eds.
      Women in Israel
      New Brunswick, NJ: Transaction Books, 1993. 467 pp.

514. Biale, Rachel
      Women and Jewish Law: An Exploration of Women's Issues in Halakhic Sources
      New York, NY: Schocken Books, 1984. 293 pp.

515. Bitton-Jackson, Livia
      Madonna or Courtesan? The Jewish Woman in Christian Literature
      Somers, CT: Seabury Press, 1982. 138 pp.

516. Broner, Esther M.
     The Telling
     San Francisco, CA: Harper & Row, 1993. 192 pp.

517. Davidman, Lynn
     Tradition in a Rootless World: Women Turn to Orthodox Judaism
     Berkeley, CA: University of California Press, 1991. 265 pp.

518. Farber, Norma
     Shekkinah
     Tucson, AZ: Capstone Editions, 1984. 96 pp.

519. Fishman, Sylvia Barack
     A Breath of Life: Feminism in the American Jewish Community
     New York, NY: The Free Press, 1993. 300 pp.

520. Frankiel, Tamar
     The Voice of Sarah: Feminine Spirituality and Traditional Judaism
     San Francisco, CA: Harper & Row, 1990. 176 pp.

521. Greenberg, Blu
     On Women and Judaism: A View from Tradition
     Philadelphia, PA: Jewish Publication Society of America, 1981. 178 pp.

522. Harris, Lis
     Holy Days: The World of a Hasidic Family
     New York, NY: Summit Books, 1985. 266 pp.

523. Henry, Sondra, and Emily Taitz
     Written Out of History: Our Jewish Foremothers
     Fresh Meadows, NY: Biblio Press, 1988. 291 pp.

524. Heschel, Susannah, ed.
     On Being a Jewish Feminist: A Reader
     New York, NY: Schocken Books, 1983. 288 pp.

525.   Isaacson, Judith Magyar
        Seed of Sarah: Memoirs of a Survivor
        Champaign, IL: University of Illinois Press, 1990. 184
        pp.

526.   Kaufman, Debra
        Rachel's Daughters: Newly Orthodox Women
        New Brunswick, NJ: Rutgers University Press, 1991.
        184 pp.

527.   Kaye/Kantrowitz, Melanie, and Irena Klepfisz, eds.
        The Tribe of Dina: A Jewish Woman's Anthology
        Boston, MA: Beacon Press, 1989. 352 pp.

528.   Koltun, Elizabeth, ed.
        The Jewish Woman: New Perspectives
        New York, NY: Schocken Books, 1976. 294 pp.

529.   Kuzmack, Linda Gordon
        *Women's Cause: The Jewish Women's Movement in England
            and the United States, 1881–1933*
        Columbus, OH: Ohio State University Press, 1990. 300
        pp.

530.   Laska, Vera, ed.
        *Women in the Resistance and in the Holocaust: The Voices of
            Eyewitnesses*
        Westport, CT: Greenwood Press, 1983. 330 pp.

531.   Levine, Elizabeth Resnick
        *Ceremonies Sampler: New Rites, Celebrations, and Obser-
            vances of Jewish Women*
        San Diego, CA: Women's Institute for Continuing
        Jewish Education, 1991. 127 pp.

532.   Mazow, Julia W., ed.
        *Women Who Lost Their Names: Selected Writings by Ameri-
            can Jewish Women*
        San Francisco, CA: Harper & Row, 1981. 222 pp.

533. Morton, Leah
     I Am a Woman—and a Jew
     New York, NY: Marcus Weiner, 1986. 362 pp.

534. Ochs, Vanessa L.
     Words on Fire: One Woman's Journey into the Sacred
     New York, NY: Harcourt Brace Jovanovich, 1990. 328
     pp.

535. Schneider, Susan Weidman
     Jewish and Female: Choices and Changes in Our Lives Today
     New York, NY: Simon & Schuster, 1984. 649 pp.

536. Schwertfeger, Ruth
     Women of Theresienstadt: Voices from a Concentration Camp
     Manchester, U.K.: Manchester University Press, 1989.
     162 pp.

537. Sochen, June
     *Consecrate Every Day: The Public Lives of Jewish-American
     Women, 1880–1980*
     Albany, NY: State University of New York Press, 1981.
     167 pp.

538. Swajger, Adina Blady
     *I Remember Nothing More: The Warsaw Children's Hospital
     and the Women's Resistance*
     New York, NY: Pantheon Books, 1991. 184 pp.

539. Swirski, Barbara, and Marilyn Safir
     Calling the Equality Bluff: Women in Israel
     New York, NY: Macmillan, 1991. 352 pp.

540. no entry

541. Teubal, Savina J.
     Hagar the Egyptian
     San Francisco, CA: Harper & Row, 1990. 192 pp.

542.   Tolley, Jacqueline, ed.
       On Our Spiritual Journey: A Creative Shabbat Service
       San Diego, CA: Women's Institute for Continuing
          Jewish Education, 1984. 74 pp.

543.   Umansky, Ellen M.
       *Lily Montagu and the Advancement of Liberal Judaism:
          From Vision to Vocation*
       Lewiston, NY: The Edwin Mellen Press, 1984. 305 pp.

544.   Umansky, Ellen M., ed.
       Four Centuries of Jewish Women's Spirituality: A Sourcebook
       Boston, MA: Beacon Press, 1992. 340 pp.

545.   Walden, Daniel, ed.
       *Studies in American Jewish Literature, vol. 3: Jewish Women
          Writers and Women in Jewish Literature*
       Albany, NY: State University of New York Press, 1980.
          239 pp.

546.   Wegner, Judith Romney
       Chattel or Person? The Status of Women in the Mishnah
       Oxford, U.K.: Oxford University Press, 1988. 272 pp.

547.   Weinberg, Sydney Stahl
       *The World of Our Mothers: The Lives of Jewish Immigrant
          Women*
       Chapel Hill, NC: University of North Carolina Press,
          1988. 325 pp.

548.   Weinstein, Frida Scheps
       A Hidden Childhood, 1942–1945
       New York, NY: Hill & Wang, 1985. 151 pp.

549.   Wiseman, Adele
       Old Woman at Play
       Toronto, Ont.: Clarke, Irwin, & Co., 1978. 148 pp.

Modern Christian Women

550. Aronica, Michele Teresa
Beyond Charismatic Leadership (Catholic Worker Movement)
New Brunswick, NJ: Transaction Books, 1987. 197 pp.

551. Bacon, Margaret Hope
Mothers of Feminism: The Story of Quaker Women in America
San Francisco, CA: Harper & Row, 1989. 288 pp.

552. Banta, Martha
Imaging American Women: Ideas and Ideals in Cultural History
New York, NY: Columbia University Press, 1987. 844 pp.

553. Barker, Eileen, ed.
Of Gods and Men: New Religious Movements in the West
Macon, GA: Mercer University Press, 1984. 347 pp.

554. Beecher, Maureen U., and Lavina F. Anderson, eds.
Sisters in Spirit: Mormon Women in Historical and Cultural Perspective
Champaign, IL: University of Illinois Press, 1987. 281 pp.

555. Bendroth, Mary Lamberts
Fundamentalism and Gender, 1875 to the Present
New Haven, CT: Yale University Press, 1993. 179 pp.

556. Boyd, Lois A., and R. Douglas Brackenridge
Presbyterian Women in America: Two Centuries of a Quest for Status
Westport, CT: Greenwood Press, 1983. 308 pp.

557.   Boylan, Anne M.
       *Sunday School: The Formation of an American Institution,
       1790–1880*
       New Haven, CT: Yale University Press, 1988. 256 pp.

558.   Brandon, Ruth
       *The Spiritualists: The Passion for the Occult in the Nine-
       teenth and Twentieth Centuries*
       Buffalo, NY: Prometheus Books, 1984. 315 pp.

559.   Braude, Ann
       *Radical Spirits: Spiritualism and Women's Rights in Nine-
       teenth-Century America*
       Boston, MA: Beacon Press, 1991. 268 pp.

560.   Brown, Elizabeth Potts, and Susan M. Stuard
       Witnesses for Change: Quaker Women Over Three Centuries
       New Brunswick, NJ: Rutgers University Press, 1984.
       190 pp.

561.   Brumberg, Joan Jacobs
       *Mission for Life: The Judson Family and American Evangeli-
       cal Culture*
       New York, NY: Columbia University Press, 1984. 302
       pp.

562.   Caskey, Marie
       Chariot of Fire: Religion and the Beecher Family
       New Haven, CT: Yale University Press, 1978. 442 pp.

563.   Chilcote, Paul Wesley
       John Wesley and the Women Preachers of Early Methodism
       Metuchen, NJ: Scarecrow Press, 1991. 375 pp.

564.   Chmielewski, Wendy E., Louis Kern, and Marilyn
       Klee-Hartzell, eds.
       *Women in Spiritual and Communitarian Societies in the
       United States*
       Syracuse, NY: Syracuse University Press, 1993. 320 pp.

565. Corrigan, D. Felicitas
The Nun, the Infidel and the Superwoman (Dame Laurentia McLachlan)
Chicago, IL: University of Chicago Press, 1985. 148 pp.

566. Crews, Clyde F.
English Catholic Modernism: Maude Petre's Way of Faith
Notre Dame, IN: Notre Dame University Press, 1984. 156 pp.

567. DeBerg, Betty A.
Ungodly Women: Gender and the First Wave of American Fundamentalism
Philadelphia, PA: Fortress Press, 1990. 144 pp.

568. Foster, William
Women, Family and Utopia: Communal Experiments of the Shakers, the Oneida Community, and the Mormons
Syracuse, NY: Syracuse University Press, 1991.

569. Friedman, Jean
The Enclosed Garden: Women and Community in the Evangelical South
Chapel Hill, NC: University of North Carolina Press, 1985. 180 pp.

570. Fuller, Margaret, ed. Larry Reynolds and S. B. Belasco
"These Sad but Glorious Days": Dispatches from Europe, 1846–50
New Haven, CT: Yale University Press, 1991. 320 pp.

571. Gaston, Paul
Women of Fair Hope
Athens, GA: University of Georgia Press, 1984. 143 pp.

572. Greaves, Richard L., ed.
Triumph over Silence: Women in Protestant History
Westport, CT: Greenwood Press, 1985. 295 pp.

573. Grimke, Sarah, ed. Elizabeth Ann Bartlett
Letters on the Equality of the Sexes and Other Essays
New Haven, CT: Yale University Press, 1988. 176 pp.

574. Guyot, Charles, trans. Deidre Cavanagh
The Legend of the City of Ys
Amherst, MA: University of Massachusetts Press, 1979.
88 pp.

575. Hardesty, Nancy A.
*Women Called to Witness: Evangelical Feminism in the
Nineteenth Century*
Nashville, TN: Abingdon Press, 1984. 176 pp.

576. Harrison, Barbara G.
*Visions of Glory: A History and Memory of Jehovah's Wit-
nessses*
New York, NY: Simon & Schuster, 1978. 413 pp.

577. Hill, Patricia R.
*The World Their Household: The American Woman's For-
eign Mission Movement and Cultural Transformation*
Ann Arbor, MI: University of Michigan Press, 1984.
231 pp.

578. Humez, Jean M., ed.
*Mother's First-Born Daughters: Early Shaker Writings on
Women and Religion*
Bloomington, IN: Indiana University Press, 1993. 294
pp.

579. James, Janet Wilson, ed.
Women in American Religion
Philadelphia, PA: University of Pennsylvania Press,
1980. 280 pp.

580. Karlsen, Carol F.
*The Devil in the Shape of a Woman: Witchcraft in Colonial
New England*
New York, NY: W. W. Norton, 1988. 360 pp.

581. Keller, Rosemary Skinner, ed.
     *Spirituality and Social Responsibility: Vocational Vision of
     Women in the United Methodist Tradition*
     Nashville, TN: Abingdon Press, 1993. 294 pp.

582. Kenneally, James J.
     The History of American Catholic Women
     New York, NY: Crossroad/Continuum, 1990. 288 pp.

583. Kennelly, Karen, ed.
     American Catholic Women: A Historical Explanation
     New York, NY: Macmillan, 1989. 251 pp.

584. Lagerquist, L. Deane
     *From Our Mothers' Arms: A History of Women in the
     American Lutheran Church*
     Minneapolis, MN: Fortress/Augsburg, 1988. 224 pp.

585. Lang, Amy Schrager
     *Prophetic Woman: Anne Hutchinson and the Problem of
     Dissent in the Literature of New England*
     Berkeley, CA: University of California Press, 1987. 237
     pp.

586. Larner, Christine
     Enemies of God
     Cambridge, MA: Blackwell, 1983. 244 pp.

587. Lawless, Elaine J.
     *Handmaidens of the Lord: Pentecostal Women Preachers and
     Traditional Religon*
     Philadelphia, PA: University of Pennsylvania Press,
     1988. 294 pp.

588. Lebsock, Suzanne
     *The Free Women of Petersburg: Status and Culture in a
     Southern Town, 1784–1860*
     New York, NY: W. W. Norton, 1984. 326 pp.

589. McDonnell, Colleen
     The Christian Home in Victorian America, 1840–1900

Bloomington, IN: Indiana University Press, 1986. 193 pp.

590. Mercadante, Linda A.
Gender, Doctrine, and God: The Shakers and Contemporary Theology
Nashville, TN: Abingdon Press, 1990. 208 pp.

591. Owen, Alex
The Darkened Room: Women, Power and Spiritualism in Late Victorian England
Philadelphia, PA: University of Pennsylvania Press, 1989. 336 pp.

592. Peterson, Susan Carol, and C. A. Vaughn-Roberson, eds.
Women with Vision: The Presentation Sisters of South Dakota, 1880–1985
Champaign, IL: University of Illinois Press, 1988. 334 pp.

593. Porterfield, Amanda
Feminine Spirituality in America: From Sarah Edwards to Martha Graham
Philadelphia, PA: Temple University Press, 1980. 238 pp.

594. Procter-Smith, Marjorie
Women in Shaker Community: A Feminist Analysis of Uses of Religious Symbolism
Lewiston, NY: The Edwin Mellen Press, 1985. 253 pp.

595. Rooney, Lucy, and Robert Farley
Mary, Queen of Peace: Is the Mother of God Appearing in Medjugorhe?
Dearborn, MI: Alba, 1985. 98 pp.

596. Sasson, Diane
The Shaker Spiritual Narrative
Knoxville, TN: University of Tennessee Press, 1986. 232 pp.

597. Sizer, Sandra S.
    Gospel Hymns and Social Religion: The Rhetoric of Nine-teenth-Century Revivalism
    Philadelphia, PA: Temple University Press, 1979. 222 pp.

598. Springer, Marlene
    A Study of the Correspondence of Harriet Beecher Stowe and Nineteenth-Century Women of Letters
    Ann Arbor, MI: UMI Research Press, 1990. 200 pp.

599. Stepsis, M. V., and D. Lipstat, eds.
    Pioneer Healers: The History of Women Religious in American Health Care
    New York, NY: Crossroad Publishing, 1988. 376 pp.

600. Sweet, Leonard
    The Minister's Wife: Her Role in Nineteenth-Century Evangelism
    Philadelphia, PA: Temple University Press, 1983. 337 pp.

601. Taves, Ann, ed.
    Religion and Domestic Violence in Early New England: The Memoirs of Abigail Abbot Bailey
    Bloomington, IN: Indiana University Press, 1989. 198 pp.

602. Thomas, Hilah K., Rosemary S. Keller, and L. L. Queen
    Women in New Worlds: Historical Perspectives on Wesleyan Tradition, 2 vols.
    Nashville, TN: Abingdon Press, 1982. 448 pp.

603. Tucker, Cynthia Grant
    Prophetic Sisterhood: Liberal Women Ministers of the Frontier, 1880–1930
    Boston, MA: Beacon Press, 1990. 304 pp.

604. Tyrell, Ian
    Women's World/Women's Empire: The Women's Christian

Temperance Union in International Perspective, 1880–
1930
Chapel Hill, NC: University of North Carolina Press,
1991. 420 pp.

605. Ulrich, Laurel T.
*Good Wives: Images and Reality in the Lives of Women in
Northern New England, 1650–1750*
Oxford, U.K.: Oxford University Press, 1983. 330 pp.

606. Valenze, Deborah M.
*Prophetic Sons and Daughters: Female Preaching and Popu-
lar Religion*
Princeton, NJ: Princeton University Press, 1985. 344
pp.

607. Waller, Altina L.
*Reverend Beecher and Mrs. Tilton: Sex and Class in Victo-
rian America*
Amherst, MA: University of Massachusetts Press, 1982.
192 pp.

608. Zweip, Mary
*Pilgrim Path: The First Company of Women Missionaries to
Hawaii*
Madison, WI: University of Wisconsin Press, 1991. 376
pp.

Native American Women

609. Allen, Paula Gunn
Shadow Country
Los Angeles, CA: University of California—Los Ange-
les, 1982. 149 pp.

610. Allen, Paula Gunn
The Woman Who Owned the Shadows
San Francisco, CA: Spinsters Ink, 1983. 213 pp.

611. Allen, Paula Gunn
The Sacred Hoop: Recovering the Feminine in American Indian Traditions
Boston, MA: Beacon Press, 1986. 311 pp.

612. Allen, Paula Gunn
Grandmothers of the Light: A Medicine Woman's Sourcebook
Boston, MA: Beacon Press, 1991. 246 pp.

613. Allen, Paula Gunn, ed.
Spider Woman's Granddaughters: Traditional Tales and Contemporary Writing
Boston, MA: Beacon Press, 1988. 320 pp.

614. Bataille, Gretchen M., and Kathleen M. Sands
American Indian Women: Telling Their Lives
Lincoln, NE: University of Nebraska Press, 1984. 209 pp.

615. Behar, Ruth
Translated Woman: Crossing the Border with Esperanza's Story
Boston, MA: Beacon Press, 1993. 372 pp.

616. Blackman, Margaret B.
During My Time: Florence Davidson, a Haida Woman
Seattle, WA: University of Washington Press, 1985. 172 pp.

617. Blackman, Margaret B.
Sadie Brower Neakok, an Inupiaq Woman (Eskimo)
Seattle, WA: University of Washington Press, 1989. 304 pp.

618. Brant, Beth, ed.
A Gathering of Spirit: Writing and Art by North American Indian Women
Rockland, ME: Sinister Wisdom Books, 1985. 238 pp.

619. Cameron, Anne
      Daughters of Copper Woman
      Vancouver, B.C.: Press Gang Publishers, 1981. 150 pp.

620. Cameron, Anne
      Dzelarhons: Myths of the Northwest Coast
      Maidereia Park, B.C.: Harborn Publishing Co., 1986.
      160 pp.

621. Cruikshank, Julie, with Angela Sidney, Kitty Smith,
      and Annie Ned
      *Life Lived Like a Story: Life Stories of Three Yukon Native
      Elders*
      Lincoln, NE: University of Nebraska Press, 1991. 404
      pp.

622. Green, Rayna
      *That's What She Said: Contemporary Poetry and Fiction by
      Native American Women*
      Bloomington, IN: Indiana University Press, 1984. 329
      pp.

623. Hungry Wolf, Beverly
      The Ways of My Grandmothers
      New York, NY: William Morrow, 1980. 256 pp.

624. Kelley, Jane Holden
      Yaqui Women: Contemporary Life Histories
      Lincoln, NE: University of Nebraska Press, 1991. 272
      pp.

625. Lindeman, Frank B.
      Pretty-shield, Medicine Woman of the Crows
      Lincoln, NE: University of Nebraska Press, 1989. 256
      pp.

626. Lurie, Nancy O., ed.
      *Mountain Wolf Woman, Sister of Crashing Thunder: The
      Autobiography*
      Ann Arbor, MI: University of Michigan Press, 1961.
      142 pp.

627. Moon, Sheila
Changing Woman and Her Sisters: Feminine Aspects of Selves and Deities
San Francisco, CA: Guild for Psychological Studies Publishing House, 1985. 232 pp.

628. Mourning Dove, ed. Jay Miller
A Salishan Autobiography
Lincoln, NE: University of Nebraska Press, 1990. 246 pp.

629. Mullett, G. M.
Spider Woman Stories: Legends of the Hopi Indians
Tucson, AZ: University of Arizona Press, 1979. 142 pp.

630. Neithammer, Carolyn
Daughters of the Earth: The Lives and Legends of American Indian Women
New York, NY: Macmillan, 1977. 300 pp.

631. Powers, Marla N.
Ogala Women: Myth, Ritual, and Reality
Chicago, IL: University of Chicago Press, 1986. 241 pp.

632. Reyer, Carolyn
Canto ohitaka Win (Brave-hearted women): Images of Lakota Women from the Pine Ridge Reservation, South Dakota
Vermillion, SD: University of South Dakota Press, 1991. 88 pp.

633. Sams, Jamie, and Twylah Nitsch
Other Council Fires Were Here Before Ours
San Francisco, CA: Harper & Row, 1991. 128 pp.

634. Silko, Leslie M.
Ceremony
New York, NY: Viking Press, 1977. 275 pp.

635. Silko, Leslie M.
Storyteller
New York, NY: Seaver Books, 1981. 277 pp.

636. Steiner, Stan, ed.
     *Spirit Woman: The Diaries and Paintings of Bonita Wa Wa
        Calachaw Nunez*
     San Francisco, CA: Harper & Row, 1980. 243 pp.

637. Stephen, Lynn
     Zapotec Women
     Austin, TX: University of Texas Press, 1992. 272 pp.

638. Tooker, Elisabeth
     *Native North American Spirituality of the Eastern Wood-
        lands*
     Ramsey, NJ: Paulist Press, 1979. 302 pp.

639. Trambley, Estela Portillo
     Trini (novel about a Tarahumara woman)
     Tempe, AZ: Bilingual Press, 1986. 245 pp.

640. Walters, Anna Lee
     The Sun Is Not Merciful (short stories)
     Ithaca, NY: Firebrand Books, 1985. 136 pp.

641. Weigle, Marta
     Spiders and Spinsters: Women and Mythology
     Albuquerque, NM: University of New Mexico Press,
        1982. 340 pp.

642. Wong, Hertha D.
     *Sending My Heart Back Across the Years: Tradition and
        Innovation in Native American Autobiography*
     Oxford, U.K.: Oxford University Press, 1992. 256 pp.

African-American Women

643. Andrews, William L., ed.
     *Sisters of the Spirit: Three Black Women's Autobiographies of
        the Nineteenth Century*

Bloomington, IN: Indiana University Press, 1986. 245 pp.

644. Bogin, Ruth
Black Women in Nineteenth-Century American Life
University Park, PA: Pennsylvania State University Press, 1976. 355 pp.

645. Brown, Karen McCarthy
Mama Lola: A Vodou Priestess in Brooklyn
Berkeley, CA: University of California Press, 1991. 426 pp.

646. Bush, Barbara
Slave Women in Caribbean Society, 1650–1832
Bloomington, IN: Indiana University Press, 1989. 320 pp.

647. Caraway, Nancie
Segregated Sisterhood: Racism and the Politics of American Feminism
Knoxville, TN: University of Tennessee Press, 1991. 280 pp.

648. Crawford, Vicki, Jacqueline Ann Rouse, and Barbara Woods, eds.
Women in the Civil Rights Movement: Trailblazers and Torchbearers, 1941–1965
Brooklyn, NY: Carlson Publications, 1990. 225 pp.

649. Fields, Mamie Garvin, and Karen Fields
Lemon Swamp and Other Places: A Carolina Memoir
New York, NY: The Free Press, 1983. 250 pp.

650. Giddings, Paula
When and Where I Enter: The Impact of Black Women on Race and Sex in America
New York, NY: William Morrow, 1984. 408 pp.

651. Gordon, Vivian V.
      *Black Women, Feminism, and Black Liberation: Which
         Way?*
      Chicago, IL: Third World Press, 1987. 66 pp.

652. Guy-Sheftall, Beverly
      *"Daughters of Sorrow": Attitudes Towards Black Women,
         1880–1920*
      Brooklyn, NY: Carlson Publications, 1990. 250 pp.

653. Higginbotham, Evelyn Brooks
      *Righteous Discontent: The Women's Movement in the Black
         Baptist Church, 1880–1920*
      Cambridge, MA: Harvard University Press, 1993. 306
         pp.

654. Hine, Darlene Clark, ed.
      *Black Women in American History, vols. 1–4: Colonial to
         Nineteenth Century*
      Brooklyn, NY: Carlson Publications, 1990. 554 pp.

655. Hine, Darlene Clark, ed.
      *Black Women in American History, vols. 5–8: Twentieth
         Century*
      Brooklyn, NY: Carlson Publications, 1990. 717 pp.

656. Hine, Darlene Clark, ed.
      Black Women's History, vols. 9–10: Theory and Practice
      Brooklyn, NY: Carlson Publications, 1990. 353 pp.

657. hooks, bell
      Talking Back: Thinking Feminist, Thinking Black
      Boston, MA: South End Press, 1988. 200 pp.

658. hooks, bell
      Yearning: Race, Gender and Cultural Politics
      Boston, MA: South End Press, 1991. 224 pp.

659. hooks, bell, and Cornel West
      Breaking Bread: Insurgent Black Intellectual Life
      Boston, MA: South End Press, 1991. 120 pp.

660. Hull, Gloria T., and Barbara Smith, eds.
      But Some of Us Are Brave: Black Women's Studies
      Old Westbury, NY: The Feminist Press, 1982. 432 pp.

661. Hurston, Zora Neale
      The Sanctified Church
      Berkeley, CA: Turtle Island Press, 1981. 107 pp.

662. Hurston, Zora Neale, ed. Alice Walker
      I Love Myself When I Am Laughing
      Old Westbury, NY: The Feminist Press, 1979. 320 pp.

663. Jackson, Rebecca, Jean M. Humez, ed.
      *Gifts of Power: The Writings of Rebecca Jackson, Black
      Visionary, Shaker Eldress*
      Amherst, MA: University of Massachusetts Press, 1987.
      376 pp.

664. Jones-Jackson, Patricia
      When Roots Die: Endangered Traditions on the Sea Islands
      Athens, GA: University of Georgia Press, 1987. 189 pp.

665. Jordan, June
      *Technical Difficulties: African-American Notes on the State
      of the Union*
      New York: NY: Pantheon Books, 1992. 228 pp.

666. Lawson, Ellen N.
      *The Three Sarahs: Documents of Antebellum Black College
      Women*
      Lewiston, NY: The Edwin Mellen Press, 1985. 335 pp.

667. Loewenberg, Bert James, and Ruth Bogin, eds.
      *Black Women in Nineteenth-Century American Life: Their
      Words, Their Thoughts, Their Feelings*
      University Park, PA: Pennsylvania State University
      Press, 1987. 368 pp.

668. Malson, Micheline R., E. Mudimbe-Boyi, J. O. Barr,
      and M. Wyer, eds.

Black Women in America: Social Science Perspective
Chicago, IL: University of Chicago Press, 1990. 348 pp.

669. Neverdon-Morton, Cynthia
Afro-American Women of the South and the Advancement of the Race, 1895–1925
Knoxville, TN: University of Tennessee Press, 1989. 288 pp.

670. Noble, Jeanne
Beautiful Also Are the Souls of My Black Sisters: A History of Black Women in America
Englewood Cliffs, NJ: Prentice-Hall, 1978. 128 pp.

671. Richardson, Marilyn, ed.
Maria W. Stewart: America's First Black Woman Political Writer
Bloomington, IN: Indiana University Press, 1987. 160 pp.

672. Russell, Sandi
Render Me My Song: African-American Women Writers from Slavery to the Present
New York, NY: St. Martin's Press, 1990. 230 pp.

673. Scott, Kesho
The Habit of Surviving: Black Women in America
New Brunswick, NJ: Rutgers University Press, 1991. 225 pp.

674. Shockley, Ann Allen, ed.
Afro-American Women Writers, 1746–1933
New York, NY: New American Library, 1989. 465 pp.

675. Simms, Margaret, and Julianne Malveaux, eds.
Slipping Through the Cracks: The Status of Black Women
New Brunswick, NJ: Transaction Books, 1986. 302 pp.

676. Smith, Barbara, ed.
Home Girls: A Black Feminist Anthology

New York, NY: Kitchen Table: Women of Color Press, 1983. 370 pp.

677. Steady, Filomina Chioma, ed.
      The Black Woman Cross-Culturally
      Rochester, VT: Schenkman, 1981. 645 pp.

678. Sterling, Dorothy, ed.
      We Are Your Sisters: Black Women in the Nineteenth Century
      New York, NY: W. W. Norton, 1984. 535 pp.

679. Tate, Claudia, ed.
      Black Women Writers at Work: Conversations
      Seabury, NY: Continuum Publishing Co., 1984. 213 pp.

680. Wallace, Michelle
      Invisibility Blues: From Pop Theory Towards a Black Feminist Cultural Criticism
      New York, NY: Verso/Cond, 1990. 256 pp.

681. Washington, Mary Helen, ed.
      Invented Lives: Narratives of Black Women (1860–1960)
      Garden City, NY: Doubleday & Co., 1987. 447 pp.

682. Wilson, Emily Herring
      Hope and Dignity: Older Black Women of the South
      Philadelphia, PA: Temple University Press, 1983. 234 pp.

Hispanic/Latina Women

683. Acosta Belen, Edna
      The Puerto Rican Woman: Perspectives on Culture, History and Society
      New York, NY: Praeger, 1986. 208 pp.

684. Alvarado, Elvia, ed. and trans. Medea Benjamin
      *Don't Be Afraid, Gringo: A Honduran Woman Speaks from
          the Heart*
      New York, NY: Harper & Row, 1989. 192 pp.

685. Andreas, Carol
      When Women Rebel: The Rise of Popular Feminism in Peru
      Westport, CT: Lawrence Hill & Co., 1987. 320 pp.

686. Anzaldua, Gloria
      Borderlands/La Frontera: The New Mestiza
      San Francisco, CA: Spinsters Ink, 1987. 203 pp.

687. Blea, Irene I.
      La Chicana and the Intersection of Race, Class, and Gender
      New York, NY: Praeger, 1992. 192 pp.

688. Bronstein, Audrey
      The Triple Struggle: Latin American Peasant Women
      Boston, MA: South End Press, 1983. 268 pp.

689. Cabrera, Lydia, trans. Morton Marks
      El Monte (novel)
      New York, NY: Methuen, 1985. 564 pp.

690. Carter, B., and K. Insko, eds.
      A Dream Compels Us: Salvadoran Women Speak Out
      Boston, MA: South End Press, 1989. 214 pp.

691. Elasser, Nan, Kyle MacKenzie, and Y Tixier Y Vigil
      Las Mujeres: Conversations from a Hispanic Community
      Old Westbury, NY: The Feminist Press, 1980. 162 pp.

692. Flusche, Della M., and Eugene Korth
      *Forgotten Females: Women of African and Indian Descent in
          Colonial Chile, 1535–1800*
      Detroit, MI: Blaine Ethridge, 1983. 112 pp.

693. Franco, Jean
      Plotting Women: Gender and Representation in Mexico

New York, NY: Columbia University Press, 1989. 244 pp.

694.   Frisch, Michael, ed.
       *Oral History and Puerto Rican Women: Special Issue of the
       Oral History Review*
       New York, NY: Oral History Association, SUNY, 1988.
       100 pp.

695.   Garfield, Evelyn Picon, ed.
       Women's Voices from Latin America
       Detroit, MI: Wayne State University Press, 1986. 188
       pp.

696.   Gomez, Alma, C. Moraga, and M. Romo-Carmona
       Cuentos: Stories by Latinas
       New York, NY: Kitchen Table: Women of Color Press,
       1983. 241 pp.

697.   Holt-Seeland, Inger, trans. E. H. Lacoste
       Women of Cuba
       Westport, CT: Lawrence Hill & Co., 1981. 109 pp.

698.   Horno-Delgado, Asuncion, et al.
       Breaking Boundaries: Latina Writing and Critical Readings
       Amherst, MA: University of Massachusetts Press, 1989.
       336 pp.

699.   Kita, Bernice
       What Prize Awaits Us: Letters from Guatemala
       Maryknoll, NY: Orbis Books, 1988. 200 pp.

700.   Miller, Beth, ed.
       Women in Hispanic Literature: Icons and Fallen Idols
       Berkeley, CA: University of California Press, 1984. 383
       pp.

701.   Mirande, Alfredo, and Evangelina Enriquez
       La Chicana: The Mexican-American Woman
       Berkeley, CA: University of California Press, 1979. 283
       pp.

702. Mohr, Nicholasa
      Rituals of Survival: A Woman's Portfolio
      Houston, TX: Arte Publico Press, 1985. 158 pp.

703. Moraga, Cherrie
      Loving in the War Years: Lo que nunca pasa por sus labios
      Boston, MA: South End Press, 1983. 152 pp.

704. Patai, Daphne
      Brazilian Women Speak: Contemporary Life Stories
      New Brunswick, NJ: Rutgers University Press, 1987.
         396 pp.

705. Silverblatt, Irene
      *Moon, Sun, and Witches: Gender Ideologies and Class in
         Inca and Colonial Peru*
      Princeton, NJ: Princeton University Press, 1987. 266
         pp.

706. Torre, Adela de la, and Beatriz Pesquera, eds.
      *Building with Our Hands: New Directions in Chicana
         Studies*
      Berkeley, CA: University of California Press, 1993. 246
         pp.

Asian Women

707. Ariyoshi, Sawako, trans. Mildred Tahara
      The Twilight Years
      New York, NY: Kodansha International, 1984. 216 pp.

708. Asian Women United of California, ed.
      *Making Waves: An Anthology of Writings by and About
         Asian Women*
      Boston, MA: Beacon Press, 1989. 481 pp.

709. Bingham, Marjorie W., E. Gross, and J. Donaldson
      Women in Japan: From Ancient Times to Present

St. Louis Park, MN: Glenhurst Publishers, 1987. 317 pp.

710. no entry

711. Cho Wha Soon, ed. Sun Ai and A. S. Nim
Let the Weak Be Strong: A Woman's Struggle for Justice
Oak Park, IL: Meyer-Stone, 1988. 176 pp.

712. Cleary, Thomas, trans. and ed.
Immortal Sisters: Secrets of Taoist Women
Boulder, CO: Shambala Press, 1989. 99 pp.

713. Condon, Jane
A Half Step Behind: Japanese Women of the Eighties
New York, NY: Dodd, Mead, 1985. 319 pp.

714. Croll, Elisabeth
Chinese Women Since Mao
London, U.K.: Zed Books, 1983. 129 pp.

715. Daiyun, Yue, and Caroline Wakeman
To the Storm: The Odyssey of a Revolutionary
Berkeley, CA: University of California Press, 1985. 405 pp.

716. Delza, Sophia
T'ai Chi Ch'uan: Body and Mind in Harmony
Albany, NY: State University of New York Press, 1985. 244 pp.

717. Guisso, Richard W., and Stanley Johannesen, eds.
Women in China: Current Direction in Historical Scholarship
Youngstown, PA: Philo Press, 1981. 238 pp.

718. Honig, Emily, and Gail Hershatter
Personal Voices: Chinese Women in the 1980's
Palo Alto, CA: Stanford University Press, 1988. 387 pp.

719. Hossain, Rokeya Sakhawat, ed. and trans. Roushan
      Jahan
      "Sultana's Dream" and Selections from "The Secluded Ones"
      Old Westbury, NY: The Feminist Press, 1988. 90 pp.

720. Jaini, Padmanabh S.
      *Gender and Salvation: Jaina Debates on the Spiritual Libera-
      tion of Women*
      Berkeley, CA: University of California Press, 1991. 250
      pp.

721. Janelli, Roger L., and Dawnhee Yim Janelli
      Ancestor Worship and Korean Society
      Palo Alto, CA: Stanford University Press, 1982. 228 pp.

722. Kanda, Mikio, ed. and trans. Taeko Midoikawa
      *Widows of Hiroshima: The Life Stories of Nineteen Peasant
      Wives*
      New York, NY: St. Martin's Press, 1988. 199 pp.

723. Kendall, Laurel
      *Shamans, Housewives and Other Restless Spirits: Women in
      Korean Ritual Life*
      Honolulu, HI: University of Hawaii Press, 1985. 234
      pp.

724. Kendall, Laurel
      The Life and Hard Times of a Korean Shaman
      Honolulu, HI: University of Hawaii Press, 1988. 157
      pp.

725. Khaing, Mi Mi
      The World of Burmese Women
      London, U.K.: Zed Books, 1984. 198 pp.

726. King, Sallie B.
      *Passionate Journey: The Spiritual Autobiography of Satomi
      Myodo*
      Boulder, CO: Shambala Press, 1987. 212 pp.

727. Kingston, Maxine Hong
The Woman Warrior
New York, NY: Alfred A. Knopf, 1977. 209 pp.

728. Kingston, Maxine Hong
China Men
New York, NY: Alfred A. Knopf, 1980. 308 pp.

729. Kristeva, Julia, trans. Anita Barrows
About Chinese Women
New York, NY: Marion Boyars, 1977. 211 pp.

730. Kwok, Pui-lan
Chinese Women and Christianity, 1860–1927
Alpharetta, GA: Scholars Press, 1992. 235 pp.

731. Lebra, Takie Sugiyama
Japanese Women: Constraint and Fulfillment
Honolulu, HI: University of Hawaii Press, 1984. 345 pp.

732. Ling, Ding, ed. Tani Barlow, with Gary Bjorge
I Myself Am a Woman
Boston, MA: Beacon Press, 1989. 320 pp.

733. Matsubara, Hisako
Cranes at Dusk (Shinto virtues and survival)
Garden City, NY: Dial Press, Doubleday, 1985. 254 pp.

734. Mumtaz, Khawar, and Farida Shaheed
Women of Pakistan
London, U.K.: Zed Books, 1987. 256 pp.

735. Peck, Stacey
Halls of Jade, Walls of Stone: Women in China Today
New York, NY: Franklin Watts, 1985. 321 pp.

736. Risseeuw, Carla
The Fish Don't Talk About the Water: Gender Transformation, Power and Resistance Among Women in Sri Lanka
Leiden, Neth.: E. J. Brill, 1988. 399 pp.

737. Robins-Mowry, Dorothy
      The Hidden Sun: Women of Modern Japan
      Boulder, CO: Westview, 1983. 394 pp.

738. Setouchi, Harumi, trans. Janine Beichman
      The End of Summer (novel)
      New York, NY: Kodansha International, 1989. 114 pp.

739. Ueda, Makoto, ed.
      The Mother of Dreams and Other Stories
      New York, NY: Kodansha International, 1986. 279 pp.

740. Yayori, Matsui
      Women's Asia
      London, U.K.: Zed Books, 1989. 172 pp.

Hinduism and Women

741. Dehejia, Vidya
      Antal and Her Path of Love: Poems of a Woman Saint from South India
      Albany, NY: State University of New York Press, 1990. 192 pp.

742. Eck, Diana L.
      Banaras, City of Light
      Princeton, NJ: Princeton University Press, 1983. 427 pp.

743. Feldhaus, Anne
      The Religious Systems of the Mahanubhara Sect
      Columbia, MO: South Asia Books, 1983. 285 pp.

744. Feldhaus, Anne, ed.
      The Deeds of God in Rddhipur
      Oxford, U.K.: Oxford University Press, 1984. 209 pp.

745. Gatwood, Lynn E.
      *Devi and the Spouse Goddess: Women, Sexuality and Mar-
      riage in India*
      Riverdale, MD: Riverdale Co., 1985. 206 pp.

746. Harlan, Lindsey
      *Religion and Rajput Women: The Ethic of Protection in
      Contemporary Narratives*
      Berkeley, CA: University of California Press, 1991. 286
      pp.

747. Jayakar, Pupul
      The Earth Mother
      San Francisco, CA: Harper & Row, 1990. 229 pp.

748. Kramrisch, Stella
      The Presence of Siva
      Princeton, NJ: Princeton University Press, 1981. 514
      pp.

749. Leslie, Julia, ed.
      Roles and Rituals for Hindu Women
      Cranbury, NJ: Fairleigh Dickinson University Press,
      1992. 256 pp.

750. Marglin, Frederique Apffel
      Wives of the God-King: The Rituals of the Devadasis of Puri
      Oxford, U.K.: Oxford University Press, 1985. 388 pp.

751. Mitter, Sara S.
      *Dharma's Daughters: Contemporary Indian Women and
      Hindu Culture*
      New Brunswick, NJ: Rutgers University Press, 1991.
      220 pp.

752. O'Flaherty, Wendy Doniger
      Women, Androgynes and Other Mythical Beasts
      Chicago, IL: University of Chicago Press, 1980. 382
      pp.

753. O'Flaherty, Wendy Doniger
     Shiva: The Erotic Ascetic
     Oxford, U.K.: Oxford University Press, 1981. 400 pp.

754. Sangari, Kumkum
     Recasting Women in India: Essays in Colonial History
     New Brunswick, NJ: Rutgers University Press, 1990.
         372 pp.

755. Vandana, Sister
     Waters of Fire
     Warwick, NY: Amity House, 1987. 192 pp.

756. Waghorne, Joanne Punzo, ed.
     *Gods of Flesh, Gods of Stone: The Embodiment of Divinity in
         India*
     Chambersburg, NY: Anima Publications, 1985. 208 pp.

Buddhism and Women

757. Allione, Tsultrim
     Women of Wisdom (Tibetan women saints)
     Boston, MA: Pandora/Routledge & Kegan Paul, 1984.
         282 pp.

758. Bennett, Lynn
     *Dangerous Wives and Sacred Sisters: Roles of High-Caste
         Women in Nepal*
     New York, NY: Columbia University Press, 1983. 353
         pp.

759. Boucher, Sandy
     *Turning the Wheel: American Women Creating the New
         Buddhism*
     San Francisco, CA: Harper & Row, 1988. 256 pp.

760. David-Neel, Alexandra, and Lama Yongden, trans. J.
     van Wetering

The Power of Nothingness
Boston, MA: Houghton Mifflin, 1982. 134 pp.

761. Friedman, Lenore
Meetings with Remarkable Women: Buddhist Teachers in America
Boulder, CO: Shambala Press, 1987. 250 pp.

762. Gross, Rita
Buddhism After Patriarchy: A Feminist History, Analysis, and Reconstruction of Buddhism
Albany, NY: State University of New York Press, 1993. 365 pp.

763. Havnevik, Hanna
Tibetan Buddhist Nuns: History, Cultural Norms and Social Reality
Oxford, U.K.: Oxford University Press, 1990. 282 pp.

764. Hopkinson, Deborah, Michele Hill, and Eileen Kiera, eds.
Not Mixing Up Buddhism: Essays on Women in Buddhist Practice
Freedom, NY: White Pine Press, 1986. 116 pp.

765. Khema, Ayya
Being Nobody, Going Nowhere
Boston, MA: Wisdom Publications, 1989. 192 pp.

766. Kleunick, Linda (Sujata), and Richard Hayes (Mubul), eds.
Women and Buddhism (triple issue of Spring World)
Ann Arbor, MI: Spring World, 1986. 400 pp.

767. Paul, Diana
The Buddhist Feminine Ideal: Queen Srimala and the Tathagatagarbha
Alpharetta, GA: Scholars Press, 1980. 246 pp.

768.   Paul, Diana
       *Women in Buddhism: Images of the Feminine in the Mahay-
          ana Tradition*
       Berkeley, CA: University of California Press, 1985. 333
          pp.

769.   Richman, Paula
       *Women Branch Stories and Religious Rhetoric in a Tamil
          Buddhist Text* (So. Asian Series #12)
       Syracuse, NY: Syracuse University Press, 1989. 288 pp.

770.   Shaw, Miranda
       Passionate Enlightenment: Women in Tantric Buddhism
       Princeton, NJ: Princeton University Press, 1994. 312 pp.

771.   Tsomo, Karuna Lekslte, ed.
       Sakyadhita: Daughters of the Buddha
       Ithaca, NY: Snow Lion Publishers, 1988. 346 pp.

772.   Willis, Janis, ed.
       Feminine Ground: Essays on Women in Tibet
       Ithaca, NY: Snow Lion Publishers, 1990. 200 pp.

773.   Willson, Martin, ed.
       In Praise of Tara: Songs to the Saviouress
       Boston, MA: Wisdom Publications, 1986. 496 pp.

Islam and Women

774.   Abouzeid, Leila, trans. Barbara Parmenter
       *Year of the Elephant: A Moroccan Woman's Journey Toward
          Independence*
       Austin, TX: University of Texas Press, 1990. 129 pp.

775.   Ahmed, Leila
       *Women and Gender in Islam: Historical Roots of a Modern
          Debate*
       New Haven, CT: Yale University Press, 1992. 320 pp.

776. Atiya, Nayra
Khul-Khaal: Five Egyptian Women Tell Their Stories
Syracuse, NY: Syracuse University Press, 1990. 216 pp.

777. Cloudsley, Anne
Women of Omduran: Life, Love and the Cult of Virginity
New York, NY: St. Martin's Press, 1985. 181 pp.

778. El Saadawi, Nawal
The Hidden Face of Eve: Women in the Arab World
London, U.K.: Zed Books, 1980. 212 pp.

779. Fernea, Elizabeth Warnock, and Basima Qattan Bezir-
gan, eds.
Middle Eastern Muslim Women Speak
Austin, TX: University of Texas Press, 1977. 452 pp.

780. Fernea, Elizabeth Warnock, ed.
*Women and the Family in the Middle East: New Voices of
Change*
Austin, TX: University of Texas Press, 1985. 368 pp.

781. Friedl, Erica
Women of Deh Koh
Washington, DC: Smithsonian, 1989. 257 pp.

782. Hall, Marjorie, and Bakhita Amin Ismail
Sisters Under the Sun: The Story of Sudanese Women
White Plains, NY: Longman, 1981. 264 pp.

783. Hussain, Freeda, ed.
Muslim Women: The Ideal and the Contextual Realities
New York, NY: St. Martin's Press, 1984. 232 pp.

784. Jeffrey, Patricia
Frogs in a Well: Indian Women in Purdah
London, U.K.: Zed Books, 1979. 187 pp.

785. Keddie, Nikki R., and Beth Baron, eds.
*Women in Middle Eastern History: Shifting Boundaries in
Sex and Gender*
New Haven, CT: Yale University Press, 1992. 352 pp.

786. Mernissi, Fatima, trans. Mary Jo Lakeland
      *The Veil and the Male Elite: A Feminist Interpretation of
      Women's Rights in Early Islam*
      Reading, MA: Addison-Wesley Publishing Company,
      1991. 225 pp.

787. Metcalf, Barbara Daly, ed.
      *Moral Conduct and Authority: The Peace of Adab in South
      Asian Islam*
      Berkeley, CA: University of California Press, 1984. 389
      pp.

788. Nagata, Judith
      *The Reflowering of Islam: Modern Religious Radicals and
      Their Roots*
      Vancouver, B.C.: University of British Columbia Press,
      1984. 282 pp.

789. Reeves, Minou
      *Female Warriors of Allah: Women and the Islamic Revolu-
      tion of Iran*
      New York, NY: Paragon, 1990. 218 pp.

790. Sabbah, Fatma A., trans. Mary Jo Lakeland
      Woman in the Muslim Unconscious
      Elmsford, NY: Pergamon Press, 1984. 140 pp.

791. Schimmel, Annemarie
      Mystical Dimensions of Islam
      Chapel Hill, NC: University of North Carolina Press,
      1975. 506 pp.

792. Schimmel, Annemarie
      As Through a Veil: Mystical Poetry in Islam
      New York, NY: Columbia University Press, 1982. 359 pp.

793. Schimmel, Annemarie
      *And Mohammed Is His Messenger: The Veneration of the
      Prophet in Islamic Piety*

Chapel Hill, NC: University of North Carolina Press, 1985. 377 pp.

794. Shaarwi, Huda
Harem Years: The Memoirs of an Egyptian Feminist, 1879–1924
Old Westbury, NY: The Feminist Press, 1987. 158 pp.

795. Shabban, Bouthaina
Both Right and Left Handed Arab Women Talk About Their Lives
Bloomington, IN: Indiana University Press, 1991. 256 pp.

796. Smith, Jane I., ed.
Women in Contemporary Muslim Societies
Cranbury, NJ: Bucknell University Press, 1980. 259 pp.

797. Smith, Margaret
Rabia: The Mystic and Her Fellow Saints
Cambridge, U.K.: Cambridge University Press, 1984. 219 pp.

798. Walther, Wiebke
Women in Islam
New York, NY: World, 1982. 204 pp.

799. Wikan, Unni
Behind the Veil in Arabia: Women in Oman
Chicago, IL: University of Chicago Press, 1991. 328 pp.

800. Zuhur, Sherifa
Revealing Reveiling: Islamic Gender Ideology in Contemporary Egypt
Albany, NY: State University of New York Press, 1992. 250 pp.

Women of Africa

801. Amadivme, Ifi
Male Daughters, Female Husbands: Gender and Sexism in African Society
London, U.K.: Zed Books, 1987. 272 pp.

802. Boddy, Janice
Wombs and Alien Spirits: Women, Men and the Zar Cult in Northern Sudan
Madison, WI: University of Wisconsin Press, 1989. 384 pp.

803. Creider, Jane Tapsubei
Two Lives: My Spirit and I (Kenyan)
London, U.K.: Women's Press, 1986. 178 pp.

804. Emecheta, Buchi
The Bride Price: Young Ibo Girl's Love (novels)
New York, NY: George Braziller, 1976. 168 pp.

805. Emecheta, Buchi
The Joys of Motherhood (novel)
New York, NY: George Braziller, 1979. 224 pp.

806. Emecheta, Buchi
Second-Class Citizen (novel)
New York, NY: George Braziller, 1983. 175 pp.

807. Emecheta, Buchi
The Rape of Shavi (novel)
New York, NY: George Braziller, 1985. 178 pp.

808. Gleason, Judith
Oya: In Praise of the Goddess (Yoruba goddess)
Boulder, CO: Shambala Press, 1987. 256 pp.

809. Head, Bessie
When Rain Clouds Gather (novel)
Harmondsworth, U.K.: Penguin, 1971. 188 pp.

810. Head, Bessie
     Maru (novel)
     London, U.K.: Heinemann, 1972. 127 pp.

811. Kuzwayo, Ellen
     Call Me Woman (South African)
     San Francisco, CA: Spinsters Ink, 1985. 288 pp.

812. Lipman, Beata
     We Make Freedom: Women in South Africa
     Boston, MA: Pandora/Routledge & Kegan Paul, 1984.
     141 pp.

813. Makeba, Miriam, with James Smith
     Makeba: My Story
     New York, NY: New American Library, 1988. 249 pp.

814. Marks, Shula, ed.
     *Not Either an Experimental Doll: The Separate Worlds of
     Three South African Women*
     Bloomington, IN: Indiana University Press, 1987. 217
     pp.

815. Mirza, Sarah, and Margaret Strobel, eds.
     Three Swahili Women: Life Histories from Mombasa, Kenya
     Bloomington, IN: Indiana University Press, 1989. 157
     pp.

816. Oosthuizen, Ann, ed.
     Sometimes When It Rains: Writings by South African Women
     Boston, MA: Pandora/Routledge & Kegan Paul, 1987.
     184 pp.

817. Richards, Audrey
     Chisungu: A Girl's Initiation Ceremony Among the Bemba
     London, U.K.: Tavistock, 1982. 224 pp.

818. Robertson, Claire C.
     *Sharing the Same Bowl: A Socio-economic History of Women
     and Class*

Bloomington, IN: Indiana University Press, 1984. 299 pp.

819.   Robertson, Claire C., and Martin Klein, eds.
       Women and Slavery in Africa
       Madison, WI: University of Wisconsin Press, 1983. 380 pp.

820.   Romero, Patricia, ed.
       Life Histories of African Women
       Atlantic Highlands, NJ: Humanities Press, 1988. 200 pp.

821.   Russell, Diana E. H.
       Lives of Courage: Women for a New South Africa
       New York, NY: Basic Books, 1989. 352 pp.

822.   Schreiner, Olive, ed. Carol Barash
       An Olive Schreiner Reader: Writings on Women and South Africa
       Boston, MA: Pandora/Routledge & Kegan Paul, 1987. 200 pp.

823.   Shostak, Marjorie
       Nisa: The Life and Worlds of a !Kung Woman
       Cambridge, MA: Harvard University Press, 1981. 402 pp.

824.   Thiam, Awa, trans. Dorothy Blair
       Black Sisters, Speak Out: Feminism and Oppression in Black Africa
       London, U.K.: Pluto Press, 1986. 160 pp.

Women in Primal Culture

825.   Bell, Diane
       Daughters of the Dreaming (Australian aboriginal)
       London, U.K.: Allen & Unwin, 1984. 297 pp.

826. Brock, Peggy, ed.
      *Women Rites and Sites: Aboriginal Women's Cultural
          Knowledge*
      Boston, MA: Pandora/Routledge & Kegan Paul, 1989.
          208 pp.

827. Fay, Gayle, ed.
      We Are Bosses Ourselves (Australian aboriginal)
      Atlantic Highlands, NJ: Humanities Press, 1983. 175
          pp.

828. Gutmanis, June
      Na Pule Kahiko: Ancient Hawaiian Prayers
      Honolulu, HI: Editors Limited, 1983. 124 pp.

829. Meigs, Anna S.
      Food, Sex, and Pollution: A New Guinea Religion
      New Brunswick, NJ: Rutgers University Press, 1984.
          196 pp.

830. Phaigh, Betha
      Gestalt and the Wisdom of the Kahunas (Hawaiian)
      Marina del Rey, CA: De Vorss & Co., 1983. 112 pp.

831. Smith, Jean
      Tapu Removal in Maori Religion
      Wellington, N.Z.: Polynesian Society, 1974. 96 pp.

832. Strathern, Marilyn
      *The Gender of Gift: Problems with Women and Problems with
          Society in Melanesia*
      Berkeley, CA: University of California Press, 1988. 422
          pp.

833. White, Isobel, D. Barwick, and B. Meehan, eds.
      Fighters and Singers: The Lives of Some Aboriginal Women
      London, U.K.: Allen & Unwin, 1985. 226 pp.

4. FEMINIST PSYCHOLOGY

The psychological insights of women who have called into question the assumptions of the forefathers of modern psychology permeate studies located within this chapter. While the field of "personality sciences" is vast and the literature is immense, there are a number of highly relevant studies by women concerned with human development and behavior that color understanding of spirituality. I have divided this chapter into two parts, identifying studies attached to Jungian understandings as distinctive. In the first section a variety of approaches are represented which can be generally understood as Freudian, neo-Freudian, object relations, and clinical psychology orientations. Many of these studies address questions of maturation and healthy integration for women, critiquing earlier studies which served to narrow prospects for women and limit the notion of full human expression. Certain authors suggest the importance of French postmodern thought (especially the influence of Lacan's reading of Freud); others are concerned with relationships, especially of the mother to her sons and daughters. Nancy Chodorow's recent collection of essays is particularly noteworthy.

The contribution of writers who have developed spiritual insight from Jung's writing is significant. A decade ago there were a number of women and men elaborating upon men's and women's spiritual experience within this tradition, including Anne Ulanov; today the list is long and impressive. Among concerns discussed by Jungians are the functions of dream and myth as well as the "shadow."

General

834. Alpert, Judith L., ed.
Psychoanalysis and Women: Contemporary Reappraisals
Hillsdale, NJ: The Analytic Press (Bernay), 1986. 336 pp.

835. Ashurst, Pamela, and Zaida Hall, eds.
Understanding Women in Distress
New York, NY: Routledge, 1989. 272 pp.

836. Baruch, Elaine Hoffman, and L. Serrano
Women Analyze Women
New York, NY: New York University Press, 1988. 424 pp.

837. Bauer, Jan
Alcoholism and Women: The Background and the Psychology
Toronto, Ont.: Inner City Books, 1982.

838. Belenky, Mary, B. Clinchy, N. Goldberger, and J. Tarule
Women's Ways of Knowing: The Development of Self, Voice and Mind
New York, NY: Basic Books, 1986. 256 pp.

839. Bernay, Toni, and Dorothy Cantor, eds.
The Psychology of Today's Woman: New Psychoanalytical Visions
Hillsdale, NJ: The Analytic Press (Bernay), 1986. 377 pp.

840. Bregman, Lucy
The Rediscovery of Inner Experience
Chicago, IL: Nelson-Hall, 1982. 194 pp.

841. Brennan, Teresa
Between Feminism and Psychoanalysis
New York, NY: Routledge, 1989. 224 pp.

842. Caprio, Betsy
*The Woman Sealed in the Tower: Psychological Approach to
Feminine Spirituality*
Ramsey, NJ: Paulist Press, 1982. 105 pp.

843. Chinnici, Rosemary
Can Women Re-Image the Church?
Ramsey, NJ: Paulist Press, 1992. 110 pp.

844. Chodorow, Nancy
Feminism and Psychoanalytic Theory
New Haven, CT: Yale University Press, 1989. 186 pp.

845. Clement, Catherine
The Weary Sons of Freud
New York, NY: Verso/Cond, 1987. 144 pp.

846. DeMarinis, Valerie M.
Critical Caring: A Feminist Model for Pastoral Psychology
Louisville, KY: Westminster/John Knox Press, 1993.
208 pp.

847. Dinnerstein, Dorothy
*The Mermaid and the Minotaur: Sexual Arrangements and
Human Malaise*
New York, NY: Harper & Row, 1976. 288 pp.

848. Dooley, Anne Marie
*A Quest for Religious Maturity: Obsessive-Compulsive Per-
sonality* (counseling)
Washington, DC: University Press of America, 1981.
111 pp.

849. Downing, Christine
*Mysteries of Women: Glimpses into the Psychology of
Women—and Beyond*
New York, NY: Crossroad/Continuum, 1992. 252 pp.

850. Eichenbaum, Luise, and Susie Orbach
*Between Women: Love, Envy and Competition in Women's
Friendships*
New York, NY: Viking Press, 1987. 223 pp.

851. Eichenbaum, Luise, and Susie Orbach
      What Do Women Want: Exploding the Myth of Dependency
      New York, NY: Coward-McCann, 1983. 240 pp.

852. Feldstein, Richard, and Judith Roof, eds.
      Feminism and Psychoanalysis
      Ithaca, NY: Cornell University Press, 1989. 392 pp.

853. Flax, Jane
      *Thinking Fragments: Psychoanalysis, Feminism, and
          Postmodernism in the Contemporary West*
      Berkeley, CA: University of California Press, 1989. 286
          pp.

854. Freeman, Lucy, and Herbert S. Strean
      Freud and Women
      New York, NY: Crossroad Publishing, 1981. 283 pp.

855. Gallop, Jane
      The Daughter's Seduction: Feminism and Psychoanalysis
      Ithaca, NY: Cornell University Press, 1982. 164 pp.

856. George, Diana Hume
      Blake and Freud
      Ithaca, NY: Cornell University Press, 1980. 253 pp.

857. Gilligan, Carol
      In a Different Voice
      Cambridge, MA: Harvard University Press, 1982. 184
          pp.

858. Goldenberg, Naomi
      *Returning Words to Flesh: Feminism, Psychoanalysis, and
          the Resurrection of the Body*
      Boston, MA: Beacon Press, 1990. 256 pp.

859. Greenspan, Miriam
      A New Approach to Women and Therapy
      New York, NY: McGraw-Hill Book Co., 1983. 355 pp.

860. Houston, Jean
The Search for the Beloved: Journeys in Mythology and Sacred Psychology
Los Angeles, CA: Jeremy Tarcher Books, 1989. 252 pp.

861. Jordan, Judith, Jean Baker, Alexandra Kaplan et al., eds.
Women's Growth in Connection: Writings from the Stone Center
New York, NY: Guilford Press, 1991. 310 pp.

862. Josselson, Ruthellen
Finding Herself: Pathways to Identity Development in Women
San Francisco, CA: Jossey-Bass, 1987. 230 pp.

863. Klein, Viola
The Feminine Character
New York, NY: Routledge, 1989. 200 pp.

864. Lerman, Hannah
A Mote in Freud's Eye: From Psychoanalysis to the Psychology of Women
New York, NY: Spring Publishing, 1986. 228 pp.

865. Miller, Alice, trans. Hildegarde Hannum and Hunter Hannum
Thou Shalt Not Be Aware
New York, NY: Farrar, Straus & Giroux, 1984. 331 pp.

866. Miller, Alice, trans. Hildegarde Hannum and Hunter Hannum
For Your Own Good: Hidden Cruelty in Child-Rearing and the Roots of Violence
New York, NY: Farrar, Straus & Giroux, 1985. 284 pp.

867. Mitchell, Juliet, and Jacqueline Rose, eds.
Feminine Sexuality: Jacques Lacan and the Ecole Freudienne
New York, NY: Pantheon Books, 1983. 187 pp.

868. Olivier, Christiane
      Jocasta's Children: The Imprint of the Mother
      New York, NY: Routledge, 1989. 192 pp.

869. Robbins, Joan Hamerman, and Rachel J. Siegel, eds.
      *Women Changing Therapy: New Assessments, Values and
      Strategies in Feminist Therapy*
      New York, NY: Harrington Park Press, 1985. 240 pp.

870. Robbins, Martha Ann
      *Midlife Women and the Death of Mother: A Study of
      Psychohistorical and Spiritual Transformation*
      New York, NY: Peter Lang, 1990. 340 pp.

871. Roith, Estelle
      *The Riddle of Freud: Jewish Influences on His Theory of
      Female Sexuality*
      London, U.K.: Tavistock, 1987. 250 pp.

872. Saussy, Caroll
      *God Images and Self Esteem: Empowering Women in a
      Patriarchal Society*
      Louisville, KY: Westminster/John Knox Press, 1991.
      192 pp.

873. Sayers, Janet
      *Sexual Contradictions: Psychology, Psychoanalysis, and Fem-
      inism*
      London, U.K.: Tavistock, 1986. 250 pp.

874. Squire, Corinne
      Significant Differences: Feminism in Psychology
      New York, NY: Routledge, 1989. 176 pp.

875. Van Herik, Judith
      Freud on Femininity and Faith
      Berkeley, CA: University of California Press, 1982. 217
      pp.

876. Vaughan, Frances
The Inward Arc: Healing and Wholeness in Psychotherapy and Spirituality
Boulder, CO: Shambala Press, 1985. 238 pp.

877. Walsh, Mary Roth, ed.
The Psychology of Women: Ongoing Debates
New Haven, CT: Yale University Press, 1987. 484 pp.

878. Wolff-Salin, Mary
No Other Light: Points of Convergence in Psychology and Spirituality
New York, NY: Crossroad Publishing, 1986. 234 pp.

Jungian Perspectives

879. Bertine, Eleanor
Human Relationships: In the Family, in Friendship, in Love
White Plains, NY: Longman, 1958. 237 pp.

880. Brewi, Janice, and Anne Brennan
Celebrate Mid-Life: Jungian Archetypes and Mid-Life Spirituality
New York, NY: Crossroad Publishing, 1989. 306 pp.

881. Carlson, Kathie
In Her Image: The Unhealed Daughter's Search for Her Mother
Boulder, CO: Shambala Press, 1989. 152 pp.

882. Clift, Jean Dalby, and Wallace B. Clift
Symbols of Transformation in Dreams
New York, NY: Crossroad Publishing, 1984. 155 pp.

883. Colegrave, Sukie
The Spirit of the Valley: Androgyny and Chinese Thought
London, U.K.: Virago Press, 1979. 244 pp.

884.   DeCastillejo, Irene Claremont
       Knowing Woman
       New York, NY: Putnam Books, 1973. 188 pp.

885.   Downing, Christine
       Mirrors of the Self: Archetypal Images That Shape Your Life
       Los Angeles, CA: Jeremy Tarcher Books, 1991. 284 pp.

886.   Dunne, Carrin
       Behold Woman: A Jungian Approach to Feminist Theology
       Wilmette, IL: Chiron, 1989. 112 pp.

887.   Englesman, Joan Chamberlain
       The Feminine Dimension of the Divine
       Wilmette, IL: Chiron, 1987. 203 pp.

888.   Grant, W. Harold, Magdala Thompson, and T. Clarke
       *From Image to Likeness: A Jungian Path in the Gospel
          Journey*
       Ramsey, NJ: Paulist Press, 1980. 249 pp.

889.   Gregory, Eileen
       Summoning the Familiar: Powers and Rites of Common Life
       Dallas, TX: The Dallas Institute, 1984. 90 pp.

890.   Hall, Nor
       *The Moon and the Virgin: Reflections on the Archetypal
          Feminine*
       New York, NY: Harper & Row, 1980. 284 pp.

891.   Hannah, Barbara
       *Encounters with the Soul: Active Imagination as Developed
          by C. G. Jung*
       Santa Monica, CA: Sigo Press, 1981. 254 pp.

892.   Harding, M. Esther
       The Way of All Women
       New York, NY: Harper Colophon Books, 1970. 314 pp.

893. Harding, M. Esther
      Woman's Mysteries, Ancient and Modern
      New York, NY: Harper & Row, 1971. 256 pp.

894. Howes, Elizabeth Boyden
      Jesus' Answer to God
      San Francisco, CA: Guild for Psychological Studies
          Publishing House, 1984. 257 pp.

895. Howes, Elizabeth Boyden
      Intersection and Beyond
      San Francisco, CA: Guild for Psychological Studies
          Publishing House, 1985. 198 pp.

896. Jaffe, Aniela
      The Myth of Meaning
      New York, NY: Penguin Books, 1975. 186 pp.

897. Jung, Emma, trans. C. F. Baynes
      Anima and Animus
      New York, NY: Spring Publishing, 1981. 94 pp.

898. Lauter, Estella, and Carol Schrier Rupprecht, eds.
      *Feminist Archetypal Theory: Interdisciplinary Re-visions of
          Jungian Thought*
      Knoxville, TN: University of Tennessee Press, 1985.
          296 pp.

899. Leonard, Linda Schierse
      *The Wounded Woman: Healing the Father-Daughter Rela-
          tionship*
      Boulder, CO: Shambala Press, 1983. 179 pp.

900. Leonard, Linda Schierse
      *On the Way to the Wedding: Transforming the Love Relation-
          ship*
      Boulder, CO: Shambala Press, 1986. 261 pp.

901. Leonard, Linda Schierse
      Witness to the Fire: Creativity and the Veil of Addiction
      Boulder, CO: Shambala Press, 1989. 384 pp.

902. Lichtman, Susan A.
Life Stages of Women's Heroic Journey: A Study of the Origins of the Great Goddess Archetype
Lewiston, NY: The Edwin Mellen Press, 1991. 108 pp.

903. Luke, Helen M.
Woman, Earth and Spirit: The Feminine in Symbol and Myth
New York, NY: Crossroad Publishing, 1984. 102 pp.

904. Luke, Helen M.
The Voice Within: Love and Virtue in the Age of the Spirit
New York, NY: Crossroad Publishing, 1984. 118 pp.

905. Paris, Ginette, trans. G. Moor
Pagan Meditations: The Worlds of Aphrodite, Artemis and Hestia
New York, NY: Spring Publishing, 1986. 204 pp.

906. Qualls-Corbett, Nancy
The Sacred Prostitute: Eternal Aspects of the Feminine
Toronto, Ont.: Inner City Books, 1988. 171 pp.

907. Singer, June
The Boundaries of the Soul: The Practice of Jung's Psychology
Garden City, NY: Doubleday & Co., 1972. 420 pp.

908. Singer, June
Androgyny: Toward a New Theory of Sexuality
Garden City, NY: Anchor Press, Doubleday, 1976. 371 pp.

909. Stroud, Joanne, and Gail Thomas, eds.
Images of the Untouched: Virginity in Psyche, Myth, and Community
New York, NY: Spring Publishing, 1985. 201 pp.

910. Ulanov, Ann
The Feminine in Jungian Psychology and in Christian Theology

Evanston, IL: Northwestern University Press, 1971. 347 pp.

911. Ulanov, Ann
Picturing God
Cambridge, MA: Cowley Publishing, 1986. 198 pp.

912. Ulanov, Ann, and Barry Ulanov
Cinderella and Her Sisters: The Envied and the Envying
Louisville, KY: Westminster/John Knox Press, 1983. 186 pp.

913. Von Franz, Marie-Louise
The Feminine in Fairy Tales
New York, NY: Spring Publishing, 1972. 200 pp.

914. Von Franz, Marie-Louise
Patterns of Creativity Mirrored in Creation Myths
New York, NY: Spring Publishing, 1972. 250 pp.

915. Wagner, Kathleen
Unlocking Secrets of the Feminine: The Path Beyond Sexism
Kansas City, MO: Sheed & Ward, 1986. 156 pp.

916. Wehr, Demaris S.
Jung and Feminism: Liberating Archetypes
Boston, MA: Beacon Press, 1987. 160 pp.

917. Welsh, John
Spiritual Pilgrims: Carl Jung and Teresa of Avila
Ramsey, NJ: Paulist Press, 1982. 228 pp.

918. Whitmont, Edward C.
Return of the Goddess
New York, NY: Crossroad Publishing, 1984. 272 pp.

919. Wickes, Frances G.
The Inner World of Choice
Englewood Cliffs, NJ: Prentice-Hall, 1963. 318 pp.

920. Young-Eisendrath, Polly
      *Hags and Heroes: A Feminist Approach to Jungian Psycho-
         therapy with Couples*
      Toronto, Ont.: Inner City Books, 1982. 184 pp.

921. Wheelwright, Jane Hollister, et al.
      The Death of a Woman
      New York, NY: St. Martin's Press, 1981. 287 pp.

5. STORIES: WOMEN'S AUTOBIOGRAPHIES, BIOGRAPHIES, AND JOURNEYS

"Telling our stories" is a phrase heard with great frequency among feminist women and, in truth, proves to be a major activity in women's groups. In the assembly of autobiographical and biographical materials which constitute the first section of this chapter, I have attempted to present some of the most exciting authors who have reflected on the question, What is pivotal in the narrative of a woman's life? Unlike the hagiographical titles presented in some accounts, which enumerate biographies that celebrate a life without critical discernment, the titles within this rubric offer clear-sighted accounts which courageously go forward into another's life. Several writers have taken up the critical inquiry of autobiographical effort, probing the relationship between subject and author. In addition to *Between Women* (edited by Ascher, DeSalvo, and Ruddick), I think that Heilbrun's recent analysis, as well as *Interpreting Women's Lives* (edited by the Personal Narratives Group), are stimulating presentations.

The journey accounts of women are equally informing with respect to women's reflection. The incorporation of titles under this heading is designed to encourage reading which enables understanding of movement and pilgrimage. Earlier periods have known the adventures of male travellers; we are now in possession of published accounts of women's journeys.

Autobiographies and Biographies

922. Bateson, Mary Catherine
       Composing a Life
       New York, NY: Atlantic Monthly, 1989. 241 pp.

923.   Blanchard, Paula
       Margaret Fuller: From Transcendentalism to Revolution
       Reading, MA: Addison-Wesley Publishing Company,
       1987. 371 pp.

924.   Blanchard, Paula
       The Life of Emily Carr
       Seattle, WA: University of Washington Press, 1987. 331
       pp.

925.   Blovin, Andree
       My Country Africa: The Autobiography of the Black Pasion-
       aria
       New York, NY: Praeger, 1983. 294 pp.

926.   Blumkofer, Edith
       Aimee Semple McPherson: Everybody's Sister
       Grand Rapids, MI: William B. Eerdmans Publishing
       Co., 1993. 431 pp.

927.   Bok, Sissela
       Alva Myrdal: A Daughter's Memoir
       Reading, MA: Addison-Wesley Publishing Company,
       1991. 375 pp.

928.   Borden, Ruth
       Frances Willard: A Biography
       Chapel Hill, NC: University of North Carolina Press,
       1986. 294 pp.

929.   Braxton, Joanne M.
       Black Women Writing Autobiography: A Tradition Within a
       Tradition
       Philadelphia, PA: Temple University Press, 1989. 240
       pp.

930.   Bryher
       The Heart to Artemis: A Writer's Memoirs
       New York, NY: Harcourt Brace Jovanovich, 1962. 316
       pp.

931. Buhrig, Marga
Woman Invisible: A Personal Odyssey in Christian Feminism
Philadelphia, PA: Trinity International Press, 1993.
126 pp.

932. Burgos-Debray, Elizabeth, ed., trans. A. Wright
I . . . Rigoberta Menchu: An Indian Woman in Guatemala
New York, NY: Verso/Cond, 1984. 251 pp.

933. Caldwell, Elizabeth
The Mysterious Mantle: The Biography of Hulda Niebuhr
New York, NY: Pilgrim Press, 1992. 160 pp.

934. Campion, Nardi Reeder
Mother Ann Lee: Morning Star of the Shakers
Hanover, NH: University Presses of New England,
1990. 128 pp.

935. Carrigan, Ana
Salvador Witness: The Life and Calling of Jean Donovan
New York, NY: Simon & Schuster, 1985. 317 pp.

936. Chevigny, Bell Gale, ed.
*The Woman and the Myth: Margaret Fuller's Life and
Writings*
Old Westbury, NY: The Feminist Press, 1976. 500 pp.

937. Coles, Robert
Simone Weil: A Modern Pilgrimage
Reading, MA: Addison-Wesley Publishing Company,
1987. 179 pp.

938. Coles, Robert
Dorothy Day: A Radical Devotion
Reading, MA: Addison-Wesley Publishing Company,
1987. 182 pp.

939. Corcoran, Theresa
Vida Dutton Scudder
Boston, MA: Twayne Publishers, 1982. 150 pp.

940. Culkey, Margo, ed.
American Women's Fea(s)ts of Memory
Madison, WI: University of Wisconsin Press, 1992. 321 pp.

941. Day, Dorothy
The Long Loneliness: An Autobiography
San Francisco, CA: Harper & Row, 1981. 288 pp.

942. Deegan, Mary Jo
Jane Addams and the Men of the Chicago School, 1892–1918
New Brunswick, NJ: Transaction Books, 1988. 352 pp.

943. Dillard, Annie
An American Childhood
New York, NY: Harper & Row, 1987. 255 pp.

944. Durr, Virginia Foster, ed. Hollin Barnard
Outside the Magic Circle: The Autobiography of Virginia Durr
University, AL: University of Alabama Press, 1985. 360 pp.

945. Egan, Eileen
Such a Vision of the Street: Mother Teresa—The Spirit and the Work
Garden City, NY: Doubleday & Co., 1985. 434 pp.

946. Endicott, Marion
Emily Carr: The Story of an Artist
Toronto. Ont.: Women's Press, 1981. 64 pp.

947. Evans, Mary
Simone de Beauvoir: A Feminist Mandarin
New York, NY: Methuen, 1985. 142 pp.

948. Fiori, Gabriella
Simone Weil: An Intellectual Biography
Athens, GA: University of Georgia Press, 1989. 380 pp.

949. Fisk, Erma J.
The Peacocks of Baboquivari
New York, NY: W. W. Norton, 1987. 284 pp.

950. Fletcher, Sheila
Maude Royden
Oxford, U.K.: Oxford University Press, 1989. 256 pp.

951. Forest, Jim
Love Is the Message: A Biography of Dorothy Day
Ramsey, NJ: Paulist Press, 1986. 224 pp.

952. Foster, Barbara, and Michael Foster
Forbidden Journey: The Life of Alexandra David-Neel
San Francisco, CA: Harper & Row, 1987. 363 pp.

953. Fries, Adelaide L., ed.
The Road to Salem (Moravian)
Chapel Hill, NC: University of North Carolina Press,
1988. 316 pp.

954. Garland, Anne Witte
Women Activists
Old Westbury, NY: The Feminist Press, 1988. 176 pp.

955. Glassman, Steve, and Kathryn Lee Seidel, eds.
Zora in Florida
Tallahassee, FL: University of Central Florida Press,
1991. 197 pp.

956. Gornick, Vivian
Fierce Attachments: A Memoir
New York, NY: Farrar, Straus & Giroux, 1987. 204 pp.

957. Graham, E., H. Hinds, E. Hobby, and H. Wilcox, eds.
*Her Own Life: Autobiographical Writings of Seventeenth
Century English Women*
New York, NY: Routledge, 1989. 224 pp.

958.   Griffith, Elisabeth
       In Her Own Right: The Life of Elizabeth Cady Stanton
       Oxford, U.K.: Oxford University Press, 1984. 304 pp.

959.   Hanley, Mary Laurence, and O. A. Bushnell
       Pilgrimage and Exile: Mother Marianne of Moloka'i
       Honolulu, HI: University of Hawaii Press, 1991. 464
       pp.

960.   Harrison, Nancy
       Winnie Mandela
       New York, NY: George Braziller, 1986. 181 pp.

961.   Heilbrun, Carolyn G.
       Writing a Woman's Life
       New York, NY: W. W. Norton, 1988. 144 pp.

962.   Hemenway, Robert E.
       Zora Neale Hurston: A Literary Biography
       Champaign, IL: University of Illinois Press, 1977. 371
       pp.

963.   Henricksen, Louise L., with Jo Ann Boydston
       Anzia Yezierska: A Writer's Life
       New Brunswick, NJ: Rutgers University Press, 1988.
       327 pp.

964.   Herbstrith, Waltraud
       Edith Stein: The Untold Story
       San Francisco, CA: Harper & Row, 1985. 127 pp.

965.   Heyward, Carter
       A Priest Forever
       New York, NY: Harper & Row, 1976. 146 pp.

966.   Hill, Mary A.
       Charlotte Perkins Gilman: The Making of a Radical Feminist, 1860–1896
       Philadelphia, PA: Temple University Press, 1981. 362
       pp.

967. Hillesum, Etty, trans. Arno Pomerans
      *An Interrupted Life: The Diaries of Etty Hillesum, 1941–
      1943*
      New York, NY: Pantheon Books, 1983. 226 pp.

968. Hillesum, Etty, trans. Arno Pomerans
      Letters from Westerbork
      New York, NY: Pantheon Books, 1986. 156 pp.

969. Hollyday, Joyce
      Turning Toward Home
      San Francisco, CA: Harper & Row, 1989. 208 pp.

970. Hosmer, Rachel, ed. Joyce Glover
      My Life Remembered: Nun, Priest, Feminist
      Cambridge, MA: Cowley Publishing, 1991. 200 pp.

971. Howard, Jane
      Margaret Mead: A Life
      New York, NY: Fawcett Crest Books, 1985. 527 pp.

972. Howard, Lillie
      Zora Neale Hurston
      Boston, MA: Twayne Publishers, 1980. 192 pp.

973. Hurston, Zora Neale
      Dust Tracks on a Road: An Autobiography
      Champaign, IL: University of Illinois Press, 1984. 384
      pp.

974. Ishimoto, Baroness Shidzue
      Facing Two Ways: The Story of My Life
      Palo Alto, CA: Stanford University Press, 1984. 387 pp.

975. Jelinek, Estelle C.
      *Her Self: Women's Autobiography from Antiquity to the
      Present*
      Boston, MA: Twayne Publishers, 1986. 242 pp.

976. Johnson, Sonia
      From Housewife to Heretic
      Garden City, NY: Doubleday & Co., 1981. 406 pp.

977. Jones, Adrienne Lash
      Jane Edna Hunter: A Case Study of Black Leadership,
      1910–1950
      Brooklyn, NY: Carlson Publications, 1990. 225 pp.

978. Jones, Beverly Washington
      Quest for Equality: The Life and Writings of Mary Eliza
      Church Terrell, 1863–1954
      Brooklyn, NY: Carlson Publications, 1990. 250 pp.

979. Kazel, Dorothy C.
      Alleluia Women (biography of woman murdered by
      Salvadorian soldiers)
      Cleveland, OH: Chapel Publications, 1988. 64 pp.

980. Kennedy, Adrienne
      People Who Led to My Plays
      New York, NY: Alfred A. Knopf, 1987. 125 pp.

981. Lightfoot, Sara Lawrence
      Balm in Gilead: Journey of a Healer (Dr. Margaret Law-
      rence, black psychiatrist)
      Reading, MA: Addison-Wesley Publishing Company,
      1989. 321 pp.

982. Lincoln, Victoria
      Teresa: A Woman—A Biography of Teresa of Avila
      Albany, NY: State University of New York Press, 1985.
      440 pp.

983. Logan, Onnie Lee
      Motherwit: An Alabama Midwife's Story
      New York, NY: E. P. Dutton, 1989. 256 pp.

984. Lorde, Audre
      Zami: Biomythography
      Trumansburg, NY: Crossing Press, 1985. 256 pp.

985.   Lovell, Mary J.
       Straight on Till Morning: The Biography of Beryl Markham
       New York, NY: St. Martin's Press, 1987. 408 pp.

986.   Mabee, Carleton, with Susan Mabee Newhouse
       Sojourner Truth: Slave, Prophet, Legend
       New York, NY: New York University Press, 1993. 320 pp.

987.   Mandela, Winnie, ed. Anne Benjamin
       Part of My Soul Went with Him
       New York, NY: W. W. Norton, 1985. 164 pp.

988.   Markham, Beryl
       West with the Night
       Berkeley, CA: North Point, 1983. 293 pp.

989.   Martin, Ralph G.
       Golda: Golda Meir—The Romantic Years
       New York, NY: Macmillan, 1988. 422 pp.

990.   Meadow, Mary J., and Carole A. Rayburn, eds.
       *A Time to Weep, a Time to Laugh: Faith Stories of Women
            Scholars of Religion*
       Somers, CT: Seabury Press, 1985. 250 pp.

991.   Meir, Golda
       My Life
       New York, NY: Putnam Books, 1975. 480 pp.

992.   Miller, William D.
       Dorothy Day: A Biography
       San Francisco, CA: Harper & Row, 1982. 527 pp.

993.   Moon, Sheila
       Dreams of a Woman
       Santa Monica, CA: Sigo Press, 1983. 207 pp.

994.   Moorehead, Caroline
       Freya Stark
       New York, NY: Penguin Books, 1985. 128 pp.

995. Murray, Pauli
      Proud Shoes: The Story of an American Family
      New York, NY: Harper & Row, 1956. 280 pp.

996. Murray, Pauli
      Song in a Weary Throat: An American Pilgrimage
      New York, NY: Harper & Row, 1987. 451 pp.

997. Newell, Linda King, and Valeen T. Avery
      Mormon Enigma: Emma Hale Smith
      Garden City, NY: Doubleday & Co., 1984. 394 pp.

998. O'Connor, Flannery, ed. Sally Fitzgerald
      The Habit of Being
      New York, NY: Farrar, Straus & Giroux, 1979. 617 pp.

999. Peacock, Sandra J.
      Jane Ellen Harrison: The Mark of the Self
      New Haven, CT: Yale University Press, 1988. 283 pp.

1000. Personal Narratives Group, ed.
       *Interpreting Women's Lives: Feminist Theory and Personal
       Narratives*
       Bloomington, IN: Indiana University Press, 1989. 277
       pp.

1001. Rice, Sarah, ed. Louise Westling
       He Included Me: The Autobiography of Sarah Rice
       Athens, GA: University of Georgia Press, 1989. 181
       pp.

1002. Roberts, Nancy L.
       Dorothy Day and the Catholic Worker
       Albany, NY: State University of New York Press, 1984.
       226 pp.

1003. Robinson, Roxana
       Georgia O'Keeffe: A Life
       San Francisco, CA: Harper & Row, 1989. 639 pp.

1004. Salomon, Charlotte, trans. Leila Vennewitz
       Charlotte: Life or Theatre?
       New York, NY: Viking Press, 1983. 784 pp.

1005. Scott-Maxwell, Florida
       The Measure of My Days
       Harmondsworth, U.K.: Penguin, 1968. 158 pp.

1006. Smith, Sidonie, and Julia Watson, eds.
       *De/Colonizing the Subject: The Politics of Gender in
       Women's Autobiographies*
       Minneapolis, MN: University of Minnesota Press,
       1992. 484 pp.

1006a. Sterling, Dorothy
       Black Foremothers: Three Lives
       Old Westbury, NY: The Feminist Press, 1988. 224 pp.

1007. Teresa, Mother, ed. J. L. Gonzalez-Balado and Janet
       Playfoot
       My Life for the Poor
       San Francisco, CA: Harper & Row, 1985. 107 pp.

1008. Turner, Edith
       The Spirit and the Drum: A Memoir of Africa
       Tucson, AZ: University of Arizona Press, 1987. 165
       pp.

1009. Wade-Gayles, Gloria
       Pushed Back to Strength: A Black Woman's Journey Home
       Boston, MA: Beacon Press, 1993. 276 pp.

1010. Walters, Dorothy
       Flannery O'Connor
       Boston, MA: Twayne Publishers, 1971. 172 pp.

1011. Wessinger, Catherine L.
       Annie Besant and Progressive Messianism (1847–1933)
       Lewiston, NY: The Edwin Mellen Press, 1988. 380 pp.

1012.   Whitman, Ruth, with Livia Roth Kirchen
        The Testing of Hanna Senesh
        Detroit, MI: Wayne State University Press, 1986. 115
        pp.

Journeys

1013.   Angelou, Maya
        All God's Children Need Traveling Shoes
        New York, NY: Random House, 1986. 210 pp.

1014.   Bender, Sue
        Plain and Simple: A Woman's Journey to the Amish
        San Francisco, CA: Harper & Row, 1989. 160 pp.

1015.   Boucher, Sandy
        Heartwomen: An Urban Feminist's Odyssey Home
        San Francisco, CA: Harper & Row, 1982. 401 pp.

1016.   David-Neel, Alexandra
        My Journey to Lhasa
        Boston, MA: Beacon Press, 1986. 310 pp.

1017.   Davidowicz, Lucy S.
        From That Place and Time
        New York, NY: W. W. Norton, 1989. 333 pp.

1018.   Freemantle, Anne
        Woman's Way to God
        New York, NY: St. Martin's Press, 1977. 255 pp.

1019.   Galland, China
        *Longing for Darkness: Tara and the Black Madonna—A
          Ten-Year Journey*
        New York, NY: Viking Press, 1990. 392 pp.

1020.   Ginter, Barbara
        The Long Haul: Journal and Letters from Nicaragua,
        1983–1986
        Latham, NY: Sisters of St. Joseph Carondelet, 1987.
        74 pp.

1021.   McDaniel, Judith
        Sanctuary: A Journey
        Ithaca, NY: Firebrand Books, 1987. 171 pp.

1022.   Miller, Luree
        On Top of the World: Five Women Explorers in Tibet
        Seattle, WA: The Mountaineers, 1984. 222 pp.

1023.   Ochs, Vanessa L.
        Words on Fire: One Woman's Journey into the Sacred
        New York, NY: Harcourt Brace Jovanovich, 1990. 328
        pp.

1024.   Slater, Candace
        Trail of Miracles: Stories from Pilgrimage in Northeast
        Brazil
        Berkeley, CA: University of California Press, 1986.
        289 pp.

1025.   Stark, Freya
        The Valleys of the Assassins and Other Persian Tales
        Los Angeles, CA: Jeremy Tarcher Books, 1983. 364
        pp.

1026.   Varawa, Joan McIntyre
        Changes in Latitude: An Uncommon Anthropology (Poly-
        nesian account)
        New York, NY: Atlantic Monthy, 1989. 274 pp.

6. SPIRITUALITY OF THE GODDESS

A decade ago there was little in the way of titles concerned with goddess spirituality and the contribution of neopagan writers. I have placed the two approaches together, although authors in one section of this chapter might seem inappropriate to the second section. My reason for this organization is related to the types of inquiries I have heard from students interested in contemporary non-Western or nontraditional religions. A number of scholarly works on goddesses are listed in the first section, indicating that a comparative interest is slowly emerging that understands cross-cultural and transhistorical devotion to a female divinity, or "mother worship," as significant. Elinor Gadon's study on the historical ubiquity of goddess belief and worship offers an unusually comprehensive perspective. Her reading of visual texts demonstrates the value of approaching goddess understanding with an embrace of nonverbal as well as written evidence.

The neopagan movement is well recognized today and has been instrumental in the creation of spiritual celebrations, workshops, journals, enterprises, and so on. No name is so well known to this movement as Starhawk, a leader who combines the issues of justice and social change with ecology and personal growth in her approach to spirituality. Her *Spiral Dance* was first published a decade ago and was reissued in 1989. I have included some fiction in this section because it is best identified in this context—an indication of the effectiveness of imaginative treatment to this subject.

Historical Approaches

1027.   Agrawala, Prithvi Kumar
        Goddesses in Ancient India

Atlantic Highlands, NJ: Humanities Press, 1982. 145 pp.

1028. Begg, Ean
       The Cult of the Black Virgin
       New York, NY: ARK Publishing, Routledge, Chapman & Hall, 1985. 289 pp.

1029. Birnbaum, Lucia Chiavola
       Black Madonnas
       Boston, MA: Northeastern University Press, 1993. 273 pp.

1030. Blofeld, John
       The Bodhisattva of Compassion: The Mystical Tradition of Kuan Yin
       Boulder, CO: Shambala Press, 1978. 158 pp.

1031. Bolon, Carol Radcliffe
       Forms of the Goddess Lajja Gauri in Indian Art
       University Park, PA: Pennsylvania State University Press, 1992. 184 pp.

1032. Brown, C. Mackenzie
       The Triumph of the Goddess: The Canonical Models and Theological Visions of the Devi-Bhagavata Purana
       Albany, NY: State University of New York Press, 1990. 384 pp.

1033. Cles-Reden, Sibylle von
       The Realms of the Great Goddess
       Englewood Cliffs, NJ: Prentice-Hall, 1962. 328 pp.

1034. Coburn, Thomas B.
       Encountering the Goddess: A Translation of Devi-Mahatmya and the Study of Its Interpretation
       Albany, NY: State University of New York Press, 1991. 384 pp.

1035. Condren, Mary
       The Serpent and the Goddess: Women, Religion, and Power in Celtic Ireland
       San Francisco, CA: Harper & Row, 1989. 256 pp.

1036. Gadon, Elinor
       The Once and Future Goddess: A Symbol for Our Time
       San Francisco, CA: Harper & Row, 1989. 352 pp.

1037. Gimbutas, Marija
       The Gods and Goddesses of Old Europe, 6500–3500 BCE
       Berkeley, CA: University of California Press, 1982. 304 pp.

1038. Gimbutas, Marija
       The Language of the Goddess
       San Francisco, CA: Harper & Row, 1989. 388 pp.

1039. Gufstafson, Fred
       The Black Madonna
       Santa Monica, CA: Sigo Press, 1990. 150 pp.

1040. Harper, Katherine Anne
       Seven Hindu Goddesses of Spiritual Transformation: The Iconography of the Saptamatrikas
       Lewiston, NY: The Edwin Mellen Press, 1990. 336 pp.

1041. Hawley, John S., and Donna M. Wulff, eds.
       The Divine Consort: Radha and the Goddesses of India
       Berkeley, CA: Berkeley Religious Studies Series, 1982. 414 pp.

1042. Hurtado, Larry, ed.
       Goddesses in Religions and Modern Debate
       Alpharetta, GA: Scholars Press, 1990. 236 pp.

1043. Johnson, Buffie
       Lady of the Beasts: Ancient Images of the Goddess and Her Sacred Animals
       San Francisco, CA: Harper & Row, 1988. 386 pp.

1044.   Kinsley, David
        Hindu Goddesses: Visions of the Divine Feminine in Hindu Religious Tradition
        Berkeley, CA: University of California Press, 1987. 320 pp.

1045.   Kinsley, David
        The Goddesses' Mirror: Visions of the Divine from East and West
        Albany, NY: State University of New York Press, 1988. 320 pp.

1046.   Markale, Jean
        Women of the Celts
        Rochester, VT: Inner Traditions International, 1986. 315 pp.

1047.   Matthews, Caitlin
        Sophia, Goddess of Wisdom: The Divine Feminine Form from Black Goddess to World Soul
        Winchester, MA: Unwin Hyman, 1990. 378 pp.

1048.   Obeyesekere, Ganath
        The Cult of the Goddess Pattini
        Chicago, IL: University of Chicago Press, 1984. 629 pp.

1049.   Olson, Carl, ed.
        The Book of the Goddess, Past and Present: An Introduction to Her Religion
        New York, NY: Crossroad Publishing, 1985. 259 pp.

1050.   Patai, Raphael
        The Hebrew Goddess
        New York, NY: Discus Books, Avon, 1967. 342 pp.

1051.   Preston, James
        The Cult of the Goddess: Social and Religious Change in a Hindu Temple
        Prospect Heights, IL: Waveland Press, 1985. 109 pp.

1052.   Preston, James, ed.
        Mother Worship: Themes and Variations

Chapel Hill, NC: University of North Carolina Press,
1982. 360 pp.

1053. Ross, Anne
Everyday Life of the Pagan Celts
New York, NY: Putnam Books, 1986. 160 pp.

1054. Shafer, Edward H.
The Divine Woman: Dragon Ladies and Rain Maidens
Berkeley, CA: North Point, 1980. 239 pp.

1055. Sjoestedt, Marie-Louise, trans. Miles Dillon
Gods and Heroes of the Celts
Berkeley, CA: Turtle Island Press, 1982. 104 pp.

1056. Spretnak, Charlene
*Lost Goddesses of Early Greece: A Collection of Pre-Hellenic
Myths*
Boston, MA: Beacon Press, 1981. 132 pp.

1057. Stone, Merlin
When God Was a Woman
New York, NY: Harvest/Harcourt Brace Jovanovich,
1976. 265 pp.

1058. Stone, Merlin
Ancient Mirrors of Womanhood
Boston, MA: Beacon Press, 1984. 425 pp.

1059. Wolkstein, Diane, and Samuel Noah Kramer
Inanna: Queen of Heaven and Earth
New York, NY: Harper & Row, 1983. 227 pp.

Contemporary Expressions

1060. Adler, Margot
*Drawing Down the Moon: Witches, Druids, Goddess-
Worshippers and Other Pagans in America Today*
Boston, MA: Beacon Press, 1981. 455 pp.

1061.   Andrews, Lynn V.
Medicine Woman
San Francisco, CA: Harper & Row, 1981. 204 pp.

1062.   Andrews, Lynn V.
The Flight of the Seventh Moon: The Teaching of the Shields
San Francisco, CA: Harper & Row, 1984. 203 pp.

1063.   Andrews, Lynn V.
Jaguar Woman and the Wisdom of the Butterfly Tree
San Francisco, CA: Harper & Row, 1986. 194 pp.

1064.   Andrews, Lynn V.
Star Woman
New York, NY: Warner Books, 1986. 256 pp.

1065.   Austen, Hallie Iglehart
*The Heart of the Goddess: Art, Myth and Meditations on
the World's Sacred Feminine*
Berkeley, CA: Wingbow Press, 1990. 174 pp.

1066.   Bolen, Jean Shinoda
Goddesses in Everywoman: A New Psychology of Women
San Francisco, CA: Harper & Row, 1984. 334 pp.

1067.   Bradley, Marion Zimmer
The Mists of Avalon (novel)
New York, NY: Alfred A. Knopf, 1983. 876 pp.

1068.   Brindel, June R.
Phaedra: A Novel of Ancient Athens
New York, NY: St. Martin's Press, 1985. 227 pp.

1069.   Brindel, June R.
Ariadne: A Novel of Ancient Crete
New York, NY: St. Martin's Press, 1980. 246 pp.

1070.   Budapest, Zsuzsanna E.
The Holy Book of Women's Mysteries
Los Angeles, CA: Susan B. Anthony Coven, 1979. 135
pp.

1071.   Budapest, Zsuzsanna E.
       The Grandmother of Time: A Women's Book of Celebrations, Spells and Sacred Objects for Every Month of the Year
       San Francisco, CA: Harper & Row, 1989. 192 pp.

1072.   Cabot, Laurie, with Tom Cowan
       Power of the Witch: The Earth, the Moon, and the Magical Path to Enlightenment
       New York, NY: Delacort Press/Seymour Lawrence, 1989. 256 pp.

1073.   Cameron, Anne
       Tales of the Cairds
       Cambridge, MA: Harbour Press, 1989. 191 pp.

1074.   Canan, Janine, ed.
       She Rises Like the Sun: Invocations of the Goddess by Contemporary American Women Poets
       Trumansburg, NY: Crossing Press, 1989. 226 pp.

1075.   Christ, Carol P.
       Laughter of Aphrodite: Reflections on a Journey to the Goddess
       San Francisco, CA: Harper & Row, 1987. 240 pp.

1076.   Daly, Mary
       Webster's First New Intergalactic Wickedary of the English Language
       Boston, MA: Beacon Press, 1987. 310 pp.

1077.   Dexter, Miriam Robbins
       Whence the Goddesses: A Sourcebook
       Elmsford, NY: Pergamon Press, 1990. 280 pp.

1078.   Downing, Christine
       The Goddess: Mythological Images of the Feminine
       New York, NY: Crossroad Publishing, 1984. 250 pp.

1079. Forfreedom, Ann, and Julie Ann, eds.
       Book of the Goddess
       Sacramento, CA: Temples of the Goddess Within,
          1980. 346 pp.

1080. Forrest, Katherine V.
       Daughters of a Coral Dawn (novel of Mother Goddess)
       Tallahassee, FL: Naiad Press, 1983. 226 pp.

1081. George, Demetra
       *Mysteries of the Dark Moon: The Healing Power of the Dark
          Goddess*
       San Francisco, CA: Harper & Row, 1992. 298 pp.

1082. Getty, Alice
       Goddess: Mother of Living Nature
       New York, NY: Thames & Hudson, 1990. 96 pp.

1083. Iglehart, Hallie
       WomanSpirit: A Guide to Women's Wisdom
       San Francisco, CA: Harper & Row, 1983. 176 pp.

1084. Kinstler, Clysta
       The Moon Under Her Feet (a novel)
       San Francisco, CA: Harper & Row, 1989. 315 pp.

1085. Koltuv, Barbara Black
       The Book of Lilith
       York Beach, ME: Nicole-Hays, 1987. 127 pp.

1086. Laura, Judith
       She Lives! The Return of Our Great Mother (myths,
          rituals, meditations, and music)
       Freedom, CA: Crossing Press, 1989. 141 pp.

1087. Mascetti, Manuela Dunn
       The Song of Eve: Mythology and Symbols of the Goddess
       New York, NY: Simon & Schuster, 1990. 239 pp.

1088. Masters, Robert
The Goddess Sekmet and Her Way of the Five Bodies
Oak Park, IL: Meyer-Stone, 1988. 192 pp.

1089. Monaghan, Patricia
The Book of Goddesses and Heroines
New York, NY: E. P. Dutton, 1981. 318 pp.

1090. Nicholson, Shirley, ed.
The Goddess Reawakening: The Feminine Principle Today
Wheaton, IL: Theosophical Publishing House, 1989.
314 pp.

1091. Noble, Vicki
*Motherpeace: A Way to the Goddess Through Myth, Art,
and Tarot*
San Francisco, CA: Harper & Row, 1982. 276 pp.

1092. Noble, Vicki
Shakti Woman
San Francisco, CA: Harper & Row, 1991. 224 pp.

1093. Oda, Mayumi
Goddesses
Berkeley, CA: Asian Humanities Press, 1982. 78 pp.

1094. Orenstein, Gloria
*Journeys and Cycles of Power: The Reflowering of the
Goddess in Western Culture*
Elmsford, NY: Pergamon Press, 1989. 256 pp.

1095. Orlock, Carol
The Goddess Letters (Demeter-Persephone myth)
New York, NY: St. Martin's Press, 1987. 220 pp.

1096. Paris, Ginette
*Pagan Grace: Dionysos, Hermes, and Goddess Memory in
Daily Life*
New York, NY: Spring Publishing, 1990. 152 pp.

1097. Perera, Sylvia Brinton
Descent to the Goddess: A Way of Initiation for Women
Toronto, Ont.: Inner City Books, 1981. 112 pp.

1098. Pirani, Alex, ed.
The Absent Mother: Restoring the Goddess of Judaism and Christianity
New York, NY: HarperCollins, 1991. 256 pp.

1099. Purce, Jill
The Mystic Spiral: Journey of the Soul
New York, NY: Thames & Hudson, 1980. 128 pp.

1100. Reis, Patricia
Through the Goddess: A Woman's Way of Healing
New York, NY: Crossroad/Continuum, 1991. 224 pp.

1101. Rufus, Anneli, and Kristin Lawson
Goddess Sites: Europe
San Francisco, CA: Harper & Row, 1991. 304 pp.

1102. No entry.

1103. Sjoo, Monica, and Barbara Mor
The Great Cosmic Mother: Rediscovering the Religion of the Earth
San Francisco, CA: Harper & Row, 1987. 416 pp.

1104. Starhawk
Dreaming the Dark: Magic, Sex and Politics
Boston, MA: Beacon Press, 1982. 242 pp.

1105. Starhawk
Truth or Dare: Encounters with Power, Authority, and Mystery
San Francisco, CA: Harper & Row, 1987. 370 pp.

1106. Starhawk
The Spiral Dance: A Rebirth of the Ancient Religion of the Great Goddess
San Francisco, CA: Harper & Row, 1989. 218 pp.

1107. Stein, Diane
The Kwan Yin Book of Changes
St. Paul, MN: Llewellyn Publishers, 1985. 231 pp.

1108. Stein, Diane
The Woman's Spirituality Book
St. Paul, MN: Llewellyn Publishers, 1987. 262 pp.

1109. Stein, Diane
Casting the Circle: A Woman's Book of Ritual
Trumansburg, NY: Crossing Press, 1991. 300 pp.

1110. Stein, Diane
The Goddess Celebrates: An Anthology of Women's Rituals
Trumansburg, NY: Crossing Press, 1991. 259 pp.

1111. Teish, Luisah
Jambalaya: The Natural Woman's Book of Personal Charms and Practical Rituals
San Francisco, CA: Harper & Row, 1985. 268 pp.

1112. Thorsten, Geraldine
God Herself: The Feminine Roots of Astrology
New York, NY: Avon, 1980. 414 pp.

1113. Valiente, Doreen
The Rebirth of Witchcraft
London, U.K.: Robert Hale, 1989. 236 pp.

1114. Walker, Barbara G.
The Crone: Woman of Age, Wisdom and Power
San Francisco, CA: Harper & Row, 1985. 160 pp.

1115. Walker, Barbara G.
The I-Ching of the Goddess
San Francisco, CA: Harper & Row, 1986. 113 pp.

1116. Walker, Barbara G.
The Skeptical Feminist: Discovering the Virgin, Mother and Crone
San Francisco, CA: Harper & Row, 1987. 224 pp.

1117.   Warren, Patricia N.
        One Is the Sun (novel about the earth goddess of
            India)
        New York, NY: Ballantine, 1991. 536 pp.

1118.   Whitaker, Kay Cordell
        *The Reluctant Shaman: A Woman's First Encounters with
            the Unseen Spirits of the Earth*
        San Francisco, CA: Harper & Row, 1991. 224 pp.

1119.   Woolger, Jennifer Barber, and Roger Woolger
        *The Goddess Within: A Guide to the Eternal Myths That
            Shape Women's Lives*
        New York, NY: Bantam Books, 1989. 483 pp.

7. WOMEN'S MINISTRY AND SPIRITUAL PRACTICE

In looking back at earlier accounts of women's ministry, much attention was given to the matter of ordination and formal acceptance of women's public role in religious structures a decade ago. Although studies continue to take up these issues, in recent years women writing about ministry have been more concerned with the viability of their vocation and its particular shape. This development signals a move away from defensive strategems and expressions to a confident expression of determination regarding women's ministerial presence in the church today. I have incorporated titles that expand the traditions of role-defined minister, indicating that much professional effort, heretofore unrecognized, is ministry. One question emerges with respect to this section: Does gender make a difference in the routine life of professional religious leadership?

The second section offers a variety of approaches to spiritual practice, including devotional literature and worship materials. Several volumes are listed which either anthologize women's sermons or describe the character of women's liturgical work. Chris Smith's study is noteworthy in presenting careful analysis of gender and the language and imagery of women's sermons. Exceptional work is being created in the women's center WATER (Silver Spring, Maryland), especially through the efforts of Diann Neu, in women's liturgy and ritual. I have included titles from this program.

Ministry

1120.   Bozarth, Alla Renee
        Womanpriest: A Personal Odyssey
        San Diego, CA: LuraMedia, 1988. 217 pp.

1121.   Brewer, Eileen Mary
        Nuns and the Education of American Catholic Women
        Chicago, IL: Loyola University Press, 1987. 217 pp.

1122.   Canham, Elizabeth
        Pilgrimage to Priesthood
        Somers, CT: Seabury Press, 1984. 113 pp.

1123.   Carroll, Jackson, and Barbara J. Hargrove
        Women of the Cloth: New Opportunity for the Churches
        New York, NY: Harper & Row, 1983. 276 pp.

1124.   Chittister, Joan
        Woman, Ministry, and the Church
        Ramsey, NJ: Paulist Press, 1983. 130 pp.

1125.   Chittister, Joan
        Winds of Change: Women Challenge Church
        Kansas City, MO: Sheed & Ward, 1986. 237 pp.

1126.   Chittister, Joan
        WomanStrength: Modern Church, Modern Women
        Kansas City, MO: Sheed & Ward, 1990. 190 pp.

1127.   Clarke, Rita-Lou
        Pastoral Care of Battered Women
        Louisville, KY: Westminster/John Knox Press, 1986.
           130 pp.

1128.   Cuneen, Sally
        *Mother Church: What the Experience of Women Is Teaching
           Her*
        Ramsey, NJ: Paulist Press, 1991. 222 pp.

1129.   Curran, Patricia
        *Grace Before Meals: Food Rituals and Body Discipline in
           Convent Culture*

Urbana, IL: University of Illinois Press, 1989. 168 pp.

1130. Darin, Marcy, ed.
Stories from the Circle: Women's Leadership in Community
Wilton, CT: Morehouse, 1991..

1131. Denman, Rose Mary
Let My People In: A Lesbian Minister Tells of Her Struggles . . .
New York, NY: William Morrow, 1990. 261 pp.

1132. Donovan, Mary Ann
Sisterhood as Power: Women Religious as Catalysts of the Future
New York, NY: Crossroad Publishing, 1989. 150 pp.

1133. Donovan, Mary Sudman
A Different Call: Women's Ministries in the Episcopal Church
Wilton, CT: Morehouse, 1986. 216 pp.

1134. Elizondo, Virgil, and Norbert Greinacher, eds.
Women in a Man's Church
Somers, CT: Seabury Press, 1980. 135 pp.

1135. Fiand, Barbara
Living the Vision: Religious Vows in an Age of Change
New York, NY: Crossroad/Continuum, 1990. 176 pp.

1136. Field-Bibb, Jacqueline
Women Towards Priesthood: Ministerial Politics and Feminist Praxis
Cambridge, U.K.: Cambridge University Press, 1991. 352 pp.

1137. Flemming, Leslie A., ed.
Women's Work for Women: Missionaries and Social Change in Asia
Boulder, CO: Westview, 1989. 170 pp.

1138.   Fortune, Marie M.
        Is Nothing Sacred? When Sex Invades the Pastoral Relationship
        San Francisco, CA: Harper & Row, 1989. 192 pp.

1139.   Fortune, Marie M.
        Family Violence: Workshop Curriculum for Clergy and Other Helpers
        New York, NY: Pilgrim Press, 1991. 160 pp.

1140.   Franklin, Margaret Ann, ed.
        The Force of the Feminine: Women, Men and the Church
        London, U.K.: Allen & Unwin, 1986. 208 pp.

1141.   Furlong, Monica, ed.
        Mirror to the Church
        London, U.K.: S.P.C.K., 1988. 135 pp.

1142.   Giltner, Fern, ed.
        Women's Issues in Religious Education
        Birmingham, AL: Religious Education Press, 1985. 190 pp.

1143.   Gjerding, Iben, and Katherine Kinnamon
        No Longer Strangers: A Resource for Women and Worship
        Geneva, Switz.: World Council of Churches, 1984. 80 pp.

1144.   Glaz, Maxine, and Jeanne S. Moessner, eds.
        Women in Travail and Transition: A New Pastoral Care
        Philadelphia, PA: Fortress Press, 1990. 176 pp.

1145.   Hahn, Celia Allison
        Sexual Paradox
        New York, NY: Pilgrim Press, 1991. 244 pp.

1146.   Hannefin, Sr. Daniel
        Daughters of the Church (Daughters of Charity)
        New York, NY: New City Press, 1990. 352 pp.

1147. Harris, Maria
Women and Teaching: Themes for a Spirituality of Pedagogy
Ramsey, NJ: Paulist Press, 1988. 110 pp.

1148. Hewitt, Emily C., and Susanne R. Hiatt
Women Priests: Yes or No?
Somers, CT: Seabury Press, 1973. 128 pp.

1149. Ice, Mary Long
Clergy Women and Their World Views: Calling for a New Age
New York, NY: Praeger, 1987. 211 pp.

1150. Kleinman, Sherryl
Equals Before God: Seminarians as Humanistic Professionals
Chicago, IL: University of Chicago Press, 1984. 133 pp.

1151. Kolbenschlag, Madonna, ed.
Between God and Caesar: Priests, Sisters and Political Office in the U.S.
Ramsey, NJ: Paulist Press, 1985. 468 pp.

1152. Kolbenschlag, Madonna, ed.
Women in the Church, I
Washington, DC: Pastoral Press, 1987. 249 pp.

1153. Kolmer, Elizabeth
Religious Women in the U.S.: A Survey of the Influential Literature, 1950–1983
Wilmington, DE: Michael Glazier, 1985. 111 pp.

1154. Lawless, Elaine J.
Handmaidens of the Lord: Pentecostal Women Preachers and Traditional Religion
Philadelphia, PA: University of Pennsylvania Press, 1988. 272 pp.

1155. Lawless, Elaine J.
       Holy Women/Wholly Women: Sharing Ministries Through Life Stories
       Philadelphia, PA: University of Pennsylvania Press, 1993. 256 pp.

1156. Lebacqz, Karen
       Professional Ethics: Power and Paradox
       Nashville, TN: Abingdon Press, 1985. 189 pp.

1157. Lehman, Edward C., Jr.
       Women Clergy: Breaking Through Gender Barriers
       New Brunswick, NJ: Transaction Books, 1985. 307 pp.

1158. Lore-Kelly, Christin
       Caring Community: A Design for Ministry
       Chicago, IL: Loyola University Press, 1984. 314 pp.

1159. Mayr, Marlene, ed.
       Modern Masters of Religious Education
       Birmingham, AL: Religious Education Press, 1984. 323 pp.

1160. Milhaven, Annie Lally
       The Inside Stories: Thirteen Valiant Women Challenging the Church
       Mystic, CT: Twenty-Third Publications, 1987. 288 pp.

1161. Milhaven, Annie Lally, ed.
       Sermons Seldom Heard: Women Proclaim Their Lives
       New York, NY: Crossroad Publishing, 1991. 240 pp.

1162. Miller, Page P.
       A Claim to New Roles
       Metuchen, NJ: Scarecrow Press, 1985. 253 pp.

1163. Neal, Marie Augusta
       Catholic Sisters in Transition: From the 1960's to the 1980's
       Wilmington, DE: Michael Glazier, 1985. 173 pp.

1164. Neal, Marie Augusta
From Nuns to Sisters: An Expanding Vocation
Mystic, CT: Twenty-Third Publications, 1989. 160 pp.

1165. Noren, Carol
The Woman in the Pulpit
Nashville, TN: Abingdon Press, 1992. 176 pp.

1166. Osiek, Carolyn
Beyond Anger: On Being a Feminist in the Church
Ramsey, NJ: Paulist Press, 1986. 93 pp.

1167. Quinonez, Lora Ann
Starting Points: Six Essays Based on the Experience of U.S. Women Religious
Washington, DC: Leadership Conference of Women Religious, 1980. 151 pp.

1168. Rhodes, Lynn N.
Co-Creating: Feminist Vision of Ministry
Louisville, KY: Westminster/John Knox Press, 1987. 132 pp.

1169. Ridick, Joyce
Treasures in Earthen Vessels: The Vows
Dearborn, MI: Alba, 1984. 166 pp.

1170. Ross, Maggie
Pillars of Flame: Power, Priesthood, and Spiritual Maturity
San Francisco, CA: Harper & Row, 1988. 160 pp.

1171. Rowthorne, Anne
The Liberation of the Laity
Wilton, CT: Morehouse, 1986. 232 pp.

1172. Schaller, Lyle E., ed.
Women as Pastors
Nashville, TN: Abingdon Press, 1982. 127 pp.

1173.   Schneiders, Sandra Mane
        *New Wineskins: Re-imagining Religious Life in the Twenti-
           eth Century*
        Ramsey, NJ: Paulist Press, 1985. 309 pp.

1174.   Shannon, Margaret
        Just Because (Church Women United, 1941–75)
        Corte Madera, CA: Omega Press, 1977. 464 pp.

1175.   Stendahl, Brita
        *The Force of Tradition: A Case Study of Women Priests in
           Sweden*
        Philadelphia, PA: Fortress Press, 1985. 200 pp.

1176.   Stortz, Martha Ellen
        PastorPower
        Nashville, TN: Abingdon Press, 1993. 144 pp.

1177.   Strahan, Lynne
        *Out of Silence: A Study of a Religious Community for
           Women*
        Oxford, U.K.: Oxford University Press, 1989. 320 pp.

1178.   Swidler, Arlene Anderson, and Virginia K. Ratigan,
           eds.
        *A New Phoebe: Perspectives on Roman Catholic Women and
           the Permanent Diaconate*
        Kansas City, MO: Sheed & Ward, 1990. 120 pp.

1179.   Tucker, Cynthia G.
        *Women's Ministry: Mary Collson's Search for Reform as a
           Unitarian Minister*
        Philadelphia, PA: Temple University Press, 1984. 216
           pp.

1180.   Wallace, Ruth A.
        They Call Her Pastor: A New Role for Catholic Women
        Albany, NY: State University of New York Press, 1992.
           204 pp.

1181. Ware, Ann Patrick, ed.
Midwives of the Future: American Sisters Tell Their Story
Kansas City, MO: Leaven Press, 1985. 237 pp.

1182. Weaver, Mary Jo
New Catholic Women: The Contemporary Challenge to Traditional Religious Authority
San Francisco, CA: Harper & Row, 1988. 288 pp.

1183. Weidman, Judith, ed.
Women Ministers: How Women Are Redefining Traditional Roles
San Francisco, CA: Harper & Row, 1985. 220 pp.

1184. Wessinger, Catherine, ed.
Women's Leadership in Marginal Religions: Explorations Outside the Mainstream
Champaign, IL: University of Illinois Press, 1993. 246 pp.

1185. Wolfe, Mary Catherine, ed.
One Mind and Heart in God: Dominican Monastic Life
West Springfield, MA: Conference of Nuns of the Order of Preachers—U.S.A., 1989. 157 pp.

1186. Wolff-Salin, Mary
The Shadow Side of the Community and the Growth of the Self
New York, NY: Crossroad/Continuum, 1989. 176 pp.

Spiritual Practices

1187. Adelman, Penina V.
Miriam's Well: Rituals for Jewish Women Around the Year
Fresh Meadows, NY: Biblio Press, 1986. 143 pp.

1188. Anthony, Susan B.
       *Sidewalk Contemplatives: A Spirituality for Socially Con-
       cerned Christians*
       New York, NY: Crossroad Publishing, 1987. 160 pp.

1189. Boulding, Maria
       The Coming of God
       Collegeville, MN: Liturgical Press, 1983. 224 pp.

1190. Brennan, Anne, and Janice Brewi
       *Mid-Life Direction: Praying and Playing—Sources of New
       Dynamism*
       Ramsey, NJ: Paulist Press, 1985. 146 pp.

1191. Cady, Susan, Marian Ronan, and Hal Taussig
       Wisdom's Feast: Sophia in Study and Celebration
       San Francisco, CA: Harper & Row, 1989. 208 pp.

1192. Callahan, Sidney
       *With All Our Heart and Mind: The Spiritual Works of
       Mercy in a Psychological Age*
       New York, NY: Crossroad Publishing, 1989. 200 pp.

1193. Caron, Charlotte
       To Make and Make Again: Feminist Ritual Thealogy
       New York, NY: Crossroad Publishing, 1993. 257 pp.

1194. Chervin, Ronda, and Mary Neill
       The Woman's Tale: A Journal of Inner Exploration
       Somers, CT: Seabury Press, 1980. 146 pp.

1195. Chervin, Ronda, and Mary Neill
       *Bringing the Mother with You: Sources of Healing in
       Marian Meditation*
       Somers, CT: Seabury Press, 1982. 122 pp.

1196. Chittister, Joan, and Joan Kowakni
       Psalm Journal
       Kansas City, MO: Sheed & Ward, 1985. 104 pp.

1197. Crotwell, Helen G.
Women and the Word: Sermons
Philadelphia, PA: Fortress Press, 1978. 134 pp.

1198. Deitering, Carolyn
The Liturgy as Dance and the Liturgical Dancer
New York, NY: Crossroad Publishing, 1984. 144 pp.

1199. Duck, Ruth, and Maren Tirabassi
Touch Holiness: Resources for Worship
New York, NY: Pilgrim Press, 1989. 256 pp.

1200. Duerk, Judith
Circle of Stones: Woman's Journey to Herself
San Diego, CA: LuraMedia, 1989. 96 pp.

1201. Dyckman, Katherine Marie, and L. Patrick Carroll
*Inviting the Mystic, Supporting the Prophet: An Introduc-
tion to Spiritual Direction*
Ramsey, NJ: Paulist Press, 1981. 92 pp.

1202. Dyckman, Katherine Marie, and L. Patrick Carroll
Solitude to Sacrament
Collegeville, MN: Liturgical Press, 1982. 128 pp.

1203. Furlong, Monica
Contemplating Now
Cambridge, MA: Cowley Publishing, 1983. 124 pp.

1204. Furlong, Monica
Travelling In
Cambridge, MA: Cowley Publishing, 1984. 127 pp.

1205. Gawle, Barbara
How to Pray: Discovering Spiritual Growth Through Prayer
Englewood Cliffs, NJ: Prentice-Hall, 1984. 200 pp.

1206. Gill, Jean
*Images of Myself: Meditation Through the Jungian Imagery
in the Gospels*
Ramsey, NJ: Paulist Press, 1980. 88 pp.

1207.   Gjerding, Iben, and Katherine Kinnamon, eds.
        Women's Prayer Services
        Mystic, CT: Twenty-Third Publications, 1987. 80 pp.

1208.   Gorman, Margaret, ed.
        Psychology and Religion (esp. pt. 6: "Prayer, Symbol and
            Spirituality")
        Ramsey, NJ: Paulist Press, 1985. 324 pp.

1209.   Gratton, Carolyn
        Guidelines for Spiritual Direction
        Denville, NJ: Dimension Books, 1980. 225 pp.

1210.   Gratton, Carolyn
        Trusting: Theory and Practice
        New York, NY: Crossroad Publishing, 1982. 252 pp.

1211.   Guenther, Margaret
        Holy Listening: The Art of Spiritual Direction
        Cambridge, MA: Cowley Publishing, 1992. 146 pp.

1212.   Hackett, Charles D., ed.
        *Women of the Word: Contemporary Sermons by Women
            Clergy*
        Atlanta, GA: Susan Hunter Publishing, 1985. 142 pp.

1213.   Houston, Jean
        *The Possible Human: A Course in Extending Physical,
            Mental, Creative Abilities*
        Los Angeles, CA: J. P. Tarcher, 1982. 272 pp.

1214.   Ingram, Kristen Johnson
        With the Huckleberry Christ: A Spiritual Journey
        San Francisco, CA: Harper & Row, 1987. 96 pp.

1215.   Jessey, Cornelia
        The Prayer of COSA: Praying the Way of Francis of Assisi
        San Francisco, CA: Harper & Row, 1987. 103 pp.

1216. · Keene, Jane A.
A Winter's Song: A Liturgy for Women Seeking Healing from Sexual Abuse in Childhood
New York, NY: Pilgrim Press, 1991. 25 pp.

1217. Kirk, Martha Ann, with Coleen Fulmer
Celebrations of Biblical Women's Stories: Tears, Milk and Honey
Kansas City, MO: Sheed & Ward, 1987. 120 pp.

1218. Koontz, Christian
Connecting: Creativity and Spirituality
Kansas City, MO: Sheed & Ward, 1987. 111 pp.

1219. Levin, Ronnie, and Diann Neu
A Seder of the Sisters of Sarah
Silver Spring, MD: Water Works Press, 1986. 20 pp.

1220. Mangan, Celine
Can We Still Call God "Father"? A Woman Looks at the Lord's Prayer Today
Wilmington, DE: Michael Glazier, 1985. 110 pp.

1221. Mariechild, Diane
Crystal Visions: Nine Meditations for Personal and Planetary Peace
Trumansburg, NY: Crossing Press, 1985. 125 pp.

1222. Meehan, Bridget Mary
Exploring the Feminine Face of God: A Prayerful Journey
Kansas City, MO: Sheed & Ward, 1991. 120 pp.

1223. Milhaven, Annie Lally
Sermons Seldom Heard: Women Proclaim Their Lives
New York, NY: Crossroad/Continuum, 1991. 264 pp.

1224. Mitchell, Ella P., ed.
Those Preachin' Women: Sermons by Black Women Preachers
Valley Forge, PA: Judson, 1985. 126 pp.

1225.   Mitchell, Rosemary C., and Gail A. Ricciuti
        *Birthings and Blessings: Liberating Worship for the Inclu-
            sive Church*
        New York, NY: Crossroad/Continuum, 1991. 192 pp.

1226.   Mollenkott, Virginia Ramey, and Catherine Barry
        Views from the Intersection: Poems and Meditations
        New York, NY: Crossroad Publishing, 1985. 112 pp.

1227.   Morley, Janet
        All Desires Known: Prayers Uniting Faith and Feminism
        Wilton, CT: Morehouse, 1988. 92 pp.

1228.   Neu, Diann
        *Women Church Celebrations: Feminist Liturgies for the
            Lenten Season*
        Silver Spring, MD: Water Works Press, 1985. 70 pp.

1229.   Neu, Diann
        Feminist Celebrations
        Silver Spring, MD: Water Works Press, 1989. 22 pp.

1230.   Neufelder, Jerome, and Mary Coelho, eds.
        Writings on Spiritual Direction by Great Christian Masters
        Somers, CT: Seabury Press, 1982. 205 pp.

1231.   O'Connor, Elizabeth
        Our Many Selves: A Handbook for Self-Discovery
        New York, NY: Harper & Row, 1971. 201 pp.

1232.   Procter-Smith, Marjorie
        *In Her Own Rite: Constructing Feminist Liturgical Tradi-
            tion*
        Nashville, TN: Abingdon Press, 1990. 192 pp.

1233.   Procter-Smith, Marjorie, and Janet Walton, eds.
        *Women at Worship: Interpretations of North American
            Diversity*
        Louisville, KY: Westminster/John Knox Press, 1993.
            272 pp.

1234. Quinonez, Lora Ann, and Mary Daniel Turner
      The Transformation of American Catholic Sisters
      Philadelphia, PA: University of Pennsylvania Press,
      1992. 206 pp.

1235. Roberts, Bernadette
      The Experience of No-Self: A Contemplative Journey
      Boulder, CO: Shambala Press, 1984. 204 pp.

1236. Roller, Karen, ed.
      Women Pray
      New York, NY: Pilgrim Press, 1986. 96 pp.

1237. Ruffing, Janet
      Uncovering Stories of Faith: Spiritual Direction and Narrative
      Ramsey, NJ: Paulist Press, 1989. 179 pp.

1238. Santa-Maria, Maria
      Growth Through Meditation and Journal Writing (Jungian, Christian spirituality)
      Ramsey, NJ: Paulist Press, 1983. 157 pp.

1239. Schaffran, Janet, and Pat Kozak
      More Than Words: Prayer and Ritual for Inclusive Communities
      Oak Park, IL: Meyer-Stone, 1988. 192 pp.

1240. Schmitt, Mary Kathleen Speegle
      Seasons of the Feminine Divine: Christian Feminist Prayers for the Liturgical Cycle
      New York, NY: Crossroad Publishing, 1993. 129 pp.

1241. Schneiders, Sandra Mane
      Women and the Word
      Ramsey, NJ: Paulist Press, 1986. 81 pp.

1242. Smith, Christine M.
      Weaving the Sermon: Preaching in a Feminist Perspective
      Louisville, KY: Westminster/John Knox Press, 1989. 164 pp.

1243. Smith, Delia
       A Journey into God
       San Francisco, CA: Harper & Row, 1989. 240 pp.

1244. Spiegel, Marcia Cohn, and D. Kremsdorf, eds.
       Women Speak to God: The Prayers and Poems of Jewish Women
       Los Angeles, CA: Women's Institute of Jewish Education, 1987. 90 pp.

1245. Teresa, Mother
       A Gift of God: Prayers and Meditations
       San Francisco, CA: Harper & Row, 1975. 78 pp.

1246. Teresa, Mother, ed. Eileen Egan and Kathleen Egan
       Prayertimes with Mother Teresa
       Garden City, NY: Doubleday & Co., 1989. 128 pp.

1247. Teresa, Mother, of Calcutta and Brother Roger of Taize
       Meditations on the Way of the Cross
       New York, NY: Pilgrim Press, 1986. 60 pp.

1248. Teresa, Mother, of Calcutta and Brother Roger of Taize
       Mary, Mother of Reconciliations
       Ramsey, NJ: Paulist Press, 1989. 72 pp.

1249. Walker, Barbara G.
       Women's Ritual: A Sourcebook
       San Francisco, CA: Harper & Row, 1990. 224 pp.

1250. Weber, Christin Lore
       Blessings: Living a WomanChrist Spirituality
       San Francisco, CA: Harper & Row, 1989. 256 pp.

1251. Wenner, Hilda E., and Elizabeth Freilicher
       Here's to the Women: One Hundred Songs for and About American Women
       Syracuse, NY: Syracuse University Press, 1987. 313 pp.

1252. Winter, Miriam Therese
        Womanprayer, Womansong: Resources for Ritual
        Oak Park, IL: Meyer-Stone, 1987. 254 pp.

1253. Winter, Miriam Therese
        *Womanword: A Feminist Lectionary and Psalter on Women
        in the New Testament*
        New York, NY: Crossroad Publishing, 1990. 350 pp.

1254. Winter, Miriam Therese
        *Womanwisdom: Feminist Lectionary and Psalter—Women
        of the Hebrew Scriptures: Pt. 1*
        New York, NY: Crossroad/Continuum, 1991. 352 pp.

1255. Winter, Miriam Therese
        *Womanwitness: A Feminist Lectionary and Psalter—
        Women of the Hebrew Scriptures, Pt. 2*
        New York, NY: Crossroad/Continuum, 1991. 352 pp.

1256. Withers, Barbara, and David Ng, eds.
        An Inclusive Language Lectionary: Readings for Year A
        Louisville, KY: Westminster/John Knox Press, 1983.
        160 pp.

1257. Withers, Barbara, and David Ng, eds.
        An Inclusive Language Lectionary: Readings for Year B
        Louisville, KY: Westminster/John Knox Press, 1984.
        256 pp.

1258. Wolf, Barbara
        Journey in Faith: An Inquirer's Program
        Somers, CT: Seabury Press, 1982. 144 pp.

1259. Women Speak from the Pulpit, ed.
        Spinning a Sacred Yarn
        New York, NY: Pilgrim Press, 1982. 230 pp.

8. SPIRITUALITY AS CREATIVE EXPRESSION

Although this chapter heading defies definition and raises the greatest difficulty regarding boundaries of inclusion, I regard it as one of the pivotal classifications of this bibliography. Resources in literature and the visual and musical arts abound, and my list offers a sampler of those titles most pertinent to spirituality. I have divided the list into four clusters. The first indicates how poetry from a woman's pen can enrich our lives. The second offers novelists and essayists who merit recognition within the discussion of women's spiritual sensibility. The critical appreciation of women artists in the visual and musical fields constitutes the third section, while the fourth assembles titles from the feminist literary critical sphere.

It is to the last that I direct additional comment, because women working in religion have discovered this approach particularly inspiring. Literary criticism offers a methodology for analysis in the first place. While this is helpful to the academic feminist in religious studies, I hasten to note that this approach is more encompassing and larger in import. How text is "inscribed" and read by and for women is central to many authors in this section, suggesting that written expression requires a radical eye. The implications for spirituality liberated from prevailing canons of suitable expression are far-reaching. Certainly, the contribution of French feminists must be noted for their radicalism. I have offered a few titles related to this approach; however, the list is principally constituted of studies that examine the contribution of particular writers.

I am aware that this section is most reflective of my taste and discernment. My hope is that it prompts interest in the reader and encourages critical reflection on what artistic (visual and ceremonial as well as literary) works best exemplify a spirituality that is feminist.

Poetry and Plays

1260.   Amrani, Nora Harwit, ed.
        American Indian Women Poets: Women Between the Worlds
        New York, NY: Vintage, 1993. 451 pp.

1261.   Bass, Ellen
        Our Stunning Harvest
        Oak Park, IL: Meyer-Stone, 1988. 90 pp.

1262.   Bogin, Meg
        The Women Troubadours
        New York, NY: W. W. Norton, 1980. 190 pp.

1263.   Brant, Beth
        Mohawk Trail
        Ithaca, NY: Firebrand Books, 1985. 94 pp.

1264.   Broumas, Olga
        Beginning with O
        New Haven, CT: Yale University Press, 1977. 74 pp.

1265.   Clampitt, Amy
        Archaic Figure
        New York, NY: Alfred A. Knopf, 1987. 113 pp.

1266.   Gilbert, Sandra
        Emily's Bread: Poems
        New York, NY: W. W. Norton, 1984. 103 pp.

1267.   Giovanni, Nikki
        Cotton Candy on a Rainy Day
        New York, NY: William Morrow, 1978. 93 pp.

1268.   Golden, Renny, and Sheila Collins
        Struggle Is a Name for Hope
        Minneapolis, MN: West End Press, 1982. 47 pp.

1269.   Grahn, Judy
        The Queen of Swords (myth of Inanna)
        Boston, MA: Beacon Press, 1987. 178 pp.

1270.   Grahn, Judy
        The Queen of Wands (Myth of Helen in ancient
            Greece)
        Boston, MA: Beacon Press, 1987. 111 pp.

1271.   H.D., ed. Louis Martz
        Collected Poems, 1912–1944
        New York, NY: New Directions, 1983. 629 pp.

1272.   Hacker, Marilyn
        Love, Death and the Changing of the Seasons
        New York, NY: Arbor House, William Morrow & Co.,
            1986. 212 pp.

1273.   Hirschfield, Jane, ed.
        *Women in Praise of the Sacred: Forty-Three Centuries of
            Spiritual Poetry by Women*
        New York, NY: Harper & Row, 1994. 259 pp.

1274.   Jordan, June
        Passion: New Poems, 1977–1980
        Boston, MA: Beacon Press, 1980. 100 pp.

1275.   Kendrick, Delores
        The Women of Plums: Poems in the Voices of Slave Women
        New York, NY: William Morrow, 1989. 124 pp.

1276.   Kolmar, Gertrude, trans. Henry Smith
        Dark Soliloquy: Selected Poems
        Somers, CT: Seabury Press, 1975. 262 pp.

1277. Kumin, Maxine
Nurture
New York, NY: Penguin Books, 1989. 63 pp.

1278. Levertov, Denise
Oblique Prayers
New York, NY: New Directions, 1984. 87 pp.

1279. Levertov, Denise
Breathing the Water
New York, NY: New Directions, 1987. 96 pp.

1280. Lorde, Audre
The Black Unicorn
New York, NY: W. W. Norton, 1978. 122 pp.

1281. Metzger, Deena
Looking for the Faces of God
Berkeley, CA: Parallax Press, 1990. 96 pp.

1282. Moore, Honor, ed.
*The New Women's Theatre: Ten Plays by Contemporary
American Women*
New York, NY: Vintage, 1977. 357 pp.

1283. Mora, Pat
Borders
Houston, TX: Arte Publico Press, 1986. 88 pp.

1284. Oliver, Mary
New and Selected Poems
Boston, MA: Beacon Press, 1992. 256 pp.

1285. Ostricher, Alicia S.
The Mother/Child Papers
Boston, MA: Beacon Press, 1986. 62 pp.

1286. Piercy, Marge
The Moon Is Always Female
New York, NY: Alfred A. Knopf, 1981. 133 pp.

1287. Piercy, Marge, ed.
Early Ripening: American Women's Poetry Now
Boston, MA: Pandora/Routledge & Kegan Paul,
1987. 280 pp.

1288. Rich, Adrienne
The Fact of a Doorframe: Poems Selected and New, 1950–1984
New York, NY: W. W. Norton, 1985. 341 pp.

1289. Rich, Adrienne
Your Native Land, Your Life
New York, NY: W. W. Norton, 1986. 113 pp.

1290. Rich, Adrienne
Time's Power: Poems, 1985–1988
New York, NY: W. W. Norton, 1989. 58 pp.

1291. Sewell, Marilyn
Cries of the Spirit: A Celebration of Women's Spirituality
Boston, MA: Beacon Press, 1990. 340 pp.

1292. Shange, Ntozake
For Colored Girls Who Have Considered Suicide When the Rainbow Is Enuf
New York, NY: Bantam Books, 1980. 64 pp.

1293. Soelle, Dorothee
Revolutionary Patience
Maryknoll, NY: Orbis Books, 1977. 82 pp.

1294. Stetson, Erlene, ed.
Black Sister: Poetry by Black American Women, 1746–1980
Bloomington, IN: Indiana University Press, 1981. 312 pp.

1295. Strickland, Stephanie
The Red Virgin: A Poem of Simone Weil
Madison, WI: University of Wisconsin Press, 1993. 96 pp.

1296.   Walker, Alice
        Horses Make a Landscape More Beautiful
        San Diego, CA: Harcourt Brace Jovanovich, 1985. 96
        pp.

1297.   Wenkart, Henny, ed.
        Sarah's Daughters Sing: A Sampler of Poems by Jewish Women
        Hoboken, NJ: KTAV Publishers, 1990. 264 pp.

1298.   Wong, Nellie
        Dreams in Harrison Railroad Park
        Berkeley, CA: Kelsey Street Press, 1989. 46 pp.

Novels, Essays, and Short Stories

1299.   Arnow, Harriet
        The Dollmaker
        Lexington, KY: University Press of Kentucky, 1985.
        560 pp.

1300.   Ashton-Warner, Sylvia
        Spinster, a Novel
        New York, NY: Simon & Schuster, 1985. 242 pp.

1301.   Bambara, Toni Cade
        The Salt Eaters
        New York, NY: Random House, 1980. 295 pp.

1302.   Broner, Esther M.
        The Weave of Women
        Bloomington, IN: Indiana University Press, 1985. 296
        pp.

1303.   Bryant, Dorothy
        The Kin of Ata Are Waiting for You
        New York, NY: Random House, 1971. 220 pp.

1304. Bryant, Dorothy
Confessions of Madame Psyche
Berkeley, CA: ATA Books, 1986. 376 pp.

1305. Chase, Joan
During the Reign of the Queen of Persia
New York, NY: Harper & Row, 1983. 224 pp.

1306. Chernin, Kim
The Flame Bearers
Boston, MA: Pandora/Routledge & Kegan Paul, 1986. 288 pp.

1307. Clausen, Jan
Books and Life
Columbus, OH: Ohio State University Press, 1989. 192 pp.

1308. Cliff, Michelle
Abeng
Trumansburg, NY: Crossing Press, 1984. 167 pp.

1309. Cliff, Michelle
The Land of Look Behind: Prose and Poetry
Ithaca, NY: Firebrand Books, 1985. 119 pp.

1310. Cliff, Michelle
No Telephone to Heaven
New York, NY: E. P. Dutton, 1987. 211 pp.

1311. Cooper, J. California
Some Soul to Keep
New York, NY: St. Martin's Press, 1987. 211 pp.

1312. Cooper, Susan
The Dark Is Rising
New York, NY: Penguin Books, 1984. 232 pp.

1313. de Beauvoir, Simone, trans. Patrick O'Brian
When Things of the Spirit Come First
New York, NY: Pantheon Books, 1982. 212 pp.

1314.   Farmer, Penelope
        Eve: Her Story
        San Francisco, CA: Mercury House, 1988. 188 pp.

1315.   Fischer, M. F. K.
        Sister Age
        New York, NY: Alfred A. Knopf, 1983. 243 pp.

1316.   Furlong, Monica
        Wise Child
        New York, NY: Alfred A. Knopf, 1987. 228 pp.

1317.   Gearhart, Sally
        The Wanderground
        Watertown, NY: Persephone Press, 1977. 196 pp.

1318.   Go, Shizuko, trans. G. Harcourt
        Requiem
        New York, NY: Kodansha International, 1985. 128 pp.

1319.   Golden, Marita
        Long Distance Life
        Garden City, NY: Doubleday & Co., 1989. 312 pp.

1320.   Grahn, Judy
        The Highest Apple: Essays
        San Francisco, CA: Spinsters Ink, 1985. 159 pp.

1321.   Griffin, Susan
        Woman and Nature: The Roaring Inside Her
        New York, NY: Harper & Row, 1978. 263 pp.

1322.   Guy, Rosa
        My Love, My Love: On the Peasant Girl (Caribbean)
        New York, NY: Holt, Rinehart & Winston, 1985. 119
            pp.

1323.   Hawkes, Jacquetta
        A Quest of Love
        London, U.K.: Chatto & Windus, 1980. 219 pp.

1324. Hogan, Linda
Mean Spirit (Native American)
New York, NY: Atheneum, 1990. 374 pp.

1325. Hulme, Keri
The Bone People (Maori novel)
New York, NY: Penguin Books, 1986. 450 pp.

1326. Hurston, Zora Neale
Their Eyes Were Watching God
Champaign, IL: University of Illinois Press, 1978. 296
pp.

1327. Hurston, Zora Neale
Moses: Man of the Mountain
Champaign, IL: University of Illinois Press, 1984. 369
pp.

1328. Karmel, Ilona
An Estate of Memory
Old Westbury, NY: The Feminist Press, 1987. 466 pp.

1329. Kessler, Carol Farley, ed.
Daring to Dream: Utopian Stories by U.S. Women, 1836–1919
Boston, MA: Pandora/Routledge & Kegan Paul,
1984. 266 pp.

1330. Kogawa, Joy
Obasan
Boston, MA: Godine, 1982. 250 pp.

1331. Lane, Ann J., ed.
The Charlotte Perkins Gilman Reader
New York, NY: Pantheon Books, 1980. 208 pp.

1332. Laurence, Margaret
The Stone Angel
New York, NY: Bantam Books, 1981. 304 pp.

1333.   Le Guin, Ursula
        Always Come Home
        New York, NY: Bantam Books, 1987. 576 pp.

1334.   Le Guin, Ursula
        *Dancing at the Edge of the World: Thoughts on Words,
           Women, Places*
        New York, NY: Grove Press, 1989. 306 pp.

1335.   Le Seur, Meridel
        I Hear Men Talking
        Minneapolis, MN: West End Press, 1984. 243 pp.

1336.   Le Seur, Meridel, ed. Elaine Hedges
        Ripening: Selected Work
        Old Westbury, NY: The Feminist Press, 1981. 306 pp.

1337.   Leffland, Ella
        Rumors of Peace
        New York, NY: Harper & Row, 1979. 389 pp.

1338.   Lippit, Noriko M., and Kyoko Selden, eds.
        Stories by Contemporary Japanese Women Writers
        New York, NY: M. E. Sharpe, 1982. 221 pp.

1339.   Lorde, Audre
        Sister Outsider: Essays and Speeches
        Trumansburg, NY: Crossing Press, 1984. 190 pp.

1340.   Lorde, Audre
        A Burst of Light: Essays
        Ithaca, NY: Firebrand Books, 1988. 134 pp.

1341.   Mackey, Mary
        The Last Warrior Queen
        New York, NY: Berkley Publishing, 1984.

1342.   Marshall, Paule
        Brown Girl, Brownstones
        Old Westbury, NY: The Feminist Press, 1981. 324 pp.

1343. Marshall, Paule
       Praise Song for the Widow
       New York, NY: E. P. Dutton, 1984. 256 pp.

1344. Marshall, Paule
       The Chosen Place, the Timeless People
       New York, NY: Random House, 1984. 472 pp.

1345. Marshall, Paule
       Reena and Other Stories
       Old Westbury, NY: The Feminist Press, 1984. 210 pp.

1346. Metzger, Deena
       What Dinah Thought
       New York, NY: Viking Press, 1989. 375 pp.

1347. Mojtabi, A. G.
       Ordinary Time
       Garden City, NY: Doubleday & Co., 1989. 223 pp.

1348. Morrison, Toni
       Beloved
       New York, NY: New American Library, 1987. 275 pp.

1349. Naylor, Gloria
       Mama Day
       New York, NY: Ticknor & Fields, 1988. 312 pp.

1350. Nelson, Shirley
       The Last Year of the War
       San Francisco, CA: Harper & Row, 1978. 255 pp.

1351. O'Connor, Flannery
       *Three by Flannery O'Conner: Wise Blood, The Violent Bear
       It Away, A Good Man Is Hard to Find*
       New York, NY: New American Library, 1983. 460 pp.

1352. Olsen, Tillie
       Silences

New York, NY: Delacort Press/Seymour Lawrence, 1978. 306 pp.

1353.   Piercy, Marge
        Woman on the Edge of Time
        New York, NY: Alfred A. Knopf, 1976. 369 pp.

1354.   Pineda, Cecile
        Frieze
        New York, NY: Penguin Books, 1987. 224 pp.

1355.   Rich, Adrienne
        On Lies, Secrets and Silence: Selected Prose
        New York, NY: W. W. Norton, 1979. 310 pp.

1356.   Russ, Joanna
        Magic Mommas, Trembling Sisters, Puritans and Perverts: Feminist Essays
        Trumansburg, NY: Crossing Press, 1985. 119 pp.

1357.   Sarton, May
        The Magnificent Spinster
        New York, NY: W. W. Norton, 1985. 384 pp.

1358.   Shange, Ntozake
        Sassafras, Cypress and Indigo
        New York, NY: St. Martin's Press, 1982. 224 pp.

1359.   Stewart, Mary
        The Last Enchantment
        New York, NY: Fawcett Crest Books, 1980. 538 pp.

1360.   Stewart, Mary
        The Wicked Day
        New York, NY: William Morrow, 1983. 453 pp.

1361.   Walker, Alice
        In Search of Our Mothers' Gardens
        New York, NY: Harcourt Brace Jovanovich, 1979. 397 pp.

1362. Walker, Alice
The Color Purple
New York, NY: Washington Square Press/Solidus Pocketbooks, 1982. 295 pp.

1363. Walker, Alice
The Temple of My Familiar
San Diego, CA: Harcourt Brace Jovanovich, 1989. 416 pp.

1364. Webb, Mary
Precious Bane
Notre Dame, IN: Notre Dame University Press, 1983. 319 pp.

1365. Willard, Nancy
Things Invisible to See
New York, NY: Alfred A. Knopf, 1985. 265 pp.

1366. Wolf, Christa, trans. Jan van Heurck
Cassandra: A Novel and Four Essays
New York, NY: Farrar, Straus & Giroux, 1984. 320 pp.

1367. Wolkstein, Diane
The First Love Stories: From Isis and Osiris to Tristan and Iseult
New York, NY: HarperCollins, 1991. 272 pp.

1368. Yezierska, Anzia
Bread Givers
New York, NY: Persea Books, 1975. 297 pp.

1369. Yglesias, Helen
The Saviors
Boston, MA: Houghton Mifflin, 1987. 306 pp.

1370. Zahava, Irene, ed.
Hear the Silence: Stories of Myth, Magic and Renewal
Trumansburg, NY: Crossing Press, 1986. 194 pp.

Visual and Musical Arts

1371. Beckett, Wendy
       Contemporary Women Artists
       New York, NY: Universe Publications, 1988. 128 pp.

1372. Belcher, Gerald, and Margaret Belcher
       *Collecting Souls, Gathering Dust: The Struggles of Two
           American Artists, Alice Neel and Rhoda Medary*
       New York, NY: Paragon, 1991. 320 pp.

1373. Bowers, Jane, and Judith Tick, eds.
       *Women Making Music: The Western Art Tradition, 1150–
           1950*
       Urbana, IL: University of Illinois Press, 1989. 424 pp.

1374. Broude, Norma, and Mary D. Garrard, eds.
       Feminism and Art History
       New York, NY: Harper & Row, 1982. 358 pp.

1375. Chicago, Judy
       The Dinner Party: A Symbol of Our Heritage
       Garden City, NY: Anchor Press, Doubleday, 1979.
           253 pp.

1376. Chicago, Judy
       Embroidering Our Heritage: The Dinner Party Needlework
       Garden City, NY: Anchor Press, Doubleday, 1980.
           287 pp.

1377. Chicago, Judy
       The Birth Project
       Garden City, NY: Doubleday & Co., 1985. 231 pp.

1378. Chicago, Judy, with photography by Donald Wood-
           man
       Holocaust Project: From Darkness into Light
       New York, NY: Penguin Books, 1993. 205 pp.

1379. Civen, Janice Davis
Illuminations: A Modern Spiritual Alphabet
New York, NY: Dodd, Mead, 1984. 111 pp.

1380. Cohen, Aaron
International Discography of Women Composers
Westport, CT: Greenwood Press, 1984. 254 pp.

1381. Craighead, Meinrad
The Mother's Song: Images of God the Mother
Ramsey, NJ: Paulist Press, 1986. 88 pp.

1382. Craighead, Meinrad
The Litany of the Great River
Ramsey, NJ: Paulist Press, 1991. 76 pp.

1383. Dunford, Penelope A.
*A Biographical Dictionary of Women Artists in Europe and
America Since 1850*
Philadelphia, PA: University of Pennsylvania Press,
1989. 500 pp.

1384. Frasier, Jane
Women Composers: A Discography
Washington, DC: Harmonie Park Press, 1983. 300 pp.

1385. Garrard, Mary D.
*Artemisia Gentileschi: The Image of the Female Hero in
Italian Baroque Art*
Princeton, NJ: Princeton University Press, 1989. 607
pp.

1386. Greer, Germaine
*The Obstacle Race: The Fortune of Women Painters and
Their Work*
New York, NY: Farrar, Straus & Giroux, 1979. 373 pp.

1387. Herrera, Hayden
Frida: A Biography of Frida Kahlo
New York, NY: Harper & Row, 1983. 507 pp.

1388. Hoffman, Katherine
       An Enduring Spirit: The Art of Georgia O'Keeffe
       Metuchen, NJ: Scarecrow Press, 1984. 245 pp.

1389. Jezic, Diane P., foreword by Elizabeth Wood
       Women Composers: The Lost Tradition Found
       Old Westbury, NY: The Feminist Press, 1988. 180 pp.

1390. Jones, Suzanne W., ed.
       Writing the Woman Artist
       Philadelphia, PA: University of Pennsylvania Press,
       1991. 448 pp.

1391. Kaplan, Janet A.
       Unexpected Journeys: The Art and Life of Remedios Varo
       New York, NY: Abbeville Press, 1988. 286 pp.

1392. Kent, Sarah, and Jacqueline Moreau, eds.
       Women's Images of Men
       Boston, MA: Pandora/Routledge & Kegan Paul,
       1989. 200 pp.

1393. Koskoff, Ellen, ed.
       Women and Music in Cross-Cultural Perspective
       Urbana, IL: University of Illinois Press, 1989. 262 pp.

1394. Lauter, Estella
       Women as Mythmakers: Poetry and Visual Art by Twentieth-Century Women
       Bloomington, IN: Indiana University Press, 1984. 288 pp.

1395. Lippard, Lucy R.
       Overlay: Contemporary Art and the Art of Prehistory
       New York, NY: Pantheon Books, 1983. 266 pp.

1396. Munro, Eleanor
       Originals: American Women Artists
       New York, NY: Simon & Schuster, 1979. 527 pp.

1397. Nochlin, Linda
       Women, Art, and Power and Other Essays
       New York, NY: Harper & Row, 1988. 181 pp.

1398. Norwood, Vera, and Janice Monk, eds.
       *The Desert Is No Lady: Southwestern Landscapes in
       Women's Writing and Art*
       New Haven, CT: Yale University Press, 1987. 281 pp.

1399. Perry, Gillian
       Paula Modersohn-Becker
       New York, NY: Harper & Row, 1979. 149 pp.

1400. Pollock, Griselda
       *Vision and Difference: Femininity, Feminism and the Histo-
       ries of Art*
       Boston, MA: Routledge & Kegan Paul, 1988. 272 pp.

1401. Randall, Margaret
       *Women Brave in the Face of Danger: Photographs of Latin
       and North American Women*
       Trumansburg, NY: Crossing Press, 1985. 128 pp.

1402. Raven, Arlene
       Crossing Over: Feminism and the Art of Social Concern
       Ann Arbor, MI: UMI Research Press, 1988. 242 pp.

1403. Raven, Arlene, Cassandra Langer, and J. Frueh, eds.
       Feminist Art Criticism: An Anthology
       Ann Arbor, MI: UMI Research Press, 1988. 260 pp.

1404. Robinson, Hilary, ed.
       Visibly Female: Feminism and Art
       New York, NY: Universe Publications, 1988. 319 pp.

1405. Tick, Judith
       American Women Composers Before 1870
       Ann Arbor, MI: UMI Research Press, 1983. 302 pp.

1406.   Weiner, Annette B., and Jane Schneider, eds.
         Cloth and Human Experience
         Washington, DC: Smithsonian, 1989. 448 pp.

1407.   Wolff, Janet
         Feminine Sentences: Essays on Women and Culture
         Berkeley, CA: University of California Press, 1990.
             146 pp.

Literary Criticism

1408.   Abel, Elizabeth, M. Hirsch, and E. Langland, eds.
         The Voyage In: Fictions of Female Development
         Hanover, NH: University Presses of New England,
             1983. 366 pp.

1409.   Ascher, Carol, L. DeSalvo, and S. Ruddick, eds.
         *Between Women: Biographers, Novelists, Critics, Teachers
             and Artists Write About Their Work on Women*
         Boston, MA: Beacon Press, 1984. 469 pp.

1410.   Awkward, Michael
         *Inspiriting Influences: Tradition, Revision and Afro-
             American Women's Novels*
         New York, NY: Columbia University Press, 1989. 208
             pp.

1411.   Baker, Houston A., phototext by E. Alexander and P.
             Redmond
         *Workings of the Spirit: The Poetics of Afro-American
             Women's Writing*
         Chicago, IL: University of Chicago Press, 1991. 256
             pp.

1412.   Bernikow, Louise
         Among Women
         New York, NY: Harper & Row, 1980. 296 pp.

1413. Bowles, Gloria
Louise Bogan's Aesthetic of Limitation
Bloomington, IN: Indiana University Press, 1987. 156
pp.

1414. Burnett, Gary
H.D.: Between Image and Epic—The Mysteries of Her Poetic
Ann Arbor, MI: UMI Research Press, 1989. 220 pp.

1415. Campbell, Jane
Mythic Black Fiction: The Transformation of History
Austin, TX: University of Texas Press, 1986. 200 pp.

1416. Christian, Barbara
Black Women Novelists: The Development of a Tradition, 1892–1976
Westport, CT: Greenwood Press, 1985. 275 pp.

1417. Christian, Barbara
Black Feminist Criticism: Perspectives on Black Women Writers
Elmsford, NY: Pergamon Press, 1985. 261 pp.

1418. Conley, Verena Andermatt
Helene Cixous: Writing the Feminine
Lincoln, NE: University of Nebraska Press, 1984. 181
pp.

1419. Cooper, Jane Roberts, ed.
Reading Adrienne Rich: Reviews and Re-Visions, 1951–81
Ann Arbor, MI: University of Michigan Press, 1984.
367 pp.

1420. DeShazer, Mary K.
Inspiring Women: Reimagining the Muse
Elmsford, NY: Pergamon Press, 1987. 272 pp.

1421. DuPlessis, Rachel Blau
Writing Beyond the Ending: Narrative Strategies of Twentieth-Century Women Writers

Bloomington, IN: Indiana University Press, 1985. 254 pp.

1422.   Eberwein, Jane Donahue
        Dickinson: Strategies of Limitation
        Amherst, MA: University of Massachusetts Press, 1985. 320 pp.

1423.   Evans, Marie, ed.
        Black Women Writers (1950–1980): Critical Evaluation
        Garden City, NY: Anchor Press, Doubleday, 1984. 543 pp.

1424.   Fishman, Sylvia Barack
        Follow My Footprints: Challenging Images of Women in American Jewish Fiction
        Waltham, MA: Brandeis University Press, 1993. 506 pp.

1425.   Friedman, Susan Stanford
        Psyche Reborn: The Emergence of H.D.
        Bloomington, IN: Indiana University Press, 1981. 332 pp.

1426.   Fritz, Angela DiPace
        Thought and Vision: A Critical Reading of H.D.'s Poetry
        Washington, DC: Catholic University Press, 1988. 231 pp.

1427.   Fuchs, Esther
        Israeli Mythogynies: Women in Contemporary Hebrew Fiction
        Albany, NY: State University of New York Press, 1987. 147 pp.

1428.   Gates, Henry L., Jr., ed.
        Reading Black, Reading Feminist: A Critical Anthology
        New York, NY: Meridian Books, 1990. 534 pp.

1429.   Green, Gayle, and Coppelia Kahn, eds.
         Making a Difference: Feminist Literary Criticism
         New York, NY: Methuen, 1985. 273 pp.

1430.   Guest, Barbara
         Herself Defined: The Poet H.D. and Her World
         Garden City, NY: Doubleday & Co., 1984. 360 pp.

1431.   Heinemann, Marlene E.
         Gender and Destiny: Women Writers and the Holocaust
         Westport, CT: Greenwood Press, 1986. 149 pp.

1432.   Holloway, Karla C.
         *The Character of the Word: The Texts of Zora Neale
         Hurston*
         Westport, CT: Greenwood Press, 1987. 184 pp.

1433.   Holloway, Karla C., and Stephanie Demetrakopoulos
         New Dimensions of Spirituality (Toni Morrison)
         Westport, CT: Greenwood Press, 1987. 184 pp.

1434.   Honey, Maureen, ed.
         *Shadowed Dreams: Women's Poetry of the Harlem Renais-
         sance*
         New Brunswick, NJ: Rutgers University Press, 1989.
         238 pp.

1435.   Hull, Gloria T.
         *Color, Sex and Poetry: Three Women Writers of the Harlem
         Renaissance*
         Bloomington, IN: Indiana University Press, 1987. 240
         pp.

1436.   Jardine, Alice
         Gynesis: Configurations of Women and Modernity
         Ithaca, NY: Cornell University Press, 1985. 281 pp.

1437.   Keyes, Claire
         The Aesthetics of Power: The Poetry of Adrienne Rich
         Athens, GA: University of Georgia Press, 1986. 216 pp.

1438. Koppel, Gene
       The Religious Dimensions of Jane Austen's Novels
       Ann Arbor, MI: UMI Research Press, 1988. 154 pp.

1439. Kubitschek, Missy Dean
       *Claiming the Heritage: African-American Women Novelists
       and History*
       Jackson, MS: University Press of Mississippi, 1991.
       203 pp.

1440. Maitland, Sara
       Virgin Territory
       Bly, NY: Beaufort, 1984. 210 pp.

1441. Marcus, Jane
       Virginia Woolf and the Languages of Patriarchy
       Bloomington, IN: Indiana University Press, 1987. 219
       pp.

1442. Marcus, Jane
       Art and Anger: Reading Like a Woman
       Columbus, OH: Ohio State/Miami University
       Presses, 1988. 286 pp.

1443. Martin, Wendy
       *An American Triptych: Ann Bradstreet, Emily Dickinson,
       Adrienne Rich*
       Chapel Hill, NC: University of North Carolina Press,
       1984. 276 pp.

1444. McKay, Nellie, ed.
       Critical Essays on Toni Morrison
       Boston, MA: Twayne Publishers, 1988. 232 pp.

1445. Middlebrook, Diane Wood, and Marilyn Yalom, eds.
       *Coming to Light: American Women Poets in the Twentieth-
       Century*
       Ann Arbor, MI: University of Michigan Press, 1985.
       270 pp.

1446. Miller, Cristanne
Emily Dickinson: A Poet's Grammar
Cambridge, MA: Harvard University Press, 1987. 212 pp.

1447. Moi, Toril
Sexual/Textual Politics: Feminist Literary Theory
New York, NY: Methuen, 1986. 206 pp.

1448. Montefiore, Jan
Feminism and Poetry: Language, Experience and Identity in Women's Writing
New York, NY: Methuen, 1987. 210 pp.

1449. Mudge, Jean McClure
Emily Dickinson and the Image of the Home
Amherst, MA: University of Massachusetts Press, 1975. 293 pp.

1450. O'Connor, Flannery, ed. L. Zuber and C. Martin
The Presence of Grace and Other Book Reviews
Athens, GA: University of Georgia Press, 1983. 189 pp.

1451. Orr, Elaine Neil
Tillie Olsen and a Feminist Spiritual Vision
Jackson, MS: University Press of Mississippi, 1987. 208 pp.

1452. Ostricher, Alicia S.
Stealing the Language: The Emergence of Women's Poetry in America
Boston, MA: Beacon Press, 1986. 315 pp.

1453. Patterson, Rebecca, ed. Margaret H. Freeman
Emily Dickinson's Imagery
Amherst, MA: University of Massachusetts Press, 1980. 238 pp.

1454.   Paulson, Suzanne M.
         Flannery O'Connor: A Study of Short Fiction
         Boston, MA: Twayne Publishers, 1988. 232 pp.

1455.   Pope, Deborah
         A Separate Vision: Isolation in Contemporary Women's Poetry
         Baton Rouge, LA: Louisiana State University Press, 1984. 174 pp.

1456.   Pryse, Marjorie,and Hortense Spillers
         Conjuring: Black Women, Fiction, and Literary Tradition
         Bloomington, IN: Indiana University Press, 1985. 274 pp.

1457.   Radway, Janice
         Reading the Romance: Women, Patriarchy and Popular Literature
         Chapel Hill, NC: University of North Carolina Press, 1984. 274 pp.

1458.   Raine, Kathleen
         The Human Face of God: William Blake and the Book of Job
         New York, NY: Thames & Hudson, 1982. 320 pp.

1459.   Raine, Kathleen, ed. Brian Keeble
         The Inner Journey of the Poet and Other Papers
         London, U.K.: Allen & Unwin, 1982. 203 pp.

1460.   Rigney, Barbara Hill
         Lilith's Daughters: Women and Religion in Contemporary Fiction
         Madison, WI: University of Wisconsin Press, 1982. 120 pp.

1461.   Sanchez, Marta Ester
         Contemporary Chicana Poetry: A Critical Approach to an Emerging Literature

Berkeley, CA: University of California Press, 1986. 377 pp.

1462. Shapiro, Marianne
Woman, Earthly and Divine in the Comedy of Dante
Lexington, KY: University Press of Kentucky, 1975. 187 pp.

1463. Shinn, Thelma J.
Worlds Within Women: Myth and Mythmaking in Fantastic Literature by Women
Westport, CT: Greenwood Press, 1986. 214 pp.

1464. Showalter, Elaine, ed.
Speaking of Gender
New York, NY: Routledge, 1989. 335 pp.

1465. Stambaugh, Sara
The Witch and the Goddess in the Fiction of Isak Dinesen: A Feminist Reading
Ann Arbor, MI: UMI Research Press, 1988. 139 pp.

1466. Taylor, Martin C.
Gabriela Mistrail's Religious Sensibility
Berkeley, CA: University of California Press, 1968. 191 pp.

1467. Walker, Melissa
Down from the Mountaintop: Black Women's Novels in the Wake of the Civil Rights Movement, 1966–1989
New Haven, CT: Yale University Press, 1991. 226 pp.

1468. Wall, Cheryl, ed.
Changing Our Own Words: Essays on Criticism, Theory and Writing by Black Women
New Brunswick, NJ: Rutgers University Press, 1990. 240 pp.

1469.   Washington, Margaret, ed. M. Graham
        "How I Wrote Jubilee" and Other Essays on Life and Literature
        Old Westbury, NY: The Feminist Press, 1988. 200 pp.

1470.   Willis, Susan
        Specifying: Black Women Writing the American Experience
        Madison, WI: University of Wisconsin Press, 1987. 186 pp.

9. FEMINIST THEORY

It is not possible to exclude much of the current writing generally identified as feminist theory from a spirituality bibliography which is grounded in feminism. Although many of the authors included in the sections to follow might seem initially irrelevant—that is, not explicitly concerned with the spirit as such—their combined contribution to understanding woman's thought and experience is most informative. There are a number of pivotal writings listed in the first section which take up questions of woman's access to resources, of women's empowerment, of the notions of difference and gender role. Among the resources are edited collections of excellent essays that are frequently cited and serve as key expressions of feminist reflection. Alison Jagger and Dale Spender are but two names among a veritable assembly of women thinkers who have provided the reader with essential tools for analysis and understanding. All of the writers clustered here assume the importance of critical thought for the feminist project, however it might be implemented. In the past few years, attention has begun to be given to the human body. Focus on woman's body takes many forms in this section. I have included titles that tell the experience of women living with physical disability, of women who have been violated or who have body images which cause dysfunctional reaction (bulimia, for instance). Sexuality as a topic is once again emerging as singularly important for feminists. Many of the feminists writing ten years ago (Germaine Greer, for example) approached patriarchal society from the perspective of a sexual critique, but in the intervening years the language of gender studies has seemingly subsumed this focus—until recently. I have separated lesbian studies from the rest of this section because I believe it will foster greater consciousness of the diversity in feminist women's experiences.

General

1471.   Allen, Jeffner, and Iris Marion Young, eds.
        *The Thinking Muse: Feminism and Modern French Philos-
        ophy*
        Bloomington, IN: Indiana University Press, 1989. 215
        pp.

1472.   Aptheker, Bettina
        *Women's Legacy: Essays on Race, Sex, and Class in
        American History*
        Amherst, MA: University of Massachusetts Press,
        1982. 177 pp.

1473.   Aptheker, Bettina
        *Tapestries of Life; Women's Work, Women's Consciousness
        and Meaning of Daily Experience*
        Amherst, MA: University of Massachusetts Press,
        1989. 312 pp.

1474.   Belenky, Mary, B. Clinchy, N. Goldberger, and J.
        Tarule
        *Women's Ways of Knowing: The Development of Self, Voice
        and Mind*
        New York, NY: Basic Books, 1986. 256 pp.

1475.   Berry, Mary Frances
        *Why ERA Failed: Politics, Women's Rights, and the Amend-
        ing Process of the Constitution*
        Bloomington, IN: Indiana University Press, 1986. 147
        pp.

1476.   Birnbaum, Lucia Chiavola
        Liberazione della Donna: Feminism in Italy

Middletown, CT: Wesleyan University Press, 1985. 353 pp.

1477. Bluestone, Natalie H.
Women and the Ideal Society: Plato's Republic and the Modern Myths of Gender
Amherst, MA: University of Massachusetts Press, 1987. 248 pp.

1478. Bowles, Gloria, and Renate Duelli Klein, eds.
Theories of Women's Studies
Boston, MA: Routledge & Kegan Paul, 1983. 277 pp.

1479. Braidotti, Rosi, trans. E. Guild
Patterns of Dissonance: A Study of Women in Contemporary Philosophy
New York, NY: Routledge, 1991. 306 pp.

1480. Brownmiller, Susan
Femininity
New York, NY: Fawcett Crest Books, 1984. 541 pp.

1481. Bunch, Charlotte, and Sandra Pollack, eds.
Learning Our Way: Essays in Feminist Education
Trumansburg, NY: Crossing Press, 1983. 336 pp.

1482. Cixous, Helene, and Catherine Clement, trans. B. Wing
The Newly Born Woman
Minneapolis, MN: University of Minnesota Press, 1986. 169 pp.

1483. Code, Lorraine, Sheila Mullett, and Christine Overall, eds.
Feminist Perspectives: Philosophical Essays on Method and Morals
Toronto, Ont.: University of Toronto Press, 1988. 205 pp.

1484.   Collier, Jane F., and S. J. Yanagisako, eds.
        Gender and Kinship: Essays Toward a Unified Analysis
        Palo Alto, CA: Stanford University Press, 1987. 369
        pp.

1485.   Collins, Patricia Hill
        *Black Feminist Thought: Knowledge, Consciousness, and
        the Politics of Empowerment*
        Winchester, MA: Unwin Hyman, 1990. 240 pp.

1486.   Conway, Jill K., Susan Bourque, and Joan Scott, eds.
        Learning About Women: Gender, Politics and Power
        Ann Arbor, MI: University of Michigan Press, 1989.
        240 pp.

1487.   Culley, Margo, and Catherine Portuges, eds.
        Gendered Subjects: The Dynamics of Feminist Teaching
        Boston, MA: Routledge & Kegan Paul, 1985. 284 pp.

1488.   Daly, Mary
        Gyn/Ecology: The Metaethics of Radical Feminism
        Boston, MA: Beacon Press, 1978. 485 pp.

1489.   Daly, Mary
        Pure Lust: Elemental Feminist Philosophy
        San Francisco, CA: Harper & Row, 1992. 471 pp.

1490.   de Lauretis, Teresa, ed.
        Feminist Studies/Critical Studies
        Bloomington, IN: Indiana University Press, 1986. 230
        pp.

1491.   Delphy, Christine, trans. Diana Leonard
        *Close to Home: A Materialist Analysis of Women's Oppres-
        sion*
        Amherst, MA: University of Massachusetts Press,
        1984. 224 pp.

1492.   Doane, Janice, and Devon Hodges
        Nostalgia and Sexual Difference
        New York, NY: Methuen, 1987. 187 pp.

1493. Donovan, Josephine
Feminist Theory: The Intellectual Traditions of American Feminism
New York, NY: Ungar Publishing, 1987. 237 pp.

1494. Ecker, Gisela, ed., trans. H. Anderson
Feminist Aesthetics
Boston, MA: Beacon Press, 1986. 187 pp.

1495. Eisenstein, Hester
Contemporary Feminist Thought
Boston, MA: Twayne Publishers, 1984. 196 pp.

1496. Eisenstein, Hester, and Alice Jardine, eds.
The Future of Difference
New Brunswick, NJ: Rutgers University Press, 1985. 362 pp.

1497. Erikson, Victoria Lee
When Silence Speaks: Feminism, Social Theory, and Religion
Philadelphia, PA: Fortress Press, 1993. 219 pp.

1498. Farganis, Sondra
The Social Reconstruction of the Feminine Character
Totowa, NJ: Rowman & Allanheld, 1986. 260 pp.

1499. Ferguson, Ann
Blood at the Root: Motherhood, Sexuality and Male Dominance
Winchester, MA: Unwin Hyman, 1989. 380 pp.

1500. Ferguson, Kathy E.
The Feminist Case Against Bureaucracy
Philadelphia, PA: Temple University Press, 1984. 286 pp.

1501. Forman, Frieda J., with Caoran Sowton, eds.
Taking Our Time: Feminist Perspectives on Temporality
Elmsford, NY: Pergamon Press, 1988. 256 pp.

1502.   Frye, Marilyn
        The Politics of Reality: Essays in Feminist Theory
        Trumansburg, NY: Crossing Press, 1983. 176 pp.

1503.   Frye, Marilyn
        Beyond Power: On Women, Men and Morals
        New York, NY: Summit Books, 1985. 640 pp.

1504.   Gergen, Mary M.
        Feminist Thought and the Structure of Knowledge
        New York, NY: New York University Press, 1987. 320
            pp.

1505.   Gilligan, Carol, et al., eds.
        Mapping the Moral Domain
        Cambridge, MA: Harvard University Press, 1989. 432
            pp.

1506.   Gould, Carol, ed.
        *Beyond Domination: New Perspectives on Women and
            Philosophy*
        Totowa, NJ: Rowman & Allanheld, 1984. 334 pp.

1507.   Gray, Elizabeth Dodson
        Patriarchy as a Conceptual Trap
        Wellesley, MA: Roundtable Press, 1982. 142 pp.

1508.   Griffiths, Morwenna, and Margaret Whitford, eds.
        Feminist Perspectives in Philosophy
        New York, NY: Macmillan, 1988. 234 pp.

1509.   Hanen, Marsha, and Kai Nelson, eds.
        Science, Morality and Feminist Theory
        Calgary, Alta.: University of Calgary Press, 1987. 434
            pp.

1510.   Harding, Sandra, and Merrill B. Hintikka, eds.
        *Discovering Reality: Feminist Perspectives on Epistemology
            and Metaphysics*
        London, U.K.: Reidel, 1983. 332 pp.

1511. Hess, Beth B., and Myra Marx Feree, eds.
Analyzing Gender
Newbury Park, CA: Sage Publishers, 1987. 500 pp.

1512. hooks, bell
Feminist Theory: From Margin to Center
Boston, MA: South End Press, 1984. 174 pp.

1513. Hunter College Women's Studies Collective
*Women's Realities, Women's Choices: An Introduction to
Women's Studies*
Oxford, U.K.: Oxford University Press, 1983. 648 pp.

1514. Irigaray, Luce, trans. C. Porter and C. Burke
The Sex Which Is Not One
Ithaca, NY: Cornell University Press, 1985. 223 pp.

1515. Irigaray, Luce, trans. G. C. Gill
Speculum of the Other Woman
Ithaca, NY: Cornell University Press, 1985. 365 pp.

1516. Jagger, Alison
Feminist Politics and Human Nature
Totowa, NJ: Rowman & Allanheld, 1983. 416 pp.

1517. Janeway, Elizabeth
Powers of the Weak
New York, NY: Alfred A. Knopf, 1980. 350 pp.

1518. Janeway, Elizabeth
Cross Sections: From a Decade of Change
New York, NY: William Morrow, 1984. 320 pp.

1519. Jardine, Alice, and Paul Smith, eds.
Men in Feminism
New York, NY: Methuen, 1987. 288 pp.

1520. Johnson, Patricia Altenbernd, and Janet Kalven, eds.
With Both Eyes Open: Seeing Beyond Gender
New York, NY: Pilgrim Press, 1988. 201 pp.

1521.   Joseph, Gloria I., and Jill Lewis
        *Common Differences: Conflicts in Black and White Feminist
            Perspectives*
        Garden City, NY: Doubleday & Co., 1981. 300 pp.

1522.   Kittay, Eva Feder, and Diana T. Meyers, eds.
        Women and Moral Theory
        New York, NY: World, 1987. 336 pp.

1523.   Klatch, Rebecca E.
        Women of the New Right
        Philadelphia, PA: Temple University Press, 1987. 264
            pp.

1524.   Klein, Renate D., and Deborah L. Steinberg, eds.
        Radical Voices: A Decade of Feminist Resistance
        Elmsford, NY: Pergamon Press, 1989. 300 pp.

1525.   Koonz, Claudia
        *Mothers in the Fatherland: Woman, the Family and Nazi
            Politics*
        New York, NY: St. Martin's Press, 1987. 556 pp.

1526.   Kristeva, Julia, trans. L. Roudiez
        Tales of Love
        New York, NY: Columbia University Press, 1987. 414
            pp.

1527.   Kristeva, Julia, trans. L. Roudiez
        Powers of Horror: An Essay in Abjection
        New York, NY: Columbia University Press, 1985. 219
            pp.

1528.   Lenz, Elinor, and Barbara Myerhoff
        *The Feminization of America: How Women's Values Are
            Changing*
        Los Angeles, CA: Jeremy Tarcher Books, 1985. 276
            pp.

1529. Lowe, Marian, and Ruth Hubbard, eds.
Woman's Nature: Rationalizations of Inequality
Elmsford, NY: Pergamon Press, 1983. 155 pp.

1530. MacKinnon, Catharine A.
Feminism Unmodified: Discourses on Life and Law
Cambridge, MA: Harvard University Press, 1987. 328 pp.

1531. Marks, Elaine, and Isabelle de Courtivron, eds.
New French Feminisms
New York, NY: Schocken Books, 1981. 279 pp.

1532. McClung, Nellie
In Times Like These: The Rise of Feminism (Canadian)
Toronto, Ont.: University of Toronto Press, 1972. 217 pp.

1533. Midgely, Mary, and Judith Hughes
Women's Choices: The Philosophic Problems of Feminism
New York, NY: St. Martin's Press, 1984. 256 pp.

1534. Miller, Nancy, ed.
The Poetics of Gender
New York, NY: Columbia University Press, 1986. 303 pp.

1535. Mills, Patricia Jagentowicz
Woman, Nature and Psyche
New Haven, CT: Yale University Press, 1987. 266 pp.

1536. Minnich, Elizabeth Kamark
Transforming Knowledge
Philadelphia, PA: Temple University Press, 1990. 232 pp.

1537. Mitchell, Juliet, and Ann Oakley, eds.
What Is Feminism? A Re-Examination

New York, NY: Virago/Pantheon Pioneers, 1987. 241 pp.

1538. Newton, Judith, and Deborah Rosenfelt, eds.
        Feminist Criticism and Social Change
        New York, NY: Methuen, 1985. 250 pp.

1539. Noddings, Nel
        Caring: A Feminine Approach to Ethics and Moral Education
        Berkeley, CA: University of California Press, 1984. 211 pp.

1540. Noddings, Nel
        Women and Evil
        Berkeley, CA: University of California Press, 1989. 284 pp.

1541. Nye, Andrea
        Feminist Theory and the Philosophies of Man
        New York, NY: Croom Helm, 1988. 272 pp.

1542. O'Brien, Mary
        The Politics of Reproduction
        Boston, MA: Routledge & Kegan Paul, 1983. 240 pp.

1543. O'Brien, Mary
        Reproducing the World: Essays in Feminist Theory
        Boulder, CO: Westview, 1989. 306 pp.

1544. Raymond, Janice
        A Passion for Friends: Toward a Philosophy of Female Affection
        Boston, MA: Beacon Press, 1986. 275 pp.

1545. Risman, Barbara J., and Pepper Schwartz, eds.
        Gender in Intimate Relationships
        Belmont, CA: Wadsworth Press, 1989. 257 pp.

1546. Schaef, Anne Wilson
       *Women's Reality: An Emerging Female System in a White
       Male Society*
       New York, NY: Winston/Seabury, 1982. 176 pp.

1547. Sichtermann, Barbara, trans. J. Whitlam
       Femininity: The Politics of the Personal
       Minneapolis, MN: University of Minnesota Press,
       1986. 132 pp.

1548. Spelman, Elizabeth V.
       *Inessential Woman: Problems of Exclusion in Feminist
       Thought*
       Boston, MA: Beacon Press, 1988. 288 pp.

1549. Spender, Dale
       *For the Record: The Making and Meaning of Feminist
       Knowledge*
       London, U.K.: Women's Press, 1985. 246 pp.

1550. Spender, Dale, ed.
       Feminist Theorists: Three Centuries of Key Women Thinkers
       New York, NY: Pantheon Books, 1984. 402 pp.

1551. Stimpson, Catharine
       Where the Meanings Are: Feminism and Cultural Spaces
       New York, NY: Methuen, 1988. 224 pp.

1552. Trask, Haunani-Kay
       Eros and Power: The Promise of Feminist Theory
       Philadelphia, PA: University of Pennsylvania Press,
       1986. 186 pp.

1553. Walby, Sylvia
       Patriarchy: A New Theory
       Oxford, U.K.: Oxford University Press, 1989. 224 pp.

1554. Young-Bruehl, Elisabeth
       Mind and the Body Politic
       New York, NY: Routledge, 1989. 256 pp.

Women's Bodies and Sexuality

1555. Armstrong, Nancy, and Leonard Tennenhouse, eds.
       *The Ideology of Conduct: Essays in Literature and the
       History of Sexuality*
       New York, NY: Methuen, 1987. 243 pp.

1556. Barbach, Lonnie, ed.
       Pleasures: Women Write Erotica
       San Francisco, CA: Harper & Row, 1985. 246 pp.

1557. Bell, Rudolph M.
       Holy Anorexia
       Chicago, IL: University of Chicago Press, 1986. 248
       pp.

1558. Bordo, Susan
       Unbearable Weight: Feminism, Culture and the Body
       Berkeley, CA: University of California Press, 1993.
       361 pp.

1559. Brumberg, Joan Jacobs
       *Fasting Girls: The Emergence of Anorexia Nervosa as a
       Modern Disease*
       Cambridge, MA: Harvard University Press, 1988. 368
       pp.

1560. Burton, Clare
       Subordination: Feminism and Social Theory
       London, U.K.: Allen & Unwin, 1985. 168 pp.

1561. Butler, Judith
       Gender Trouble: Feminism and the Subversion of Identity
       New York, NY: Routledge, 1989. 224 pp.

1562. Campling, Jo
       Images of Ourselves: Women with Disabilities Talking
       Boston, MA: Routledge & Kegan Paul, 1981. 140 pp.

1563. Caplan, Pat, ed.
The Cultural Construction of Sexuality
London, U.K.: Tavistock, 1987. 320 pp.

1564. Cartledge, Sue, and Joanna Ryan, eds.
Sex and Love: New Thoughts on Old Contradictions
London, U.K.: Women's Press, 1983. 237 pp.

1565. Chernin, Kim
The Obsession: Reflections on the Tyranny of Slenderness
New York, NY: Harper & Row, 1981. 206 pp.

1566. Chernin, Kim
The Hungry Self: Women, Eating and Identity
New York, NY: Times Books, 1985. 213 pp.

1567. Cooey, Paula, Sharon Farmer, and M. E. Ross, eds.
Embodied Love: Sensuality and Relationship as Feminist Values
San Francisco, CA: Harper & Row, 1987. 241 pp.

1568. Deegan, Mary Jo, and Nancy Brooks, eds.
Women and Disability: The Double Handicap
New Brunswick, NJ: Transaction Books, 1985. 144 pp.

1569. Demetrakopoulos, Stephanie
Listening to Our Bodies: The Rebirth of Feminine Wisdom
Boston, MA: Beacon Press, 1983. 199 pp.

1570. Dijkstra, Bram
Idols of Perversity: Fantasies of Feminine Evil in Fin-de-Siecle Culture
Oxford, U.K.: Oxford University Press, 1986. 454 pp.

1571. Donnelly, Dorothy
Radical Love: Toward a Sexual Spirituality
New York, NY: Winston/Seabury, 1984. 135 pp.

1572.   Downing, Christine
         Journey Through Menopause: A Personal Rite of Passage
         New York, NY: Crossroad Publishing, 1987. 144 pp.

1573.   Dworkin, Andrea
         Intercourse
         New York, NY: The Free Press, 1988. 288 pp.

1574.   Ehrenreich, Barbara, E. Hess, and G. Jacobs
         Re-Making Love: The Feminization of Sex
         Garden City, NY: Doubleday & Co., 1986. 228 pp.

1575.   Fine, Michelle, and Adrienne Asch, eds.
         *Women with Disabilities: Essays in Psychology, Culture and
            Politics*
         Philadelphia, PA: Temple University Press, 1988. 368
         pp.

1576.   Freedman, Rita
         Beauty Bound: Why We Pursue the Myth in the Mirror
         Lexington, MA: Lexington Books, 1986. 268 pp.

1577.   Gallop, Jane
         Thinking Through the Body
         New York, NY: Columbia University Press, 1988. 200
         pp.

1578.   Gilbert, Harriet, and Christine Roche
         A Women's History of Sex
         Boston, MA: Pandora/Routledge & Kegan Paul,
         1988. 218 pp.

1579.   Goldstein, Laurence, ed.
         The Female Body: Figures, Styles, Speculations
         Ann Arbor, MI: University of Michigan Press, 1991.
         328 pp.

1580.   Griffin, Susan
         Pornography and Silence
         San Francisco, CA: Harper & Row, 1981. 277 pp.

1581.   Haug, Frigga, ed., trans. E. Carter
        Female Sexualization: A Collective Work of Memory
        New York, NY: Verso/Cond, 1987. 301 pp.

1582.   Hunt, Lynn, ed.
        Eroticism and the Body Politic
        Baltimore, MD: Johns Hopkins University Press,
        1990. 304 pp.

1583.   Jacobus, M., E. Fox Keller, and S. Shuttleworth, eds.
        Body/Politics
        New York, NY: Routledge, 1989. 224 pp.

1584.   Jeffreys, Sheila
        *The Spinster and Her Enemies: Feminism and Sexuality,
        1880–1930*
        Boston, MA: Pandora/Routledge & Kegan Paul,
        1985. 232 pp.

1585.   Kelley, Kathryn, ed.
        Females, Males, and Sexuality: Theories and Research
        Albany, NY: State University of New York Press, 1989.
        288 pp.

1586.   Kitch, Sally L.
        Chaste Liberation: Celibacy and Female Cultural Status
        Urbana, IL: University of Illinois Press, 1989. 225 pp.

1587.   Kitzinger, Sheila
        Women's Experience of Sex
        New York, NY: Putnam Books, 1983. 230 pp.

1588.   Laqueur, Thomas
        Making Sex: Body and Gender from the Greeks to Freud
        Cambridge, MA: Harvard University Press, 1990. 352
        pp.

1589.   Leidholdt, Dorchen, and Janice G. Raymond, eds.
        The Sexual Liberals and the Attack on Feminism
        Elmsford, NY: Pergamon Press, 1989. 256 pp.

1590. LeMoncheck, Linda
       Dehumanizing Women: Treating Persons as Sex Objects
       Totowa, NJ: Rowman & Allanheld, 1985. 192 pp.

1591. Mairs, Nancy
       Plaintext: Deciphering a Woman's Life
       San Francisco, CA: Harper & Row, 1986. 154 pp.

1592. Martin, Emily
       The Woman in the Body: A Cultural Analysis of Reproduction
       Boston, MA: Beacon Press, 1987. 296 pp.

1593. Mendus, Susan, and Jane Randall
       Sexuality and Subordination: Interdisciplinary Studies of Gender (nineteenth century)
       New York, NY: Routledge, 1989. 256 pp.

1594. Michie, Helena
       The Flesh Made Word: Female Figures and Women's Bodies
       Oxford, U.K.: Oxford University Press, 1986. 179 pp.

1595. Nead, Lynda
       Myths of Sexuality: Representation of Women in Victorian Britain
       Oxford, U.K.: Oxford University Press, 1989. 240 pp.

1596. Oleson, Virginia L., and Nancy F. Woods, eds.
       Culture, Society, and Menstruation
       New York, NY: Taylor & Francis, 1986. 186 pp.

1597. Ortner, Sherry, and Harriet Whitehead, eds.
       Sexual Meanings: The Cultural Construction of Gender and Sexuality
       Cambridge, U.K.: Cambridge University Press, 1981. 435 pp.

1598. Peiss, Kathy, and Christina Simmons, ed. Robert Padgug

Passion and Power: Sexuality in History (Radical History Review)
Philadelphia, PA: Temple University Press, 1989. 326 pp.

1599. Saxton, Marsha, and Florence Howe, eds.
With Wings: An Anthology of Literature by and About Women with Disabilities
Old Westbury, NY: The Feminist Press, 1987. 176 pp.

1600. Snitow, Ann, and Christine Stansell, eds.
Powers of Desire: The Politics of Sexuality
New York, NY: Monthly Review Press, 1983. 489 pp.

1601. Spitzack, Carole
Confessing Excess: Women and the Politics of Body Reduction
Albany, NY: State University of New York Press, 1990. 210 pp.

1602. Suleiman, Susan Rubin, ed.
The Female Body in Western Culture: Contemporary Perspectives
Cambridge, MA: Harvard University Press, 1986. 376 pp.

1603. Ussher, Jane
The Psychology of the Female Body
New York, NY: Routledge, 1989. 200 pp.

1604. Vance, Carole S., ed.
Pleasure and Danger: Exploring Female Sexuality
Boston, MA: Routledge & Kegan Paul, 1984. 462 pp.

1605. Walkowitz, Judith
Prostitution and Victorian Society: Women, Class and the State
Cambridge, U.K.: Cambridge University Press, 1980. 347 pp.

1606. Woodman, Marion
       *The Owl Was a Baker's Daughter: Obesity, Anorexia, and
       the Repressed Feminine*
       Toronto, Ont.: Inner City Books, 1980. 144 pp.

Lesbian Expressions

1607. Abbott, Sidney, and Barbara Love
       *Sappho Was a Right On Woman: A Liberated View of
       Lesbianism*
       New York, NY: Stein & Day, 1985. 251 pp.

1608. Allen, Jeffner
       Lesbian Philosophy: Explorations
       Palo Alto, CA: Institute of Lesbian Studies, 1986. 120
       pp.

1609. Allen, Jeffner, ed.
       Lesbian Philosophies and Cultures
       Albany, NY: State University of New York Press, 1990.
       512 pp.

1610. Balka, Christie, and Andy Rose, eds.
       Twice Blessed: On Being Lesbian, Gay and Jewish
       Boston, MA: Beacon Press, 1989. 320 pp.

1611. Beck, Evelyn T., ed.
       Nice Jewish Girls: A Lesbian Reader
       Trumansburg, NY: Crossing Press, 1985. 286 pp.

1612. Boston Lesbian Psychologies Collective
       Lesbian Psychologies: Explorations and Challenges
       Champaign, IL: University of Illinois Press, 1987. 361
       pp.

1613. Brooks, Virginia R.
       Minority Stress and Lesbian Women
       Lexington, MA: Lexington Books, 1981. 219 pp.

1614. Cavin, Susan
Lesbian Origins
San Francisco, CA: ISM Press, 1986. 288 pp.

1615. Clunis, D. Merilee, and G. Dorsey Green
Lesbian Couples
Seattle, WA: Seal Press, 1988. 272 pp.

1616. Curb, Rosemary, and Nancy Manahan, eds.
Lesbian Nuns: Breaking Silence
Tallahassee, FL: Naiad Press, 1985. 383 pp.

1617. Darty, Trudy, and Sandee Potter, eds.
Women—Identified Women
Mountain View, CA: Mayfield Publishing, 1984. 316
pp.

1618. Downing, Christine
Myths and Mysteries of Same—Sex Love
New York, NY: Crossroad Publishing, 1989. 348 pp.

1619. Faderman, Lillian
*Surpassing the Love of Men: Romantic Friendship and
Love Between Women*
New York, NY: William Morrow, 1981. 496 pp.

1620. Fuss, Diana
Inside/Out: Lesbian Theories, Gay Theories
New York, NY: Routledge, 1991. 288 pp.

1621. Grahn, Judy
Another Mother Tongue: Gay Words, Gay Worlds
Boston, MA: Beacon Press, 1984. 324 pp.

1622. Gramick, Jeannine, and Pat Furey
The Vatican and Homosexuality
New York, NY: Crossroad Publishing, 1986. 320 pp.

1623. Gramick, Jeannine, ed.
Homosexuality and the Catholic Church
Chicago, IL: Thomas More Press, 1983. 176 pp.

1624.   Kitzinger, Celia
        The Social Construction of Lesbianism
        Newbury Park, CA: Sage Publishers, 1988. 230 pp.

1625.   Krieger, Susan
        The Mirror Dance: Identity in a Woman's Culture
        Philadelphia, PA: Temple University Press, 1983. 224
        pp.

1626.   Loulan, JoAnn
        Lesbian Sex
        San Francisco, CA: Spinsters Ink, 1984. 309 pp.

1627.   Loulan, JoAnn
        Lesbian Passion: Loving Ourselves and Each Other
        San Francisco, CA: Spinsters Ink, 1987. 325 pp.

1628.   Loulan, JoAnn
        *The Lesbian Erotic Dance: Butch, Femme, Androgyny, and
        Other Rhythms*
        San Francisco, CA: Aunt Lute Press, 1991. 304 pp.

1629.   O'Neill, Craig, and Kathleen Ritter, eds.
        *Coming Out Within: Stages of Spiritual Awakening for
        Lesbians and Gay Men*
        San Francisco, CA: Harper & Row, 1992. 236 pp.

1630.   Penelope, Julia, and Susan Wolfe, eds.
        The Original Coming Out Stories
        Trumansburg, NY: Crossing Press, 1990. 300 pp.

1631.   Pharr, Suzanne
        Homophobia: A Weapon of Sexism
        Little Rock, AR: Women's Project, 1988. 91 pp.

1632.   Phelan, Shane
        *Identity Politics: Lesbian Feminism and the Limits of
        Community*
        Philadelphia, PA: Temple University Press, 1989. 256
        pp.

1633.   Ponse, Barbara
        *Identities in the Lesbian World: The Social Construction of
            Self*
        Westport, CT: Greenwood Press, 1978. 226 pp.

1634.   Rothblum, Esther D., and Ellen Cole, eds.
        Lesbianism: Affirming Nontraditional Roles
        New York, NY: Haworth Press, 1989. 224 pp.

1635.   Segrest, Mab
        *My Mama's Dead Squirrel: Lesbian Essays on Southern
            Culture*
        Ithaca, NY: Firebrand Books, 1985. 237 pp.

1636.   Wittig, Monique
        The Lesbian Body
        New York, NY: Avon, 1976. 159 pp.

1637.   Wittig, Monique, and Sande Zeig
        Lesbian Peoples: Material for a Dictionary
        New York, NY: Avon, 1979. 170 pp.

1638.   Zanotti, Barbara
        A Faith of One's Own: Explorations by Catholic Lesbians
        Trumansburg, NY: Crossing Press, 1986. 199 pp.

10. WOMEN AND FAMILY

This rubric is the largest in scope and only modestly illustrated by reference to text here. I felt that omission of this subject altogether would suggest that women's family life was not relevant to spirituality. On the other hand, the plethora of material available to the feminist reader at this juncture defies description. I have provided a token listing in order to bridge the subject and indicate, where it has happened, published titles that wed family and spiritual experience. The reality of birthing and motherhood has been a special subject for many women interested in the fullness and integration of their lives. Chesler's writing is noteworthy, as is Sara Ruddick's in the Trebilcot volume listed here. Clearly, one of the continuing controversies is reproductive choice for women and the decision to terminate pregnancy. The literature is vast, and I have mentioned only some of the volumes that I have found helpful in sorting out issues and values.

General

1639.   Alsdurf, James, and Phyllis Alsdurf
        *Battered into Submission: The Tragedy of Wife Abuse in the
            Christian Home*
        Downers Grove, IL: InterVarsity Press, 1989. 168 pp.

1640.   Barrett, Michele, and Mary McIntosh
        The Anti-Social Family
        New York, NY: Verso/Cond, 1982. 164 pp.

1641.   Bernard, Jessie
        The Future of Marriage
        New York, NY: World, 1972. 367 pp.

1642.   Bernard, Jessie
        Self-Portrait of a Family: Letters, with Commentary by J. Bernard
        Boston, MA: Beacon Press, 1978. 344 pp.

1643.   Cancion, Francesca M.
        Love in America: Gender and Self-Development
        Cambridge, U.K.: Cambridge University Press, 1987. 210 pp.

1644.   Carmody, Denise Lardner
        Caring for Marriage: Feminist and Biblical Reflections
        Ramsey, NJ: Paulist Press, 1985. 182 pp.

1645.   Chesler, Phyllis
        Mothers on Trial: The Battle for Children and Custody
        New York, NY: McGraw-Hill Book Co., 1986. 651 pp.

1646.   Ehrenreich, Barbara
        The Hearts of Men: American Dreams and the Flight from Commitment
        Garden City, NY: Anchor Press, Doubleday, 1984. 206 pp.

1647.   L'Engle, Madeline
        Two-Part Invention: The Story of a Marriage
        San Francisco, CA: Harper & Row, 1989. 240 pp.

1648.   Rubin, Lillian B.
        Worlds of Pain: Life in the Working-Class Family
        New York, NY: Basic Books, 1976. 268 pp.

1649.   Rubin, Lillian B.
        Women of a Certain Age: The Midlife Search for Self
        New York, NY: Harper & Row, 1979. 309 pp.

1650.   Silberman, Eileen Z.
        The Savage Sacrament: Marriage After American Feminism
        Mystic, CT: Twenty-Third Publications, 1984. 112 pp.

1651.   Thorne, Barrie, with Marilyn Yalom, eds.
        Rethinking the Family: Some Feminist Questions
        White Plains, NY: Longman, 1982. 246 pp.

Motherhood

1652.   Apter, Terri
        *Why Women Don't Have Wives: Professional Success and
          Motherhood*
        New York, NY: Schocken Books, 1985. 208 pp.

1653.   Ashford, Janet Isaacs, ed.
        Birth Stories: The Experience Remembered
        Trumansburg, NY: Crossing Press, 1984. 208 pp.

1654.   Badinter, Elisabeth
        *Mother Love, Myth and Reality: Motherhood in Modern
          History*
        New York, NY: Macmillan, 1987. 360 pp.

1655.   Berry, Mary Francis
        *The Politics of Parenthood: Child Care, Women's Rights,
          and the Myth of the Good Mother*
        New York, NY: Viking Press, 1993. 320 pp.

1656.   Carr, Anne E., and Elisabeth Schuessler Fiorenza,
          eds.
        *Motherhood: Experience, Institution, Theology (Concilium
          206)*
        Edinburgh, Scot.: T & T Clark, 1989. 140 pp.

1657.   Chernin, Kim
        In My Mother's House: A Daughter's Story
        New York, NY: Ticknor & Fields, 1983. 307 pp.

1658.   Chesler, Phyllis
        With Child: A Diary of Motherhood
        New York, NY: Berkley Publishing, 1981. 288 pp.

1659.   Chesler, Phyllis
        Sacred Bond: The Legacy of Baby M.
        New York, NY: Times Books, 1988. 212 pp.

1660.   Chodorow, Nancy
        The Reproduction of Mothering: Psychoanalysis and the Sociology of Gender
        Berkeley, CA: University of California Press, 1978. 263 pp.

1661.   Dally, Ann
        Inventing Motherhood: The Consequences of an Ideal
        New York, NY: Schocken Books, 1982. 360 pp.

1662.   Davidson, Cathy, and E. M. Brouer, eds.
        The Lost Tradition: Mothers and Daughters in Literature
        New York, NY: Ungar Publishing, 1980. 327 pp.

1663.   Glenn, Evelyn Nakano, Grace Change, and Linda R. Forcey, eds.
        Mothering: Ideology, Experience, and Agency
        New York, NY: Routledge, 1994. 387 pp.

1664.   Hebblethwaite, Margaret
        Motherhood and God
        New York, NY: Winston/Seabury, 1984. 148 pp.

1665.   Jordan, Brigitte
        Birth in Four Cultures (Yucatan, Holland, Sweden, US)
        Toronto, Ont.: Eden Press, University of Toronto Press, 1980. 109 pp.

1666.   Kaledin, Eugenia
        Mothers and More: American Women in the 1950's
        Boston, MA: Twayne Publishers, 1984. 261 pp.

1667. Margolis, Maxine L.
Mothers and Such: Views of American Women and Why They Changed
Berkeley, CA: University of California Press, 1984. 346 pp.

1668. O'Connor, Sarah
A Nine-Month Journey: A Christian Mother's Reflections on Pregnancy
Nashville, TN: Abingdon Press, 1984.

1669. Payne, Karen, ed.
Between Ourselves: Letters Between Mothers and Daughters
Boston, MA: Houghton Mifflin, 1983. 416 pp.

1670. Peck, Jane Carey
Self and Family
Louisville, KY: Westminster/John Knox Press, 1984. 118 pp.

1671. Price, Jane
Motherhood: What It Does to Your Mind
Boston, MA: Pandora/Routledge & Kegan Paul, 1989. 176 pp.

1672. Rabuzzi, Kathryn A.
Motherself: A Mythic Analysis of Motherhood
Bloomington, IN: Indiana University Press, 1988. 248 pp.

1673. Rich, Adrienne
Of Woman Born: Motherhood as Experience and Institution
New York, NY: W. W. Norton, 1976. 318 pp.

1674. Rubin, Nancy
The Mother Mirror: How a Generation of Women Is Changing Motherhood in America
New York, NY: Putnam Books, 1984. 285 pp.

1675.   Spencer, Anita
        Mothers Are People, Too: A Contemporary Analysis of Motherhood
        Ramsey, NJ: Paulist Press, 1984. 108 pp.

1676.   Trautmann, Mary Winfrey
        The Absence of the Dead Is Their Way of Appearing
        San Francisco, CA: Cleis Press, 1985. 256 pp.

1677.   Trebilcot, Joyce, ed.
        Mothering: Essays in Feminist Theory
        Totowa, NJ: Rowman & Allanheld, 1984. 336 pp.

1678.   Weigle, Marta
        Creation and Procreation: Feminist Reflections on Mythologies of Cosmogony and Parturition
        Philadelphia, PA: University of Pennsylvania Press, 1989. 304 pp.

Other Reproductive Issues

1679.   Arditti, Rita, Renate Duelli Klein, and S. Minden, eds.
        Test-Tube Women: What Future for Motherhood?
        Boston, MA: Pandora/Routledge & Kegan Paul, 1984. 350 pp.

1680.   Corea, Gena
        The Mother Machine: Reproductive Technologies from Artificial Insemination.
        New York, NY: Harper & Row, 1985. 374 pp.

1681.   Corea, Gena
        Man-Made Women: How New Reproductive Technologies Affect Women
        Bloomington, IN: Indiana University Press, 1987. 109 pp.

1682. Davis, Nanette J.
From Crime to Choice: The Transformation of Abortion in America
Westport, CT: Greenwood Press, 1985. 290 pp.

1683. Durkin, Mary G.
Feast of Love: Pope John Paul II on Human Intimacy
Chicago, IL: Loyola University Press, 1984. 248 pp.

1684. Field, Martha A.
Surrogate Motherhood
Cambridge, MA: Harvard University Press, 1988. 210 pp.

1685. Garfield, Jay L., and Patricia Hennessey, eds.
Abortion: Moral and Legal Perspectives
Amherst, MA: University of Massachusetts Press, 1984. 384 pp.

1686. Greer, Germaine
Sex and Destiny: The Politics of Human Fertility
New York, NY: Harper & Row, 1985. 539 pp.

1687. Harrison, Beverly Wildung
Our Right to Choose: Toward a New Ethic of Abortion
Boston, MA: Beacon Press, 1983. 334 pp.

1688. Joffe, Carole
The Regulation of Sexuality: Experiences of Family Planning Workers
Philadelphia, PA: Temple University Press, 1986. 196 pp.

1689. Luker, Kristin
Abortion and the Politics of Motherhood
Berkeley, CA: University of California Press, 1984. 324 pp.

1690. Oakley, Ann
The Captured Womb: A History of the Medical Care of Pregnant Women
Cambridge, MA: Blackwell, 1986. 336 pp.

1691.   Overall, Christine
        Ethics and Human Reproduction: A Feminist Analysis
        London, U.K.: Allen & Unwin, 1987. 245 pp.

1692.   Petchesky, Rosalind Pollack
        *Abortion and Woman's Choice: The State, Sexuality, and
            Reproductive Freedom*
        White Plains, NY: Longman, 1984. 404 pp.

1693.   Roberts, Helen, ed.
        Women, Health and Reproduction
        Boston, MA: Routledge & Kegan Paul, 1981. 196 pp.

1694.   Rubin, Eva R.
        *Abortion, Politics and the Courts: Roe vs. Wade and
            Aftermath*
        Westport, CT: Greenwood Press, 1987. 255 pp.

1695.   Spallone, Pat, and Deborah Steinberg, eds.
        *Made to Order: The Myth of Reproductive and Genetic
            Progress*
        Elmsford, NY: Pergamon Press, 1987. 267 pp.

1696.   Sullivan, Deborah, and Rose Weitz
        Labor Pains: Modern Midwives and Home Birth
        New Haven, CT: Yale University Press, 1988. 220 pp.

1697.   Warren, Mary Ann
        Gendercide: The Implications of Sex Selection
        Totowa, NJ: Rowman & Allanheld, 1985. 224 pp.

11. WOMEN'S ENVIRONMENT AND HEALTH

Although I began this bibliography project with an assumption that this chapter would encompass ecological and nature-advocacy titles, I have modified the scope to include women's health issues as well. My perspective is about surviving, and this chapter yields titles that indicate the way women writers have invited us to glimpse their respective engagements with health: of the environment and of the human body. Titles in the first section are concerned with the geographical realities of our experience; in the second section, with human physical vulnerability and strength. I regard Audre Lorde's *Cancer Journals* as an exceptional account of spirited survival and commend it to the reader. But there are many testimonies in this chapter that demonstrate the viability of this topic in grasping the meaning of women's spirit.

Environment

1698. Adams, Carol J., ed.
Ecofeminism and the Sacred
New York, NY: Crossroad Publishing, 1993. 250 pp.

1699. Anderson, Lorraine, ed.
Sisters of the Earth: Women's Poetry and Prose About Nature
New York, NY: Random House, 1991. 428 pp.

1700.   Bigwood, Carol
        Earth Muse: Feminism, Nature, and Art
        Philadelphia, PA: Temple University Press, 1993. 375
             pp.

1701.   Caldecott, Leonie, and Stephanie Leland, eds.
        Reclaim the Earth: Women Speak Out for Life on Earth
        London, U.K.: Women's Press, 1983. 245 pp.

1702.   Capra, Fritjof, and Charlene Spretnak
        Green Politics: The Global Promise
        New York, NY: E. P. Dutton, 1984. 255 pp.

1703.   Diamond, Irene, and Gloria Feman Orenstein, eds.
        Reweaving the World: The Emergence of Ecofeminism
        San Francisco, CA: Sierra Books, 1990. 320 pp.

1704.   Dillard, Annie
        Holy the Firm
        New York, NY: Harper & Row, 1977. 76 pp.

1705.   Dillard, Annie
        Pilgrim at Tinker Creek
        New York, NY: Bantam Books, 1981. 279 pp.

1706.   Dillard, Annie
        Teaching a Stone to Talk: Expeditions and Encounters
        New York, NY: Harper & Row, 1982. 177 pp.

1707.   Dillard, Annie
        Tickets for a Prayer Wheel
        Columbia, MO: University of Missouri Press, 1983.
             127 pp.

1708.   Ehrlich, Gretel
        Islands, the Universe, Home
        New York, NY: Viking Press, 1991. 196 pp.

1709.   Galland, China
        Women in the Wilderness
        San Francisco, CA: Harper & Row, 1982. 260 pp.

1710.   Gray, Elizabeth Dodson
Green Paradise Lost
Wellesley, MA: Roundtable Press, 1979. 166 pp.

1711.   Halkes, Catharina J. M.
New Creation: Christian Feminism and the Renewal of the Earth
Louisville, KY: Westminster/John Knox Press, 1992. 177 pp.

1712.   Houston, Jean
God Seed: The Mythic World of Christ
Oak Park, IL: Meyer-Stone, 1988. 160 pp.

1713.   Hynes, H. Patricia
The Recurring Silent Spring
Elmsford, NY: Pergamon Press, 1989. 272 pp.

1714.   Kaza, Stephanie
The Attentive Heart: Conversations with Trees
New York, NY: Fawcett/Columbine, 1993. 258 pp.

1715.   Kumin, Maxine
In Deep Country: Essays
Boston, MA: Beacon Press, 1987. 180 pp.

1716.   LaBastille, Anne
Beyond Black Bear Lake: Life at the Edge of Wilderness
New York, NY: W. W. Norton, 1987. 251 pp.

1717.   LaBastille, Anne, ed.
Women and Wilderness
San Francisco, CA: Sierra Books, 1980. 310 pp.

1718.   Macy, Joanna
World as Lover, World as Self
Berkeley, CA: Parallax Press, 1990. 224 pp.

1719.   Merchant, Carolyn
The Death of Nature
San Francisco, CA: Harper & Row, 1990. 384 pp.

1720. Merchant, Carolyn
       Ecological Revolutions: Nature, Gender, and Science in New England
       Chapel Hill, NC: University of North Carolina Press, 1990. 398 pp.

1721. Mueller, Ruth
       The Eye of the Child
       Philadelphia, PA: New Society Publishers, 1984. 225 pp.

1722. Plant, Judith, ed.
       Healing the Wounds: The Promise of Ecofeminism
       Philadelphia, PA: New Society Publishers, 1989. 262 pp.

1723. Primavesi, Anne
       From Apocalypse to Genesis: Ecology, Feminism, and Christianity
       Philadelphia, PA: Fortress Press, 1991. 312 pp.

1724. Raine, Kathleen
       Defending Ancient Springs
       Stockbridge, MA: Lindesfarne Press, 1985. 198 pp.

1725. Ruether, Rosemary Radford
       Gaia and God: An Ecofeminist Theology of Earth Healing
       San Francisco, CA: Harper & Row, 1992. 288 pp.

1726. Shiva, Vandana
       Staying Alive: Women, Ecology and Development
       London, U.K.: Zed Books, 1988. 224 pp.

1727. Spretnak, Charlene
       The Spiritual Dimension of Green Politics
       Santa Fe, NM: Bear & Co., 1986. 95 pp.

Health and Healing

1728. Achterberg, Jeanne
Imagery in Healing: Shamanism and Modern Medicine
Boulder, CO: Shambala Press, 1985. 253 pp.

1729. Atkins, Marguerite Henry
Also My Journey (Alzheimer's)
Wilton, CT: Morehouse, 1985. 160 pp.

1730. Babb, Jewel
Border Healing Woman: The Story of Jewel Babb (told to Pat E. Taylor)
Austin, TX: University of Texas Press, 1981. 134 pp.

1731. Bailey, Caroline
Living Through Personal Crisis
Chicago, IL: Thomas More Press, 1984.

1732. Bell, Marilyn J., ed.
Women as Elders: Images, Visions and Issues
New York, NY: Haworth Press, 1986. 90 pp.

1733. Blankenship, Jayne
In the Center of the Night (bereavement)
New York, NY: Putnam Books, 1985. 320 pp.

1734. Borysenko, Joan
Minding the Body, Mending the Mind
Reading, MA: Addison-Wesley Publishing Company, 1987. 192 pp.

1735. Butler, Sandra, and Barbara Rosenblum
Cancer in Two Voices
San Francisco, CA: Spinsters Ink, 1991. 275 pp.

1736. Doress, Paula B., Diana L. Siegal, et al.
Ourselves, Growing Older
New York, NY: Simon & Schuster, 1987. 511 pp.

1737.   Gibbons, Joan, ed. Elizabeth Howes
        Come Phoenix Word
        San Francisco, CA: Guild for Psychological Studies
        Publishing House, 1989. 110 pp.

1738.   Horner, Joyce
        That Time of Year: A Chronicle of Life in a Nursing Home
        Amherst, MA: University of Massachusetts Press,
        1982. 224 pp.

1739.   Humphreys, S. C.
        The Family, Women, and Death
        Boston, MA: Routledge & Kegan Paul, 1983. 210 pp.

1740.   Koblinsky, Marge, Judith Timyan, and Jay Gray, eds.
        The Heath of Women
        Boulder, CO: Westview, 1992. 291 pp.

1741.   Kreis, Bernadine, and Alice Pattee
        Up from Grief: Patterns of Recovery
        Somers, CT: Seabury Press, 1982. 146 pp.

1742.   Kushner, Rose
        *Alternatives: New Developments in the War on Breast
        Cancer*
        New York, NY: Warner Books, 1984. 448 pp.

1743.   L'Engle, Madeline
        Sold into Egypt: Joseph's Journey into Human Being
        Wheaton, IL: Harold Shaw Publications, 1988. 235
        pp.

1744.   Lewin, Ellen, and Virginia Oelsen, eds.
        Women, Health and Healing: Toward a New Perspective
        London, U.K.: Tavistock, 1985. 317 pp.

1745.   Lifshitz, Leatrice H.
        Her Soul Beneath the Bone: Women's Poetry on Breast Cancer
        Champaign, IL: University of Illinois Press, 1988. 78
        pp.

1746. Lorde, Audre
The Cancer Journals
San Francisco, CA: Spinsters Ink, 1980. 77 pp.

1747. Mankowitz, Ann
Change of Life: A Psychological Study of Dreams and the Menopause
Toronto, Ont.: Inner City Books, 1984. 128 pp.

1748. McClain, Carol Shepherd, ed.
Women as Healers: Cross-Cultural Perspectives
New Brunswick, NJ: Rutgers University Press, 1989. 269 pp.

1749. Olson, Carol T.
The Life of Illness: One Woman's Journey
Albany, NY: State University of New York Press, 1992. 160 pp.

1750. Pelgrin, Mark, ed. S. Moon and E. B. Howes
And a Time to Die
Northhampton, MA: Contact Press, 1962. 159 pp.

1751. Ratcliff, Kathryn S., ed.
Healing Technology: Feminist Perspectives
Ann Arbor, MI: University of Michigan Press, 1989. 416 pp.

1752. Richardson, Diane
Women and AIDS
New York, NY: Methuen, 1987. 160 pp.

1753. Ruzek, Sheryl B.
The Women's Health Movement: Feminist Alternatives to Medical Control
New York, NY: Praeger, 1978. 351 pp.

1754. Sarton, May
After the Stroke
New York, NY: W. W. Norton, 1988. 280 pp.

1755. Schaef, Anne Wilson
Co-Dependence: Misunderstood, Mistreated
San Francisco, CA: Harper & Row, 1986. 105 pp.

1756. Schaef, Anne Wilson
When Society Becomes an Addict
San Francisco, CA: Harper & Row, 1988. 152 pp.

1757. Taylor, Joan Leslie
In the Light of Dying: The Journals of a Hospice Volunteer
Seabury, NY: Continuum Publishing Co., 1989. 229 pp.

1758. Toor, Djohariah
The Road by the River: A Healing Journey for Women
San Francisco, CA: Harper & Row, 1987. 144 pp.

1759. V., Rachel
A Woman Like You: Life Stories of Women Recovering from Alcoholism and Addiction
San Francisco, CA: Harper & Row, 1988.

1760. Wakerman, Elyce
Father Loss: Daughters Discuss the Man That Got Away
New York, NY: Holt, Rinehart & Winston, 1984. 291 pp.

1761. Whelehan, Patricia, and contributors
Women and Health: Cross-Cultural Perspectives
Westport, CT: Bergin & Harvey, 1988. 230 pp.

1762. Young, Frances
Face to Face: A Narrative Essay in the Theology of Suffering
Edinburgh, Scot.: T & T Clark, 1990. 256 pp.

12. GLOBAL COMMUNITY

In truth, the bibliography begins and ends for me in this context. Feminist spirituality is both bounded and without boundary; it speaks to the particularity of woman's life and to the relatedness which is beginning to be realized in our writings and in friendships made between women across great distances and in spite of cultural differences. I have enumerated some of the resources that empower the reader with respect to connection in the first section. The second assembles writings by women on war and peace. The titles reflect a wide interpretation of this subject, but they share in the general concern about apathy and co-optation of women in men's wars.

Connections

1763. Amanecida Collective
Revolutionary Forgiveness: Feminist Reflections on Nicaragua
Maryknoll, NY: Orbis Books, 1986. 150 pp.

1764. Bassnett, Susan
Feminist Experiences: The Women's Movement in Four Cultures
London, U.K.: Allen & Unwin, 1986. 168 pp.

1765. Bernard, Jessie
The Female World from a Global Perspective
Bloomington, IN: Indiana University Press, 1987. 287 pp.

1766.   Brydon, Lynne, and Sylvia Chant
         *Women in the Third World: Gender Issues in Rural and
             Urban Areas*
         New Brunswick, NJ: Rutgers University Press, 1989.
             328 pp.

1767.   Bulbeck, Chilla
         One World Women's Movement
         London, U.K.: Pluto Press, 1988. 320 pp.

1768.   Bunch, Charlotte
         Passionate Politics: Feminist Theory in Action (1968–86)
         New York, NY: St. Martin's Press, 1987. 288 pp.

1769.   Cheatham, Annie, and Mary Clare Powell
         *This Way Day Break Comes: Women's Values and the
             Future*
         Philadelphia, PA: New Society Publishers, 1986. 288
             pp.

1770.   Davies, Miranda, ed.
         Third World, Second Sex
         London, U.K.: Zed Books, 1987. 304 pp.

1771.   Eck, Diana, and Devaki Jain, eds.
         *Speaking of Faith: Global Perspectives on Women, Religion
             and Social Change*
         Philadelphia, PA: New Society Publishers, 1987. 308
             pp.

1772.   Fisher, Jo
         Mothers of the Disappeared
         Boston, MA: South End Press, 1989. 224 pp.

1773.   Foster, Theodora C.
         Women, Religion, and Development in the Third World
         New York, NY: Praeger, 1984. 292 pp.

1774.   Iglitzin, Lynne, and Ruth Ross, eds.
         Women in the World, 1975–1985
         Santa Barbara, CA: ABC-CLIO, 1986. 484 pp.

1775. Kelly, Petra
      Fighting for Hope
      Boston, MA: South End Press, 1989. 121 pp.

1776. May, Melanie
      Bonds of Unity
      Alpharetta, GA: Scholars Press, 1989. 196 pp.

1777. Miles, Rosalind
      The Women's History of the World
      London, U.K.: Michael Joseph, 1988. 288 pp.

1778. Momsen, Janet, and Janet Townsend, eds.
      Geography of Gender in the Third World
      Albany, NY: State University of New York Press, 1987.
      424 pp.

1779. Morgan, Robin, ed.
      Sisterhood Is Global
      Garden City, NY: Anchor Press, Doubleday, 1984.
      815 pp.

1780. Seager, Joni, and Ann Olson
      Women in the World: An International Atlas
      New York, NY: Simon & Schuster, 1986. 128 pp.

1781. Spivak, Gayatri Chakravorty
      In Other Worlds: Essays in Cultural Politics
      Boston, MA: Routledge & Kegan Paul, 1987. 309 pp.

1782. Stokland, Torill, Mallica Vajrathon, and Davidson
      Nichol, eds.
      Creative Women in Changing Societies: A Quest for Alternatives
      Dobbs Ferry, NY: Transnational Publications, 1982.
      174 pp.

1783. Webster, John C., and Ellen Low, eds.
      The Church and Women in the Third World
      Louisville, KY: Westminster/John Knox Press, 1985.
      167 pp.

Peace and War

1784.   Accad, Evelyne
Sexuality and War: Literary Masks of the Middle East
New York, NY: New York University Press, 1991. 224
pp.

1785.   Adams, Judith Porter
Peacework: Oral Histories of Women Peace Activists
Boston, MA: Twayne Publishers, 1990. 288 pp.

1786.   Alonso, Harriet Hyman
*Peace as a Women's Issue: A History of the U.S. Movement
for World Peace and Women's Rights*
Syracuse, NY: Syracuse University Press, 1993. 340 pp.

1787.   Anglesey, Zoe, ed.
Ixok Amargo: Central American Women's Poetry for Peace
Brooklyn, NY: Granite Press, 1987. 613 pp.

1788.   Berkin, Carol R., and Clara M. Lovett, eds.
Women, War and Revolution
New York, NY: Holmes & Meier, 1980. 310 pp.

1789.   Bok, Sissela
A Strategy for Peace: Human Values and the Threat of War
New York, NY: Pantheon Books, 1989. 202 pp.

1790.   Bondurant, Joan V.
Conquest of Violence: The Gandhian Philosophy of Conflict
Princeton, NJ: Princeton University Press, 1988. 281
pp.

1791.   Brock-Utne, Birgit
Educating for Peace: A Feminist Perspective
Elmsford, NY: Pergamon Press, 1985. 192 pp.

1792.   Brock-Utne, Birgit
Feminist Perspectives on Peace and Peace Education
Elmsford, NY: Pergamon Press, 1989. 256 pp.

1793. Cambridge Women's Peace Collective
My Country Is the Whole World: An Anthology of Women's Work on Peace and War
Boston, MA: Pandora/Routledge & Kegan Paul, 1984. 306 pp.

1794. Campbell, D'Ann
Women at War with America
Cambridge, MA: Harvard University Press, 1984. 320 pp.

1795. Casey, Juliana
Where Is God Now? Nuclear Terror, Feminism, and the Search for God
Kansas City, MO: Sheed & Ward, 1987. 166 pp.

1796. Cataldo, Mima, R. Putter, B. Fireside, and E. Lytel
The Women's Encampment for a Future of Peace and Justice
Philadelphia, PA: Temple University Press, 1987. 120 pp.

1797. Cecchini, Rose Marie
Women's Action for Peace and Justice: Christian, Buddhist, and Muslim Women . . .
Maryknoll, NY: Maryknoll Sisters, 1988. 320 pp.

1798. Cook, Alice, and Gwyn Kirk
Greenham Women Everywhere: Dreams, Ideas and Actions from the Women's Peace Movement
Boston, MA: South End Press, 1983. 127 pp.

1799. Deming, Barbara, ed. Jane Meyerding
We Are All Part of One Another: A Barbara Deming Reader
Philadelphia, PA: New Society Publishers, 1984. 320 pp.

1800. Dwyer, Judith A., ed.
The Catholic Bishops and Nuclear War: A Critique and Analysis of the Pastoral "The Challenge of Peace"
Washington, DC: Georgetown University Press, 1984. 107 pp.

1801.   Elshtain, Jean Bethke
Women and War
New York, NY: Basic Books, 1987. 288 pp.

1802.   Enloe, Cynthia
Does Khaki Become You? The Militarization of Women's Lives
Boston, MA: Pandora/Routledge & Kegan Paul, 1988. 270 pp.

1803.   Florence, Mary Sargent, Catherine Marshall, and C. K. Ogden
Militarism Versus Feminism: Writings on Women and War
London, U.K.: Virago Press, 1987. 178 pp.

1804.   Gellhorn, Martha
The Face of War
New York, NY: Atlantic Monthly, 1988. 360 pp.

1805.   Gibson, Elizabeth
The Water Is Wide: Irish Conflict
Grand Rapids, MI: Zondervan Press, 1984. 299 pp.

1806.   Gioseffi, Daniela, ed.
Women on War: Essential Voices for the Nuclear Age
New York, NY: Simon & Schuster, 1988. 391 pp.

1807.   Golden, Renny, and Michael McConnell
Sanctuary: The New Underground Railroad
Maryknoll, NY: Orbis Books, 1986. 214 pp.

1808.   Griffin, Susan
A Chorus of Stones: The Private Life of War
Garden City, NY: Doubleday & Co., 1992. 363 pp.

1809.   Harford, Barbara, and Sarah Hopkins, eds.
Greenham Common: Women at the Wire
London, U.K.: Women's Press, 1985. 171 pp.

1810. Harris, Adrienne, and Ynestra King, eds.
Rocking the Ship of State: Toward a Feminist Peace Politics
Boulder, CO: Westview, 1989. 256 pp.

1811. Higonnet, Margaret R., Jane Jensen, et al., eds.
Behind the Lines: Gender and the Two World Wars
New Haven, CT: Yale University Press, 1987. 310 pp.

1812. Huddle, Norrie
Surviving: The Best Game on Earth
New York, NY: Schocken Books, 1984. 281 pp.

1813. Isaksson, Eva, ed.
Women and the Military System
New York, NY: St. Martin's Press, 1988. 440 pp.

1814. Jeffords, Susan
The Remasculinization of America: Gender and the Vietnam War
Bloomington, IN: Indiana University Press, 1989. 215 pp.

1815. Jones, Lynn, ed.
Keeping the Peace: Women's Peace Handbook
London, U.K.: Women's Press, 1983. 162 pp.

1816. Liddington, Jill
The Road to Greenham Common: Feminism and Anti-Militarism in Britain Since 1820
Syracuse, NY: Syracuse University Press, 1991. 360 pp.

1817. MacDonald, Sharon, Pat Holden, and S. Ardener, eds.
Images of Women in Peace and War: Cross-Cultural and Historical Perspectives
Madison, WI: University of Wisconsin Press, 1988. 240 pp.

1818. Macy, Joanna Rofers
Despair and Personal Power in the Nuclear Age

Philadelphia, PA: New Society Publishers, 1983. 17 pp.

1819. Marshall, Kathryn
        In the Combat Zone: An Oral History of American Wome.
        in Vietnam
        Boston, MA: Little, Brown & Co., 1987. 270 pp.

1820. McAllister, Pam
        You Can't Kill the Spirit
        Philadelphia, PA: New Society Publishers, 1988. 23͡
        pp.

1821. McAllister, Pam, ed.
        Reweaving the Web of Life: Feminism and Non-Violence
        Philadelphia, PA: New Society Publishers, 1983. 456 pp.

1822. McNeal, Patricia
        The American Catholic Peace Movement, 1928–1972
        New York, NY: Arno, 1978. 326 pp.

1823. Myrdal, Alva
        The Game of Disarmament: How the U.S. and Russia Run
        the Arms Race
        New York, NY: Pantheon Books, 1976. 392 pp.

1824. Norman, Elizabeth
        Women at War: The Story of Fifty Military Nurses Who
        Served in Vietnam
        Philadelphia, PA: University of Pennsylvania Press, 1990. 222 pp.

1825. Oldfield, Sybil
        Women Against the Iron Fist: From Sarajevo to Greenham
        Common
        Cambridge, MA: Blackwell, 1989. 224 pp.

1826. Peace Pilgrim
        Peace Pilgrim: Her Life and Work in Her Own Words
        Santa Fe, NM: Ocean Books, 1982. 198 pp.

1827. Pierson, Ruth Roach, ed.
Women and Peace: Theoretical, Historical, and Practical Perspectives
New York, NY: Croom Helm, 1987. 249 pp.

1828. Puget Sound Women's Peace Camp
We Are Ordinary Women
Seattle, WA: Seal Press, 1984. 72 pp.

1829. Rathbone, Irene
We That Were Young
Old Westbury, NY: The Feminist Press, 1988. 500 pp.

1830. Reardon, Betty
Sexism and the War System
New York, NY: Teachers College Press, Columbia University, 1985. 111 pp.

1831. Reardon, Betty
Women and Peace: Feminist Visions of Global Security
Albany, NY: State University of New York Press, 1993. 209 pp.

1832. Reardon, Betty A., ed.
Comprehensive Peace Education: Educating for Global Responsibility
New York, NY: Teachers College Press, Columbia University, 1988. 121 pp.

1833. Ridd, Rosemary, and Helen Callaway, eds.
Women and Political Conflict
New York, NY: New York University Press, 1987. 246 pp.

1834. Riley, Maria
I Am Because We Are
Washington, DC: Center for Concern, 1985. 43 pp.

1835. Ruddick, Sara
Maternal Thinking: Toward a Politics of Peace
Boston, MA: Beacon Press, 1989. 291 pp.

1836. Russell, Diana E. H., ed.
       Exposing Nuclear Phallacies
       Elmsford, NY: Pergamon Press, 1989. 350 pp.

1837. Saywell, Shelley
       Women in War
       New York, NY: Viking Press, 1985. 320 pp.

1838. Sichol, Marcia W.
       *The Making of a Nuclear Peace: The Task of Today's Just
           War Theorists*
       Washington, DC: Georgetown University Press, 1991.
           308 pp.

1839. Smith, Helen Zenna
       "Not So Quiet": Stepdaughters of War
       Old Westbury, NY: The Feminist Press, 1988. 304 pp.

1840. Soelle, Dorothee
       Of War and Love
       Maryknoll, NY: Orbis Books, 1983. 172 pp.

1841. Soelle, Dorothee
       The Arms Race That Kills Even Without War
       Philadelphia, PA: Fortress Press, 1983. 111 pp.

1842. Stiehm, Judith Hicks
       Arms and the Enlisted Woman
       Philadelphia, PA: Temple University Press, 1989. 352
           pp.

1843. Stiehm, Judith Hicks, ed.
       Women and Men's Wars
       Elmsford, NY: Pergamon Press, 1983. 134 pp.

1844. Thistlethwaite, Susan, ed.
       A Just Peace Church
       New York, NY: Pilgrim Press, 1986. 177 pp.

1845. Thompson, Dorothy, ed.
Over Our Dead Bodies: Women Against the Bomb
London, U.K.: Virago Press, 1983. 253 pp.

1846. Tuchman, Barbara
The March of Folly: From Troy to Vietnam
New York, NY: Alfred A. Knopf, 1984. 464 pp.

1847. Walker, Keith
A Piece of My Heart: The Stories of Twenty-six American Women in Vietnam
Novato, CA: Presidio, 1985. 350 pp.

1848. Wilder, Anthony
Man and Woman, War and Peace: The Strategist's Companion
New York, NY: Routledge, 1989. 328 pp.

1849. Young, Elise G.
Keepers of the History: Women and the Israeli-Palestinian Conflict
New York, NY: Macmillan, 1991. 240 pp.

13. RESOURCES

The final chapter of this bibliography provides material that connects women with one another. Under each of the headings (which are self-evident), information regarding nonbook resources is offered in the hope that readers will tap into a growing network of women. The journals listed indicate the breadth of writing routinely published under both academic and nonacademic auspices. *Signs,* for example, demonstrates the durability of feminist journal publishing, while the *Women's Review of Books* demonstrates the substantial quality and quantity of publications for, of, and by women. I am aware that the list of centers is incomplete. My hope is that readers will add to the enumeration and supply others with these data. The small presses listed in this last section are those specifically included in the bibliography. Once again, it is an incomplete list, but it offers addresses for those women's presses which are often not represented in local bookstores. Catalogues can be sent for, as can the books cited herein.

Journals

The American Voice: A Feminist Journal for Men and Women. $15/year. 332 W. Broadway Station, Suite 1215, Louisville, KY 40202.

The Ancient Arts. Quarterly. $13/individual; $15/institution. The Witching Well, P.O. Box 1490, Idaho Springs, CO 80452.

Anima: Journal of Human Experience. Twice yearly. $9.95. Wilson College, 1053 Wilson Avenue, Chambersburg, PA 17201.

At the Crossroads: Feminist Politics, Spirituality, and Science. Quarterly. Box 112-WR, St. Paul, AR 72760.

Backbone: A New Women's Literary Journal. Twice yearly. $9/individual; $12/institution. P.O. Box 95315, Seattle, WA 98145.

Belles Lettres: A Review of Books by Women. Bimonthly. $15/individual; $30/institution. P.O. Box 987, Arlington, VA 22216.

Bridges: A Journal for Jewish Feminists and Our Friends. Twice yearly. $15/individual; $25/institution. P.O. Box 18437, Seattle, WA 98118.

Broomstick: Options for Women over Forty. Four times yearly. $15/individual; $25/institution. 3543 18th Street, San Francisco, CA 94110.

Calyx: A Journal of Art and Literature by Women. Three times yearly. $10/individual; $15/institution. P.O. Box B, Corvallis, OR 97339.

Common Lives, Lesbian Lives: A Lesbian Quarterly. $15/individual; $25/institution. P.O. Box 1553, Iowa City, IA 52244.

Conditions: A Feminist Magazine. Three times yearly. $24/individual; $34/institution. Box 159046, Van Brunt Station, Brooklyn, NY 11215-9046.

Connexions: An International Women's Quarterly. Four times yearly. $15/individual; $24/institution. People's Translation Service, 4228 Telegraph Avenue, Oakland, CA 94609.

Creation Spirituality. Six times yearly. $24/individual; $32/institution. 160 Virginia Street, San Jose, CA 95112.

Critical Matrix. Twice yearly. $12/individual; $24/institution. Program in Women's Studies, 113 Dickinson Hall, Princeton University, Princeton, NJ 08544.

Cross Currents. Four times yearly. $25/individual; $32/institution. ARIL, College of New Rochelle, New Rochelle, NY 10802. 10522.

Daughters of Sarah: Journal of Christian Feminism. Four times yearly. $18/subscription. 2121 Sheridan Road, Evanston, IL 60201.

Differences: A Journal of Feminist Cultural Studies. Four times yearly. $20/individual; $40/institution. Journals Division, Indiana University Press, 10th & Morton Streets, Bloomington, IN 47405.

Disabled Women's International Newsletter, Women with Disabilities United, P.O. Box 323, Stuyvesant Station, New York, NY 10009.

Encore Magazine: Celebrating the Return of the Crone. Bimonthly. $20/year. Dynamic Communications, P.O. Box 1599, Mariposa, CA 95339.

The European Journal of Women's Studies. Twice yearly. $23/individual; $57/institution. Sage Publications, P.O. Box 5096, Newbury Park, CA 91359.

Feminist Ethics. Three times yearly. $10. University of Calgary, Faculty of General Studies, 2500 University Drive NW, Calgary, Alta. T2N IN4 Canada.

Feminist Issues. Twice yearly. $15/individual; $25/institution. Feminist Forum, Inc., c/o Transaction Periodicals Consortium, Dept. 8010, Rutgers University, New Brunswick, NJ 08903.

Feminist Studies. Three times yearly. $28/individual; $60/institution. Claire Moses, Editor and Manager, Women's Studies Program, University of Maryland, College Park, MD 20742.

Frontiers: A Journal of Women's Studies. Three times yearly. $20/individual; $33/institution. University Press of Colorado, P.O. Box 849, Niwot, CO 80544.

Gallerie (women's art). Four times yearly. $20/subscription. Gallerie Publications, 2901 Panorama Drive, North Vancouver, B.C. V7G 2A4 Canada.

Gender and Society: Sociology for Women in Society Publications. Four times yearly. $44/individual; $117/institution. Sage Publications, P.O. Box 5096, Newbury Park, CA 91359.

Genders. Three times yearly. $11/individual; $30/institution. University of Texas Press Journals, P.O. Box 7819, Austin, TX 78713.

Gnosis Magazine. Four times yearly. $20/year. P.O. Box 14217, San Francisco, CA 94114-0217.

Hecate: An Interdisciplinary Journal of Women's Liberation. Twice yearly. $8/individual; $15/institution. P.O. Box 79, St. Lucia, Brisbane, Queensland, 4067, Australia.

Helicon Nine: The Journal of Women's Arts and Letters. Three times yearly. $15/subscription. P.O. Box 22412, Kansas City, MO 64113.

Heresies: A Feminist Publication on Art and Politics. Four times yearly. $23/individual; $33/institution. Heresies Collective, Inc., P.O. Box 1306, Canal Street, New York, NY 10013.

History of Women Religious: News and Notes. Four times yearly. Conference on History of Women Religious. 1884 Randolph Avenue, St. Paul, MN 55105.

Hurricane Alice: A Feminist Quarterly. $12/year. 207 Lind Hall, 207 Church Street, Minneapolis, MN 55455.

Hypatia: A Journal of Feminist Philosophy. Three times yearly. $35/individual; $60/institution. Journals Division, Indiana University Press, 601 North Morton Street, Bloomington, IN 47404.

Isis: Feminist International Quarterly. P.O. Box 50, 1211 Geneva 2, Switzerland.

Jewish Women's Research Center Newsletter. Three times yearly. $5/subscription. c/o National Council of Jewish Women, 9 E. 69th Street, New York, NY 10021.

Journal of Feminist Studies in Religion. Twice yearly. $15/individual; $25/institution. Membership Services, P.O. Box 15288, Atlanta, GA 30333.

Journal of Hispanic/Latino Theology. Quarterly. $20/year. The Liturgical Press, Collegeville, MN 56321.

Journal of Women and Religion. Annual. Subscription included in membership. Center for Women and Religion, 2400 Ridge Road, Berkeley, CA 94709.

Kahawai: Journal of Women and Zen. Four times yearly. Diamond Sangha, 2119 Kaloa Way, Honolulu, HI 96882.

Kalliope: A Journal of Women's Art. Four times yearly. $9/individual; $15/institution. c/o Florida Community College at Jacksonville, 3939 Roosevelt Boulevard, Jacksonville, FL 32205.

Karuna: A Journal of Buddhist Meditation. Three times yearly. $15/yr.. Karuna Meditation Society, P.O. Box 24468, Station C, Vancouver, B.C. V5T 4M5 Canada.

Legacy: A Journal of Nineteenth-Century American Women Writers. Twice yearly. $15/individual; $18/institutional. Department of English, Bartlett Hall, University of Massachusetts, Amherst, MA 01003.

Lesbian Ethics. Three times yearly. $14/individual; $18/ institution. P.O. Box 4723, Albuquerque, NM 87196.

Lilith: The Jewish Women's Magazine. Four times yearly. $16/ individual. Box 3000 Department LIL, Denville, NJ 07834.

Maenad: A Woman's Literary Journal. Four times yearly. $14/ individual. Box 738, Gloucester, MA 01930.

Matrix: Explorations in Spirituality. Four times yearly. $16. P.O. Box 8375, Berkeley, CA 94707.

Mystics Quarterly. $15/individual; $20/institution. Department of English, University of Cincinnati, Cincinnati, OH 45221-0069.

New Age Woman. Six times yearly. $15/individual. P.O. Box 399, Maynard, MA 01754.

New Directions for Women (newsletter). Six times yearly. $10/ individual; $16/institution. 108 W. Palisades Avenue, Englewood, NJ 07631.

NWSA Journal (The National Women's Studies Association Journal). Three times yearly. $45/individual; $115/ institution. Journals Division, Indiana University Press, 10th and Morton Streets, Bloomington, Indiana 47405.

Of a Like Mind: Newspaper/Networking for Women and Spirituality. Four times yearly. Sliding scale: $13–$33/year. OALM, Box 6021, Madison, WI 53716.

Off Our Backs (newspaper). Eleven times yearly. $15/ subscription. 2423 18th Street, Washington, DC 20009.

Out/Look: National Lesbian and Gay Quarterly. $19/individual; $26/institution. P.O. 146430, San Francisco, CA 94114-6430.

Parabola: Magazine of Myth and Tradition. Four times yearly. $18/subscription. 656 Broadway, New York, NY 10012-2317.

Phoebe: An Interdisciplinary Journal of Feminist Scholarship, Theory and Aesthetics. Twice yearly. $15/individual; $25/institution. c/o Women's Studies, SUNY—Oneonta, NY 13820-4015.

Psychology of Women. Four times yearly. $32/individual; $80/institution. Cambridge University Press, 32 E. 57th Street, New York, NY 10022.

Radical Teacher: A Socialist and Feminist Journal on Theory and Practice of Teaching. Twice yearly. $8/individual; $11/institution. Department N, Box 102, Cambridge, MA 02142.

Reproductive and Genetic Engineering: Journal of International Feminist Analysis. Three times yearly. $25/individual; $75/institution. Pergamon Press, Fairview Park, Elmsford, NY 10523.

Resurgence (ecology and spirituality). Monthly. $44/yearly. Rodale Press, 33 E. Minor Street, Emmaus, PA 18049.

SAGE: A Scholarly Journal on Black Women. Twice yearly. $15/individual; $25/institution. SAGE, P.O. Box 42741, Atlanta, GA 30311-0741.

SageWoman. Four times yearly. $18/subscription. P.O. Box 641, Point Arena, CA 95468.

Shaman's Drum: A Journal of Experiential Shamanism. Four times yearly. $15/subscription. P.O. Box 430, Willets, CA 95496.

Shambala Sun. Bimonthly. $20/year. 1345 Spruce Street, Boulder, CO 80302-4886.

Signs: Journal of Women in Culture and Socitey. Four times yearly. $36/individual; $88/institution. University of Chicago Press, Journals Division, P.O. Box 37005. Chicago, IL 60637.

Sinister Wisdom: A Journal for the Lesbian Imagination in the Arts and Politics. Four times yearly. $17 individual; $30/ institution. P.O. Box 3252, Berkeley, CA 94703.

Sister-Words: A Journal of Women's Practical Wisdom. No price given. California Institute of Integral Studies, 765 Ashbury Street, San Francisco, CA 94121.

Snake Power: A Journal of Contemporary Female Shamanism. Four times yearly. $23. Snake Power, 5856 College Avenue, P.O. Box 138, Oakland, CA 94618.

Studia Mystica. Four times yearly. $14/individual; $18/ institution. c/o M. Giles, California State University, Sacramento, CA 95819.

Thirteenth Moon: A Feminist Literary Magazine. Box 309, Cathedral Station, New York, NY 10025.

Tricycle: The Buddhist Review. Four times yearly. $20/year. Subscription Dept. TRL, P.O. Box 3000, Denville, NJ 07834.

Trivia: A Journal of Ideas. Three times yearly. $16/individual; $18/institution. P.O. Box 9606, North Amherst, MA 01059-9606.

Tulsa Studies in Women's Literature. Twice yearly. $12/ individual; $15/institution. University of Tulsa, 600 South College Avenue, Tulsa, OK 74104-3189.

The Wise Woman: Journal of Feminist Spirituality and Goddesses. Quarterly. $15/year. 441 Cordova Street, Oakland, CA 94602.

Women: A Cultural Review. Three times yearly. $30/individual; $60/institution. Journals Marketing Dept., Oxford University Press, 200 Madison Avenue, New York, NY 10016.

Women and Environments: A Forum for Feminist Relationships with Natural, Built and Social Environments. Four times yearly. $15/individual; $25/institution. c/o Center for Urban and Community Studies, 455 Spadina Avenue, Toronto, Ont. M5S 2G8 Canada.

Women of Power: A Magazine of Feminism, Spirituality and Politics. Four times yearly. $26/subscription. P.O. Box 2785, Department 7, Orleans, MA 02653.

Women's Art Journal. Twice yearly. $13/individual; $17/institution. Women's Art, Inc., 7008 Sherwood Drive, Knoxville, TN 37919.

Women's Studies: An Interdisciplinary Journal. Four times yearly. $96/individual; $130/institution. Gordon & Beach Science Publications. One Bedford Street, London WC2 E9PP U.K.

Women's Studies in Communication. Twice yearly. $12/individual; $25/institution. J. Cashion. 2105 South Meridian Avenue, #C, Alhambra, CA 91803.

Women's Studies International Forum. Six times yearly. $40/subscription. Pergamon Press, Fairview Park, Elmsford, NY 10523.

Zone: A Feminist Journal for Women and Men. Annually. $5.50/copy. P.O. Box 803, Brookline Village, MA 02147.

Publishers

Astarte Shell Press. P.O. Box 10453, Portland, ME 04104.

ATA Books. 1928 Stuart Street, Berkeley, CA 94703.

Bear & Company. P.O. Drawer 2860, Santa Fe, NM 87504-2860

Cleis Press. P.O. Box 8933, Pittsburgh, PA 15221.

Crossing Press. 22D Roache Road, P.O. Box 1048, Freedom, CA 95019.

Eden Press. 340 Nagel Drive, Cheektowaga, NY 14225.

Feminist Press at C.U.N.Y. 311 E. 94th Street, New York, NY 10128.

Firebrand Books. 141 The Commons, Ithaca, NY 14850.

Granite Press. 286 Prospect Place, Brooklyn, NY 11238.

Institute of Lesbian Studies. P.O. Box 60242, Palo Alto, CA 94306.

Kitchen Table: Women of Color Press. P.O. Box 908, Latham, NY 12110.

Long Haul Press. P.O. Box 592, Van Brunt Station, Brooklyn, NY 11215.

LuraMedia. P.O. Box 261668, 10227 Autumn View Lane, San Diego, CA 92126-0998.

Naiad Press. P.O. Box 10543, Tallahassee, FL 32302.

National Sisters Vocational Conference. 1307 S. Wabash Avenue, Suite 350, Chicago, IL 60605.

Roundtable Press. 4 Linden Square, Wellesley, MA 02181-4709.

Seal Press. 3131 Western Avenue, No. 410, Seattle, WA 98121-1028.

Shameless Hussy Press. Box 5540, Berkeley, CA 04705.

Sinister Wisdom Books. P.O. Box 1308, Montpelier, VT 05602.

Spinsters Ink. P.O. Box 300170, Dept. C, Minneapolis, MN 55403.

Volcano Press, Inc. P.O. Box 270C, Volcano, CA 95689.

Water Works Press. 8035 13th Street, Suites 1 & 3, Silver Spring, MD 20910.

The Woman's Press. 245 W. 107 Street, Apartment 12B, New York, NY 10025.

Women's Institute for Continuing Jewish Education. 4079 54th Street, San Diego, CA 92105.

Centers

Black Women in Church and Society, Interdenominational Theological Center, 671 Beckwith Street SW, Atlanta, GA 30314. Director: Dr. Jacquelyn Grant.

Boston Theological Institute, Women in Theological Studies, 11 Garden Street, Cambridge, MA 02138.

Center for Concern, 3700 13th Street NE, Washington, DC 20017.

Center for Women and Religion, Graduate Theological Union, 2400 Ridge Road, Berkeley, CA 94709.

Committee for Gender Research, University of Michigan, 234 W. Engineering Building, University of Michigan, Ann Arbor, MI 48109.

The Grail (Grailville), 932 O'Bannonville Road, Loveland, OH 45140.

Institute for Research on Women and Gender, Stanford University, Stanford, CA 94306.

Isis International, Via Santa Maria dell' Anima 30, Rome, Italy.

National Women's Studies Association, University of Maryland, College Park, MD 20742-1325.

Quixote Center, P.O. Box 5206, Hyattsville, MD 20782.

Peace Links Connection, Women Against Nuclear War, 747 8th Street SE, Washington, DC 20003.

Reclaiming (Starhawk), P.O. Box 14404, San Francisco, CA 94114.

Shalem Institute for Spiritual Formation, Mount St. Alban, Washington, DC 20016.

Wellesley College Center for Research on Women, Wellesley College, Wellesley, MA 02181.

Wellspring House, Inc., 302 Essex Avenue, Gloucester, MA 01930.

Womancenter at Plainville, 76 Everett Skinner Road, Plainville, MD 02762. Directors: Chris Loughlin and Carolyn McDade.

Women's Alliance for Theology, Ethics and Ritual (WATER), 8035 13th Street, Suites 1 & 3, Silver Spring, MD 20910. Directors: Dr. Mary E. Hunt and Diann Neu.

Women's International Resource Exchange Services, Inc. (WIRE), 475 Riverside Drive, No. 570, New York, NY 10115.

Women's Spirituality Forum, P.O. Box 11363, Oakland, CA 94611.

Women's Theological Center, 400 The Fenway, Boston, MA 02115. Director: Donna Bivens

INDEX OF AUTHORS

The numbers in this Index refer to entry numbers, not page numbers.

ABOUT THE AUTHOR

CLARE BENEDICKS FISCHER (A.B., Hunter College; M.A., Syracuse University; Ph.D., Religion and Society, Graduate Theological Union) is on the faculty of the Starr King School for the Ministry, which is a member of the Graduate Theological Union in Berkeley, California. She holds the Aurelia Reinhardt Chair in Religion and Culture and has served as convenor of the History of Religions area of the consortium. For the past decade she has taught classes in comparative feminist approaches to religion, feminist theology, and feminist theory. She has published *Breaking Through: A Feminist Bibliography in Theology* (1980) and is currently doing research on Indonesian women and work.